THE WOLF AND THE CROSS

An Orthodox Pilgrim's History of Lithuania

ANDREW STEPHEN DAMICK

SERAPHIM RICHARD ROHLIN

ANCIENT FAITH PUBLISHING

CHESTERTON, INDIANA

Published by:
Ancient Faith Publishing
A Division of Ancient Faith Ministries
1050 Broadway, Suite 6
Chesterton, IN 46304

Unless otherwise indicated, all Scripture quotations are from the ESV® Bible (The Holy Bible, English Standard Version®), copyright © 2001 by Crossway, a publishing ministry of Good News Publishers. Used by permission. All rights reserved.

Authors' Note: When a quotation or folk story does not contain a footnote source, the quotation and/or story has been written in the authors' own words.

Photos by Bill Damick and Andrew Stephen Damick

Cover art and design by Sophie Ries

ISBN: 978-1-955890-83-0

Library of Congress Control Number: 2025938430

For
Bill Damick
Brigid Rohlin

And in Memory of
Antanas Petras Domeika and Olga Paulina Weiland
Robert, Albert, and Bertha Damick
George and Zanell Jackson

Contents

Foreword   1

Preface and Acknowledgments   6

Prologue: The Baltic Sea   10

PART I

The Wolf Before the Cross:
The Last Pagans of Europe (1009–1387)

Chapter 1   St. Bruno and the Balts   15

Chapter 2   Baltic Paganism   22

Chapter 3   Mindaugas   28

Chapter 4   The Iron Wolf   37

Chapter 5   The Metropolis of Lithuania   41

Chapter 6   The Three Martyrs of Vilnius   45

PART II

The Scepter and the Spear:
The Conversion of Lithuania (1387–1410)

Chapter 7   Pagans Between Rome and Constantinople   53

Chapter 8   Baltic Crusaders   60

Chapter 9   Christianization   65

Chapter 10   Trakai   70

Chapter 11   The Battle of Grunwald   79

PART III

The Eagle and the Knight:
The Polish-Lithuanian State (1386–1795)

Chapter 12	From Union to Commonwealth	87
Chapter 13	East, West, and the Union of Brest	92
Chapter 14	A Faithful Cry in the Dark: St. Athanasius of Brest	102
Chapter 15	St. Leontijus Karpovičius and the Monastery of the Holy Spirit	107
Chapter 16	Lithuanian Easter Eggs in American Orthodoxy	110
Chapter 17	The Gate of Dawn	114

PART IV

The Cuckoo and the Serpent:
The Legends of Lithuania

Chapter 18	Legends, Lore, and the Life of a People	123
Chapter 19	The Palemonid Dynasty	126
Chapter 20	Eglė, Queen of Serpents	131
Chapter 21	The Curonian Spit and Its Spirits	139
Chapter 22	Jūratė and Kastytis	148
Chapter 23	The Swan Queen	151

PART V

The Cross and the Empire:
Lithuania in the Russian Empire (1795–1915)

Chapter 24	Partition	157
Chapter 25	The Russian Orthodox Diocese of Lithuania	162
Chapter 26	Our Lady of Pažaislis	169
Chapter 27	Russification and National Awakening	174
Chapter 28	The Domeikai of Kudirkos Naumiestis	183
Chapter 29	St. John of Kronstadt and Fr. Pontius Rupyshev	190
Chapter 30	The Hill of Crosses	197

Contents

PART VI

The Stork and the Bear:
Lithuania in the Twentieth Century (1915–1991)

Chapter 31 From America to Lithuania: St. Tikhon   205
Chapter 32 Independence (1918–1940)   211
Chapter 33 Our Lady of Surdegis   219
Chapter 34 From Domeika to Damick   222
Chapter 35 Chiune Sugihara   229
Chapter 36 Through Communism to Freedom   235
Chapter 37 To Put Right an Old Wrong   244

PART VII

Holy Lithuania:
Orthodox Christian Saints of Lithuania

Chapter 38 The Monarch and the Monk: Vaišvilkas and
            St. Eliziejus Laurušavietis   251
Chapter 39 The Princess-Abbess: St. Charitina of Lithuania 258
Chapter 40 The Exile Convert: St. Daumantas of Pskov   260
Chapter 41 Standing Firm: St. Macarius of Kyiv   264
Chapter 42 Lithuanian Athonite: St. Anthony of Karyes   266
Chapter 43 The Protectress: St. Sofija Olelkaitė-Radvilienė 268

Epilogue: Lithuanian Orthodox Christianity   271

Appendix: A Lithuanian Synaxarion   276
Bibliography   280
Subject Index   289
About the Authors   301

Along with them the stork came back to our fair land,
And, husbandlike, atop the roof displayed his voice.
While he gazed and rejoiced, his sweet and loving spouse
Appeared upon the sill in gay and joyful mood
And met her gentle mate with glad and gleaming beak.
They found the old thatch roof much damaged and despoiled;
And even their abode, built but a year ago,
Was weather-beaten, bent, and sagging on each side.
The very walls and beams and sturdy parapets
Were torn and blown away by the relentless gales.
Doors wrecked, sills fallen off, and ev'ry window gone:
The northern wrath had wrought its havoc on their home.
And so they both at once, as good homemakers should,
With courage and in faith began to build again.
The husband fetched great loads of branches, rods, and twigs
With which his spouse patched up their home to suit her taste.
And when their long and hard repairs were fully done
The two of them flew off to a green marsh nearby;
Then having caught and gorged some fatter frogs and toads
Together gratefully they gave their thanks to God!

—Kristijonas Donelaitis, "Joys of Spring"

Foreword

IN 2020, I WAS MANAGING the social media page of what was likely the first-ever Lithuanian Orthodox parish to hold services entirely in Lithuanian. One day, an American priest began commenting on posts about the saints of Lithuania. He asked if we had a list of these saints and posed similar questions. I responded to him with a message, and word by word, a life-changing friendship began.

Father Andrew Stephen Damick turned out to be one of the hosts on Ancient Faith Radio and later became the chief content officer of Ancient Faith Ministries. This came as a great surprise to me, as I had been a listener of the station—though not specifically of Fr. Andrew's shows. One of my favorite radio personalities from AFM was Fr. Thomas Hopko, of blessed memory. Through Fr. Andrew, I became a devoted fan of *The Lord of Spirits*.

I feel that *The Wolf and the Cross* is, in some ways, a practical application of *The Lord of Spirits*. When you travel through places and contemplate not just their material reality but also the stories behind them, you begin to re-enchant the world. You start to hear and see things that remain invisible to the secular, indifferent bystander.

Gazing at the Curonian Lagoon, you can see the silhouette of the giantess Neringa, who filled her apron with sand and, standing in the Baltic Sea, spilled it into the water to form the Curonian Spit. Looking at Trakai Castle, you can sense the spirits of the great medieval dukes and the soldiers who fell defending the ancient Lithuanian state. Standing on the Hill of Three Crosses and overlooking Vilnius, with dozens of crosses adorning the rooftops of its ancient churches, you realize how many Christians have prayed here through the ages, finding their eternal resting place near the churches they loved.

When Fr. Andrew and Richard came to Lithuania, it felt almost unbelievable—America is so far away! We also didn't know if there would ever be another opportunity to show them the country. And, of course, they were preparing the documentary that would later become the foundation for this book. So we did our best to pack everything into a single trip.

The pilgrimage aimed to showcase both the history of Lithuania and its statehood—so dear to all Lithuanians—as well as the history of Orthodox Christianity in the country. This was no simple task, as Lithuania is a predominantly Catholic nation where, for many generations, Orthodoxy has been associated with Russian imperial politics.

Because Lithuania is a predominantly Roman Catholic country, its history is often presented through a Catholic lens. However, Lithuanian book culture began with the Protestant Reformation—the first book ever published in Lithuanian was a Lutheran catechism written by Pastor Martynas Mažvydas. Additionally, during the era of the Grand Duchy of Lithuania, the majority of the population was Ruthenian Orthodox. Yet today, both Protestant and Orthodox communities are small, and their historical contributions have often been overshadowed in the telling of Lithuania's history. One of the key tasks for these communities during the national revival at the end of the twentieth century was to reclaim their own Lithuanian history and reaffirm their place within Lithuanian society.

For Orthodox Christians, this task was even more challenging due to the legacy of Russian imperial history. If you consider Lithuania's past, the country has almost always been either in conflict with Russia or under its occupation.

Tensions with the Principalities of Rus' began almost immediately after the formation of the Lithuanian state, following the assassination of King Mindaugas. From the thirteenth to the eighteenth centuries, Lithuania and Moscow were in constant struggle for control over Slavic lands, trade routes, and influence in Eastern Europe. After the Union of Lublin (1569), Lithuania merged with Poland to form the Polish-Lithuanian Commonwealth, which remained a major rival to Russia. However, Russia gradually gained the upper hand, culminating in the Partitions of the Commonwealth (1772, 1793, 1795), after which most Lithuanian ethnic lands were annexed by the Russian Empire (a small portion was annexed by Prussia).

During 120 years of Russian imperial rule and colonization, Lithuanians faced Russification and repression but responded with two uprisings (1831 and 1863) and formed an underground movement to preserve their ethnic culture. After briefly regaining independence in 1918, Lithuania sought neutrality, but in 1940 it was occupied by the Soviet Union, the political successor to the Russian Empire. When Lithuania declared the restoration of independence in 1990, the Soviet regime responded with crackdowns, culminating in the bloody events of January 1991.

After the dissolution of the USSR, it seemed that the struggle was finally over. However, in 2008 the Russo-Georgian War reignited concerns, and when war broke out in Ukraine in 2014, the question arose once again: How safe is Lithuania?

Sadly, this historical background has tainted the reputation of the Orthodox Church in Lithuania. Most people know little about Orthodoxy, except that it is "the Russian faith" and that it was the religion imposed on Lithuanians by the Russian Empire. Many have also heard that during imperial times, "the Russian emperor was the head of the Orthodox Church," a reference to the synodal period when there was no patriarch and the emperor influenced a lot of decisions.

Moreover, since 2014, the close relationship between the Russian Orthodox Church and the Russian government only reinforced these negative perceptions. Many associated the local Orthodox communities of Lithuania with Russian politics.

It is true that during Fr. Andrew and Richard's pilgrimage, the only operating Orthodox Church in Lithuania was the Russian Orthodox Church (also known as the Moscow Patriarchate). But even while my brothers and sisters in Christ and I were still within the Moscow Patriarchate, it was important for us, as Lithuanian citizens, to reclaim our history from Russian imperial politics, rediscover our identity free from its influence, and tell our story anew.

This does not require artificially rewriting history. In fact, from the beginnings of Lithuanian Christianity until the seventeenth century, Orthodox Christians in Lithuania were actually under the Ecumenical Patriarchate and had their own unique culture. It was the imperial narrative that artificially rewrote the local history to fit its own agenda after the local Christians were "moved" to the Russian Church. The new narrative proposed the idea that, actually, the local communities were always Russian.

In 2023, I witnessed an extraordinary historical event: His All-Holiness Patriarch Bartholomew visited Lithuania and reestablished the presence of the Ecumenical Patriarchate. It was the first visit of an Ecumenical Patriarch to Lithuania since the visit of Patriarch Jeremias II in 1589. During his visit, His All-Holiness addressed Lithuanian politicians in the parliament, speaking about the history of Orthodoxy in these lands and helping to dismantle the harmful stereotype that Orthodoxy is exclusively Russian.

Authentic Christian mission always goes hand in hand with the process of inculturation. As His All-Holiness said in conversations with priests, no one needs to become Greek or Russian to be Orthodox. On the contrary, Orthodoxy bears witness to the gospel's universal message in different languages and cultures. That is precisely why Ss. Cyril and Methodius translated the liturgy into Slavonic. And yet, it is unfortunate that only in the past twenty years have we begun celebrating the Divine Liturgy in Lithuanian.

In this sense, although Lithuania has an ancient Orthodox history, Lithuanian Orthodoxy itself is still quite young. In this regard, I feel we have much in common with American Orthodox Christians, which is why I have always loved listening to Ancient Faith Radio.

Both in Lithuania and America, the work of translation and inculturation is an ongoing effort, and the Orthodox are a minority. In Lithuania, we exist between East and West, and the faithful of the Moscow Patriarchate live side by side with those of the Ecumenical Patriarchate, leading to an exchange of different Orthodox customs. This is evident in liturgical practices, music, and iconography, which contain elements from different cultures and also from the medieval Lithuanian Orthodox culture (which itself was a unique synthesis). When I watch broadcasts of services from America, I notice many similarities stemming from the similar cultural interchange. Additionally, one of my seminary professors was a student of Fr. Alexander Schmemann, and many of my young parishioners listen to Ancient Faith Radio programs, so we are not unfamiliar with what is going on in America.

For all these reasons, I believe this book will not only be valuable to Americans—who can embark on a pilgrimage of the mind to Orthodox

Lithuania through the centuries by reading these pages and perhaps even visiting in person someday—but also to Lithuanians seeking a fresh perspective on their history. Guided tours of Orthodox Vilnius (or Ruthenian Vilnius) have recently emerged as a new genre, attracting both tourists and locals who were previously unaware of the rich history of their Orthodox neighbors.

By the way, many of these historical Ruthenians in the past migrated to America and helped establish the Orthodox Church there, which further reinforces my belief that Orthodox Lithuania and Orthodox America are like long-separated cousins. In any case, we are truly brothers and sisters in Christ.

I hope that this book will make the spiritual ties between our communities stronger and maybe will deepen someone's faith. Lithuania has a whole heavenly community of martyrs, confessors, and other saints who inspire us even today. Through their prayers, Lord Jesus Christ our God, have mercy on us!

—The Rev. Dr. Gintaras Jurgis Sungaila
On the Day of the Re-Establishment of the Statehood of Lithuania,
February 16, 2025

Preface and Acknowledgments

THIS BOOK TOOK THREE YEARS to write, but in some sense, I have been writing it my whole life. It was not intended as a book initially but rather began its life as a podcast documentary with the same title, based on a 2022 pilgrimage I took with my daughter Evangelia and my friend Richard (now Deacon Seraphim) Rohlin. The ostensible purpose of the pilgrimage was that documentary, but its deeper purpose for me was to reconnect a cord that had been broken.

My great-grandparents Antanas and Olga Domeika (Anthony and Olga Damick) came separately to the United States from Lithuania around the turn of the twentieth century, and in short order took up the task of being Americans, cutting the cultural, linguistic, and historical cord that had bound them to their Baltic family history for untold generations. They passed almost nothing of who their families had been in Lithuania to their children, including my grandfather. So I went to see what I could discover, and along the way I found that Lithuania also had a deep, fascinating, and varied Orthodox Christian history.

That Orthodox story is one I believe Orthodox Christians in the English-speaking world need to know. It is a story of shifting borders, changing culture, ascensions and defeats, all with Orthodox Christians as a minority religious group among pagans initially and then Roman and Greek Catholics. It is also a story of adoption and adaptation, of taking whatever is good from the surrounding culture and offering it to Christ in His Holy Orthodox Church.

Because this book came from a pilgrimage and also because this story is actually many stories, its structure, while generally following a diachronic historical narrative, is not strictly linear. The book, rather, is structured like our pilgrimage itself, with introductory passages, historical context, lives of saints, legends, fairy tales, travelogue, and encounters with wonder-working icons, liminal spaces, and holy shrines. That is why many of the chapters are short and do not necessarily flow directly from the previous chapter. This book is also not a straightforward history (even religious history) of Lithuania, though I hope the reader will come away with a solid working knowledge of that history, particularly because most people in the English-speaking world have very little (if any) knowledge of Lithuania.

Certain parts of this text are written in the first-person voice, and we have indicated which of the two of us is the speaker. This matters because the book includes thoughts from both of us that are quite personal—and in certain cases we want you, the reader, to have, as much as possible, the sense that you are on pilgrimage with us. Although Richard is now Deacon Seraphim, we have used *Richard* throughout the text because that is the name he used when we were on pilgrimage.

It may seem a strange thing to mention, but we are very much aware that how one spells names of people and places can be the subject of controversy, and that is true of subjects in this book. In choosing spellings, we generally tried to use the most common versions found in English or Lithuanian, and if it was a toss-up, we chose transliterations closest to the endonyms used in the modern country in question. We are philologists and historians, not ideologues, so one shouldn't read any agenda into our orthographical choices.

It is something of a cliché to call a large project a "labor of love." This one certainly qualifies, however, and not only in the sense that we did this because we loved it. The path from pilgrimage to publication is a path of friendship and of family. In this pilgrimage, Richard and I, already friends and collaborators, became bound together with something immutable. It was also my great privilege and joy to bring my daughter along on the original pilgrimage but then two more of my children and also my father Bill on further journeys to Lithuania.

While we were in Lithuania, we met Fr. Gintaras Sungaila, his wife Justina, and many other new friends. We are indebted to all of them, but most especially to Fr. Gintaras. He is almost a coauthor of this book. He not only guided us through our 2022 pilgrimage and took up the mantle again twice more when I returned in 2023 and 2024, but he also has been a close collaborator, reading the scripts for the documentary and offering comments. If you listen to the podcast documentary version of this story, you will hear his voice many times. In this book, his voice is embedded everywhere, absorbed into the narrative. Over the past few years, we have become fast friends, knit together initially by our mutual love for Lithuanian Orthodox history but now by virtue of Christian friendship. *Labai ačiū, mano drauge. Tavo kunigystę teatmena Viešpats Dievas Savo Karalystėje visais laikais.*

As each of us, whoever and wherever we are, stand over the bones of our ancestors—even if it cannot be literally so—may we pray for them and never forget that Christ unites all of us across the sweep of history and in whatever lands we find ourselves.

—Archpriest Andrew Stephen Damick
Sunday of the Publican and Pharisee, 2025

Almost the first thing I ever read concerning the Orthodox Church was an account—written by a Protestant author—of the life of St. Seraphim of Sarov. In this account, the author mentioned that St. Seraphim had a particular icon of the Mother of God before which he prayed. Captivated by both his life and this icon, I commissioned a copy of it from an iconographer in St. Petersburg. Bear in mind, I was still a Baptist minister at the time! This was the beginning—or at least, one of several beginnings—of my journey to the Orthodox Church. It was also the beginning of my relationship with the culture, history, and people of Lithuania.

The story of that icon, and its relation to the famous wonder-working icon of Our Lady of the Gate of Dawn, is one of the stories you will read in the pages of this book. There is another story that does not come into this tale, in which my family received a miraculous healing at the Kursk Root Icon of the Mother of God, another icon with deep significance in the life of St. Seraphim. It's important to mention these encounters since unlike Fr. Andrew, I do not (to my knowledge) have any Lithuanian ancestors. When he invited me to go with him on this pilgrimage to Lithuania, I was going first and foremost to see her. It was a true pilgrimage, an opportunity to go and stand before her icon and offer thanks for the grace that God had bestowed upon us through her intercessions.

What I found, to my great surprise, was that Lithuania was exactly the place I'd always hoped existed somewhere in the world. The people, the food, the countryside, and most of all, the old town of Vilnius itself captivated my heart and imagination. I am deeply grateful to our Lithuanian friends for their hospitality and to Fr. Andrew for taking me on this adventure. Working on *The Wolf and the Cross* documentary, and on this book, has meant that Lithuanian history, culture, and the saints that hallowed it, have been a constant part of my life for the last three years.

In assisting Fr. Andrew with the task of writing this book, I have been particularly focused on the myths and legends, as well as on the stories of the Lithuanian saints and wonder-working icons. As someone whose prior religious life was so often devoid of color, beauty, and wonder, the time I have spent writing the hagiography for this book has been a deep balm for my soul and an unlooked-for fulfillment of my writer's vocation. Through their prayers, I hope to return to Lithuania one day soon and introduce my children to this land between the forest and the sea.

—Deacon Seraphim Richard Rohlin
Sunday of the Myrrhbearers, 2025

The Baltic Sea

JOURNEY WITH US IN YOUR mind to the ancient shores of the Baltic Sea. It is a cold northeastern arm of the Atlantic Ocean, resting between Scandinavia at the west and the Baltic nations to the east. Within its depths lie the remains of an ancient, primeval evergreen forest from which fossilized tree sap has washed up to the eastern shore for untold millennia. Beginning at least 3,500 years ago, a sea-born golden-reddish jewel was carried along the Amber Road south to the Mediterranean, adorning courts from the senators of Rome to the kings of Syria to the pharaohs of Egypt and throughout the world.

One hundred sixty-three miles of the eastern shore of the Baltic belongs to the modern country of Lithuania, from which amber still makes the journey out into the world. One-fifth of that coastline is protected by the *Kuršių nerija*, the Curonian Spit, a long sandbar that is said to have been thrown there by a young giantess named Neringa to ward off evil storms sent by an angry suitor.

Poised between East and West, between Orthodox and Catholics, this last of Europe's pagan nations did not forget its ancient tales of the giantess Neringa, Eglė Queen of Serpents, or the Iron Wolf, but rather remembered them, and added to them the legends of the Hill of Crosses and the miracle-working icon of Our Lady of the Gate of Dawn.

In this green northern land, history and legend have met and fused. With the martyrdom of Ss. Antanas, Eustachijus, and Jonas in 1347, the Baltic sun cross once carried by pagans became the Cross of Jesus Christ.

Lithuania was once the largest country in Europe. Its earliest Christian contacts were with the Orthodox Church, and the first church built in Lithuania was an Orthodox church.

Through centuries of history, from its first and only king Mindaugas, to the time of the grand dukes, to the union with Poland in the Commonwealth of Two Nations, to the partitioning between the empires of Eastern Europe, to early independence in the twentieth century, to invasions and occupations of both Nazis and Soviets, to becoming the first nation to break away from the Soviet Union, this proud people has kept their faith in Christ—among them, centuries of Orthodox Christians and dozens of saints.

But there is still much work to be done in this little land where Orthodox Christians are a minority. So let us now walk with them a little while on pilgrimage—to venerate at their holy places, to pray before their miraculous icons, to learn their legends, to meet their saints, and to worship our Christ.

PART I

The Wolf Before the Cross

The Last Pagans of Europe (1009–1387)

CHAPTER 1

St. Bruno and the Balts

*T*HE ANNALS OF QUEDLINBURG, WRITTEN at Quedlinburg Abbey in central Germany, say that in the year 1009 St. Bruno, also called Boniface, an archbishop and monk, was killed by pagans at the border of the Rus' Kingdom and Lithuania, along with eighteen of his companions, who entered into heaven on the ninth of March: "*Sanctus Bruno, qui cognominatur Bonifacius, archiepiscopus et monachus, XI suae conversionis anno in confinio Rusciae et Lituae a paganis capite plexus, cum suis XVIII, VII. Id. Martii petiit coelos.*"[1]

Bruno had been working as a missionary in the area for about a year, baptizing a tribal leader named Netimer, chieftain of the Yotvingians (Lith. *Jotvingiai*), an early Baltic tribe whose territory was roughly in what is now southwest Lithuania. He was beheaded by Netimer's brother Zebeden, who hanged Bruno's fellow missionaries.

This brief note of mission and martyrdom written in Latin is the earliest-known mention of the name *Lithuania*. It would be almost four hundred more years before the Christianization of Lithuania, the last pagan nation in Europe.

But in 1009, Lithuania was not even a nation. Instead, it was a collection of Baltic tribes spread along the eastern shores of the Baltic Sea—from Old Prussia, now Kaliningrad Oblast and northern Poland, up through the lands next to the Gulf of Riga in modern Latvia.

---

1   Albinus and Fabricius, *Chronicon Quedlenburgense.*

15

But where are these places? Where is the Baltic Sea? And what is the story of these people?

Father Andrew: From August 15 to 25, 2022, my friend Richard and I took a pilgrimage to Lithuania, along with my teenage daughter Evangelia. For me, this was the trip of a lifetime, though I did not know at the time that I would return multiple times in the years that followed. My great-grandparents Antanas and Olga Domeika immigrated separately from Lithuania to America around the turn of the twentieth century, and except for one visit home for Olga in 1936, no one in my family had been back to our ancestral homeland. The memory of Lithuania and its culture disappeared when they died, erased in a single generation. And with that new American generation losing touch with each other over their lifetimes, even the memory of our Lithuanian history was lost. So by the time I was born in the mid-1970s, three generations after the immigration, *Lithuania* was just a name, a word for some distant point in the past. For the first half of my life, if you had asked me what it meant to be Lithuanian, I would have had no answer to give, though I could point it out to you on a map.

Especially after I became an Orthodox Christian in early adulthood, I began to be interested in the history and especially the *Orthodox* history of Lithuania. So I made contact with Orthodox Christians in Lithuania and began to learn from them. I also began to research as best as I could the people from my family—the Domeika family—that here in America for my little branch became *Damick*.

I went to Lithuania not only to venerate its holy places and to meet its Orthodox Christians, but also to see if I could somehow heal something that had been broken, an old wound. For me, this pilgrimage wasn't about trying to become something that I am not, to claim something that I was not given. I am not one of those native-born Americans who makes a big deal out of ethnic heritage and claims it as central to their identity.

For me, the pilgrimage was about connection, both old and new. As with all pilgrimage, it was about integration; it was to receive something that God would give me, to make it now my own, and to bring it back and tell the story to those who would listen.

Richard: In August of 2022, I had the opportunity to travel with Fr. Andrew to his ancestral homeland. Now, as far as I know, none of my ancestors are from Lithuania, though some of them—Scandinavian explorers, merchants, and pirates—almost certainly sailed the Baltic. For as long as I can remember, my imaginative landscape has been dominated by the misty shores of that sea, their vast pine forests, rivers, and valleys there at the crossroads of East and West. I had gleaned these images from the literature of the Middle Ages— sagas, chronicles, romances, and heroic poetry—but until a few years ago, my impressions of that part of the world were relegated to the distant past. Then, two things happened to change that.

The first was that, for a period of time, my wife and I fostered a young girl from the Baltic states. She arrived knowing very little English, and so I made an effort to learn some words of her Latvian language so that we would be able to communicate in some basic ways. We took her into our home and our hearts, and for her part, she taught us about her culture and even introduced us to Latvian cuisine.

The second thing that happened, right around that same time, is that I (along with my wife and children) became an Orthodox Christian. With these relationships, my connection to the shores of the Baltic was more than academic: It was wrapped up in friends, adopted family, and saints my family learned to love and venerate.

My own patron saint, Seraphim of Sarov, kept a particular icon of the Mother of God in his cell. Unusually for an Eastern icon, it depicted the Theotokos without the Christ child. She is depicted from the waist up, her hands folded on her chest, her head bowed in the act of prayer and assent—for, it is said, this icon depicts her at the moment of the Annunciation, when she gives her assent, her *fiat* to the Archangel, and becomes the mother of Emmanuel, God with us. Saint Seraphim was found on his knees before this icon when he reposed.

I was captivated by this icon from the moment I first saw and read about it, and I commissioned a reproduction of it before I was even a catechumen. As it turns out, this icon is almost visually identical to (and there are reasons to believe it may be a distant copy of) an important Lithuanian icon known as Our Lady of the Gate of Dawn.

I have a personal theory that goes something like this: It is through Mary, the Mother of God, that Christ became incarnate within time and history. Therefore, a culture, a civilization, a nation is not really Christianized—has not really manifested the reality of the Incarnation—until it has its own particular icon of the Mother of God. For Lithuanians, and particularly for the people of Vilnius, Our Lady of the Gate of Dawn is that icon.

We'll say more about this beautiful wonder-working icon in a later chapter, but suffice it to say for now that this icon has been very important to me, my relationship with the Theotokos, and my journey to the Orthodox Church. So when Fr. Andrew asked what I'd be interested in seeing in Lithuania, there was really just one answer. I wanted to go and see Our Lady. Along the way, I venerated several other wonder-working icons of the Theotokos, kissed the bones of the martyrs, and encountered Christ in the faces of my brothers and sisters in the Faith—and I gained a fresh perspective on what it means to be an Orthodox Christian in the age in which we find ourselves.

WE OWE A GREAT DEBT for our pilgrimage to Fr. Gintaras Sungaila and his wife Motinėlė Justina Trinkūnaitė-Sungailienė. Father Gintaras and Motinėlė Justina generously gave us ten days of their time, traveling with us throughout Lithuania and teaching us many things along the way.

You may have noticed that Fr. Gintaras and Motinėlė Justina seem to have two different surnames—his is *Sungaila* and hers is *Trinkūnaitė-Sungailienė*. So here's one of your first lessons in Lithuanian culture.

Lithuanian men have a last name that gets altered for their daughters and their wives. So his name is *Sungaila* while hers is *Sungailienė*. That ending means it's her married name. If they had a daughter, the name would be *Sungailaitė*.

Justina's maiden name is in there, too—*Trinkūnaitė*, which is a form of *Trinkūnas*. She uses this because of her professional work as a composer and musician. Using both maiden and married names in this way is common in Lithuania.

If the Damick family used traditional Lithuanian surnames, the father and sons' surname would be *Domeika*, the wife's would be *Domeikienė*, and the daughters' would be *Domeikaitė*. So in one family you can have three different versions of one family name.

We met Fr. Gintaras through the internet a couple years before we made our pilgrimage, so we were already friends, but by the time the pilgrimage was done we had truly become fast friends, brothers in Christ. Father Gintaras was also the best possible guide for us because the story we want to tell you is framed by Lithuanian history, and he's a great historian. We pilgrims and Fr. Gintaras all love history, and Lithuanians have a sense of their history that understandably goes pretty deep.

It's impossible to transmit that same feeling for history without actually being part of a culture, but we hope that by the end of this book, you will begin to have a sense for how Lithuanians feel about the long story of their land, from ancient Baltic paganism to the modern period.

IN A MOMENT WE WILL talk about that Baltic paganism, the religion practiced in what is now Lithuania, as well as in the lands to its immediate west and north. But who are these ancient and last pagans? Where do they live?

First, this word *Baltic*—that's not a word these people applied to themselves or to their religion. When referring to these ancient people, *Baltic* is a modern academic word, though it was used to refer to the sea near which these people lived as far back as the third century BC. But now the word is used in the languages of the three Baltic states—Lithuania, Latvia, and Estonia—to refer to their region, and it's used in English that way, too.

Modern Lithuania is a small country about the size of the American state of West Virginia, home to 2.8 million people. It's at the same latitude as Newfoundland in Canada. If you look at a map of Europe, it is in the northeast, due east of Denmark and northern England, lying on the eastern coast of the Baltic Sea.

To its north is Latvia. To its southeast is Belarus. Southwest is Poland, and it shares a western border with the small Russian exclave of Kaliningrad Oblast. At various points prior to the nineteenth century, some or all of these territories were part of the Lithuanian state.

As Lithuania emerged as a state onto the global map in the early thirteenth century, two distinct Lithuanian tribes inhabited most of the region—in the east, the Aukštaitians (the highlanders), and in the west, the Samogitians (the lowlanders). But there were other Baltic tribes—the Curonians out on the coast, the Skalvians, Prussians, and Yotvingians to the southwest, and the Semigallians, Selonians, and Latgalians to the north, in what is now Latvia. Most of these groups had various subtribes, as well.

These people were the descendants of Baltic tribes that had lived in this region since about 2000 BC. In modern times, some of these tribes became ethnic groups within Lithuania, and the country's population remains one of the most genetically distinct in the world. Until the medieval period, most Baltic tribes had little contact with the outside world, and very little is known about their prehistoric life beyond a handful of archaeological finds and linguistic traces left in the names of rivers.

MANY LINGUISTS BELIEVE THAT THE languages spoken by these Baltic peoples had their ancient origins in a proto-Balto-Slavic tongue, with the Baltic languages emerging in the west and the Slavic languages in the east. Some, however, argue that the Baltic languages were never joined with the Slavic but only have similarities because of loanwords crossing between languages.

That said, while there are many Slavic languages still being spoken, such as Polish, Russian, Ukrainian, Serbian, and Bulgarian, only two Baltic languages remain—Latvian and Lithuanian. There were historically several others, including Old Prussian, a west Baltic language. The last Old Prussian speaker died in the early eighteenth century.

Lithuanian is the oldest Indo-European language still being spoken. What does that mean? The Lithuanian language preserves many archaic features that stretch far back into the Indo-European language past. This largest of the language families of the earth includes such diverse modern tongues as French, Hindi, Armenian, Persian, Greek, Danish, German, Russian, Welsh, and English.

All of these languages and many more have their origins in one ancient Proto-Indo-European language, which changed in numerous ways over thousands of years and resulted in hundreds of distinct languages. The one living language that has held onto these ancient roots most tenaciously is

Lithuanian, which is why it has many words that are very close to Sanskrit, the language of ancient India.

If you've ever learned Latin or Greek or other inflected languages, you know how difficult it can be to learn all the case endings to figure out how a word fits into a sentence. Lithuanian has two grammatical genders for nouns and three for adjectives, pronouns, numerals, and participles. There are twelve noun declensions declined in seven cases, five adjective declensions, and one participle declension. In the indicative and indirect moods, verbs can have eleven different tenses.

Accent on words is irregular and has to be learned by rote. Lithuanian uses a modified form of the Latin alphabet, with thirty-two letters. All this complexity is part of why there are not very many people who learn Lithuanian as a second language.

Not everyone in Lithuania speaks what is called "Standard Lithuanian." The Samogitians in the western part of the country speak their own dialect that is mostly mutually intelligible with the standard dialect but also has a lot in common with Latvian to the north.

CHAPTER 2

Baltic Paganism

NOT MUCH IS ACTUALLY KNOWN about the paganism of the pre-Christian Lithuanians, mainly because they were an illiterate society. Writing came to Lithuania along with Christianity.

Among Lithuanians themselves, what remains of their ancestors' pagan religion is remembered mainly in folktales, which are not reliable sources when it comes to answering the question of what the beliefs and practices of an extinct religion really included. Further, these legends and songs did not begin to get written down until the early eighteenth century, more than three hundred years after the Christianization of Lithuania.

There are no sources from ancient Lithuanian pagans themselves testifying to their religion. Everything we have about it comes either from outsiders or from stories written down in the Christian period.

In some ways, this story is parallel to the Norse pagan religion practiced by the Northmen on the other side of the Baltic Sea. While many students of Norse mythology may be familiar with the *Eddas* and similar texts, these date from centuries after the last Norse pagan was baptized and were themselves written down by Christians. We simply do not know how much of these texts truly represents authentic paganism, because there is no firsthand testimony available.

That said, we do have some pre-Christian, outsider witnesses to the spiritual character of these tribes. The ancient Greek historian Herodotus, for instance, writes of a group he calls the *Neuri* who live in the region and have been identified by historians with the Yotvingians. He writes this:

The Neuri follow Scythian customs; but one generation before the advent of Darius' army, they happened to be driven from their country by snakes; for their land produced great numbers of these, and still more came down on them out of the desolation on the north, until at last the Neuri were so afflicted that they left their own country and lived among the Budini. It may be that these people are wizards; for the Scythians, and the Greeks settled in Scythia, say that once a year every one of the Neuri becomes a wolf for a few days and changes back again to his former shape. Those who tell this tale do not convince me; but they tell it nonetheless, and swear to its truth.[1]

This same story was even repeated by the Roman geographer Pomponius Mela five centuries later, writing during the New Testament period. The Yotvingians inhabited the region where Fr. Andrew's Domeika ancestors lived. You don't want to think you're descended from wizards and werewolves, but . . . well, there it is.

The earliest-known mythological tale from Baltic paganism is the *Tale of Sovijus*, which was written down in a Russian translation in the mid-thirteenth century. It goes like this:

Sovijus went hunting one day and caught a wild boar. He began butchering it and removed its nine spleens, giving them to his children for them to cook. Instead of cooking them, however, they ate them raw. Becoming enraged, Sovijus decided to descend into the underworld, traveling through eight of the gates of Hell. He could not make it through the ninth gate, however, and so one of his sons decided to help him.

The other brothers became angry with the helpful son, who then offered to help his father Sovijus receive a proper burial. So he went down to the underworld and had dinner with his father.

That night, the son made his father a bed underground, but Sovijus slept very badly, saying that he was eaten all night by worms. On the second night, the son made him a bed in the trunk of a tree, but Sovijus again slept badly, saying that he was being stung by bees and mosquitoes all night. On the third

---

1   *Herodotus*, bk. IV, ch. 105.

night, the bed was made out of fire. The next morning, Sovijus awoke fully refreshed and said that he had slept very soundly.[2]

This myth is said to have established cremation as a funerary practice among the Lithuanians. (Also, remind me to look up whether Lithuanian boars have nine spleens.)

SO WHAT IS THE GENERAL shape of Baltic paganism? It rises from the murky mists of ancient, prehistoric Indo-European paganism. The most high god in Baltic paganism is Dievas, who creates the world and rules the heavens. In the legendary stories and in religious practice, however, he recedes into the background.

This is a normal dynamic in pagan religion—there is a father-god, the most high god, who is in the background, and a second figure, a son or servant, is the god to whom humans relate most often and to whom worship is given. In Canaanite religion, for instance, El is the most high god while Baal is his son. In Norse religion, Odin is the father while Thor is the son engaged with by Norse pagans. Often this secondary god is associated with thunder.

Christianity has a similar dynamic, with the Son of God in a sense more accessible to humanity than the Father. That said, the relationship of the Persons of the Holy Trinity is quite different from the relationships between the pagan gods. Further, the Son of God, Jesus Christ, is one with His Father, fully God, and likewise the Creator. So we can see that pagan religion is a distortion and reduction of this Christian reality known from even the Old Testament.

So who is this second figure in Lithuanian paganism? He is called Perkūnas, and like many of these secondary figures in myth, he is a storm-god, commanding the rain and thunder, associated with fire. Perkūnas was likely the primary focal point of worship for Baltic pagans, not only because he was called upon for the rain needed to make fields fertile but also because he was said to grant victory in battle. He is depicted as a son or servant of Dievas, distinct but not opposed. His name is still integral to the Lithuanian language

2   Beresnevičius, "Myth of Sovijus," 73–84.

as well. If a Lithuanian wants to refer to a thunderstorm outside, he might use the word *perkūnija*.

Like most religions, Baltic paganism also had a devil figure—Velnias (Velinas). His name comes from the Lithuanian word *vėlė*, which means "soul," because he was understood as the collector of souls, the one who brings them into the underworld and rules them there. He is thus parallel to Hades in Greek paganism or Hel in the Norse tradition, though his stories survived into the Christian period mainly to make him a trickster rather than as a dark lord of the dead. Lithuanian Christians use the name Velnias to refer to the devil of the Bible.

Another significant deity is Žemyna, who is an earth-goddess also associated with death. In some ways she is similar to Demeter in the Greek tradition.

There are many other stories we could mention, such as how the married couple of the sun-goddess Saulė and the moon-god Mėnuo had a falling out when Mėnuo had an affair with the morning star Aušrinė (who, awkwardly, might be their daughter). For this reason, the moon is cut up into pieces every month by Saulė and put back together, which is why the moon has phases, as sung in this traditional Lithuanian song:

> The Moon wedded the Sun
> In the first spring.
> The Sun arose early
> The Moon departed from her.
> The Moon wandered alone,
> Courted the Morning Star.
> Perkūnas greatly wroth
> Cleft him with a sword.
> "Wherefore dost thou depart from the Sun?
> Wandering by night alone?
> Courting the Morning Star?"
> Full of sorrow was his heart.[3]

---

3   Ralston, *Songs of the Russian People,* 89.

There is one more god we want to mention here—Ragutis. He's the god of beer, brewing, and mead. As you might imagine, there are Lithuanian pagan beer rituals. One involves a newly married couple throwing beer in each other's eyes to give a blessing for prosperity. Another, conducted at planting time, involves making the tallest girl in the village drink a whole mug of beer as a form of divination—if she can remain standing, the harvest will be a good one.

ONE THING THAT'S ESPECIALLY IMPORTANT to understand about Lithuanian paganism but also paganism in general is that the gods are not like the God of Israel. They often behave badly, and they don't fundamentally care about human beings. In Lithuanian pagan tradition, that apathy is built right into the creation story itself.

The story of the creation of humanity in Baltic paganism is bound up with the creation of the various gods by Dievas, the primordial creator god. As he is busy creating the various gods and goddesses of the earth, the smithy, the heavenly bodies, and so on, Dievas is walking along and spits onto the ground, as men sometimes do. The saliva happens to fall on fertile soil, though Dievas does not notice, and it accidentally develops into humankind, who are ignored by the high god. He simply does not care.

Why do pagans worship their gods, then? It is because they experience their presence, often in a dominating, dangerous way, and so they offer worship as a way to get on good terms with their gods and even to try to get something from them. Worship is the central act of any religion, so why are there no ancient Lithuanian pagan temples?

While the pagans of the Greco-Roman world and the Ancient Near East used the plentiful stone of their regions to construct temples, Baltic pagans did not build such structures. Rather, they worshipped their gods in forests, often in sacred groves, particularly at certain oak trees. In the very late pagan period, when the Balts had more contact with Christians who built churches, a few wooden structures might have been built for worship purposes.

SO NOW WE BEGIN TO get a sense for Lithuanian paganism—a collection of tribes near the Baltic Sea, encountering their gods in forests and mountains, gathering at sacred oaks in sacred groves to offer sacrifice to the fiery thunder-god Perkūnas, asking for his thunderous rains, his protection, and his help in battle.

Unlike how many see religion today—as being a "part" of life—for ancient people, religion was integrated into all of life, not seen as a separate activity. Thus, paganism also affected the organization of ancient Lithuanian society, determining its very structure. The three primary gods of Baltic paganism— Dievas, Perkūnas, and Velnias—are respectively interpreted as associated with three classes: priests, kings and warriors, and farmers and merchants.

All that said, we don't have a lot of sources on Lithuanian paganism, but some bits of its stories do survive in folktales, which are an unreliable source— but in many cases, the only source—for what Lithuanian pagans believed and practiced. Much of what is now presented as authentic Lithuanian paganism is actually of relatively late origin and often mixed up with syncretistic stories.

In one such story, the blacksmith god Teliavelis, who makes the sun and puts it into heaven, is replaced by the Apostle Peter. In another, Laima (or Laumė), a goddess of fate or destiny, gets associated with the Virgin Mary, and the narrative features the Virgin Mary asking God how he created Perkūnas. Because of this kind of mixing of tales, it is difficult to say for certain what Lithuanian paganism truly consisted of.

When modern Lithuanians look back on their pagan past, how do they view it? Most of them are Christians, so do they just reject it? The Lithuanian pagan heritage remains in Lithuania but not as a practiced religion (neopagan reconstructions notwithstanding). The stories of the pagan past are retained as a mythological cultural inheritance, forming part of the language and character of their national consciousness.

You should now have a very rough idea of who the ancient pagan Lithuanians were and how they are seen in modern Lithuania. This context is what forms the background for the first stories we are going to tell.

CHAPTER 3

Mindaugas

WHILE LITHUANIA WAS MENTIONED BRIEFLY in various records as far back as Herodotus, it does not really emerge onto the pages of history until the thirteenth century, well into the European medieval period. Most of Europe was Christian by this point, but Lithuania remained pagan, worshiping Perkūnas and other gods from their tribal past.

Lithuania soon came to be ruled by its first—and only—king. That man was named Mindaugas.

He was born in the year 1203. It is not known who his father was, but there is a mythic figure named Ringaudas who is identified in the sixteenth-century Palemonid legends as Mindaugas's father. If these legends are to be believed, it would make Mindaugas a descendant of ancient Romans who immigrated to Lithuania.

The first verifiable historical mention of Mindaugas is in a treaty drawn up in 1219 with the Kingdom of Galicia-Volhynia, later known as the Kingdom of Ruthenia. He would have been sixteen years old at the time, and along with his brother Dausprungas he is mentioned as one of five elder dukes in the region who signed the treaty. At sixteen years old, Mindaugas was not old, of course. The title *elder duke* meant that he occupied a high political status.

Mindaugas's realm was between the Nemunas (Neman) and Neris Rivers, roughly what is now the southeast region of modern Lithuania. The rest of Lithuania was ruled by other regional dukes and princelings in those years.

Bound loosely together by cultural, linguistic, and commercial networks, Lithuania was not yet a state. But it was about to be.

The Unification of Lithuania

WITH THE FORMATION OF THE Livonian Confederation to the north in the territory of modern Latvia and Estonia, ruled by an autonomous branch of the Catholic military monastic order the Teutonic Knights, pressure mounted on Lithuania to accept Roman Catholicism or face invasion.

The city of Riga in Latvia had been founded by Christians and was a base of operations for attempts by Western missionaries and merchants to control the area through the military power of the Sword Brothers of the Livonian Order. The Sword Brothers kept a chronicle of their deeds, known as the *Livonian Rhymed Chronicle*, which is the basis of much of what is known about the period.

They had already forced conversion through the sword upon the Curonians, one of the westernmost Lithuanian tribes living along the coasts of modern Latvia and Lithuania, as recorded in the *Livonian Rhymed Chronicle*. The *Chronicle* says that the knights attacked the Curonians at Amboten (Embūte in Latvian), forcing them to "pay the tithe." Many were killed, but the *Chronicle* justifies the action by saying that "to break a stubborn stone, one has to strike hard." They showed the Curonians "both kindness and sternness before they would make the decision to accept baptism," which they finally "grudgingly accepted." This "annoyed" Mindaugas, whom the *Chronicle* calls "King of the Lithuanians."[1]

This army was made up of the knights of the northern Crusades, who fought pagan Balts, Finns, and Slavs—and sometimes Orthodox Christians—to force their conversion to Roman Catholicism. These Crusades had begun invading Lithuania in 1208 when Mindaugas was just five years old.

Because literacy was not yet established in Lithuania in the thirteenth century, most of what we know about Mindaugas comes from the chronicles of these enemies of his, and the text reflects this antagonism. With Catholic

---

1   Smith and Urban, *Livonian Rhymed Chronicle*, 34.

pressure mounting from the north, Lithuanian dukes also battled Orthodox nobles to the east and south, and they were also feeling the threat of the Mongol Horde farther south.

Would Lithuania become Catholic or Orthodox? Would it be by peaceful conversion or military might? Could Lithuania somehow remain pagan? These questions were asked again and again over the next century and a half, and it was while surrounded by militaristic Christian states on all sides that the Lithuanian tribes finally unified.

Mindaugas came to power in 1236 as the leader of all the Lithuanian tribes, or so said the *Livonian Rhymed Chronicle*, which as we read earlier called him their king, though he was not a king in either title or power.

The reality was rather more complicated, with multiple dukes controlling different regions of Lithuania, as well as constant threat of invasion. The Livonians certainly took note of the Lithuanians in 1236, however, as they were soundly defeated by an alliance of Lithuanian dukes at the Battle of Saulė, when the Grand Master of the Livonian Order was killed.

The *Livonian Rhymed Chronicle* records their defeat: After the pagan Lithuanians arrived, the Livonian Christians tried to ride away but were bogged down in the swampy ground and could put up only a weak resistance. Many were killed easily, including the grand master and numerous horses, though the Livonians "put up a heroic defense." After that, they fought on foot and killed many pagans before their defeat. The Lithuanians then finished them off with long spears and they, "along with many other crusaders, departed this life in glory."[2] Many such incursions were turned away, pushing Christian Crusaders back to the north.

One of the many places we went on our pilgrimage was the city of Ukmergė north of Vilnius, and we climbed a great mound that had been a hill fort where the Lithuanians fought back the Crusaders. We could almost imagine the sight of those knights advancing and the local Baltic dukes rallying their men in an attempt to keep their lands and their ways intact.

Both sides would have called upon their deities for help, the Livonian Sword Brothers calling on Christ and the Lithuanians asking for aid from

---

2   Smith and Urban, 27–28.

Perkūnas. But of course we can't romanticize the warriors on either side, many of whom were buried in that hill. They were bloody men fighting in a bloody time. Mindaugas was no exception.

While the Lithuanian dukes were fighting off Christian invasions from the north, throughout the 1230s and 1240s Mindaugas also eliminated or subjugated most other local leaders. He expanded his holdings into Slavic regions to the southeast, in what is now Belarus, and he sent his son Vaišvilkas to rule those lands.

Lithuania wasn't quite unified, though. During the years 1248 to 1251, the land was essentially in a constant state of civil war, and it was Mindaugas who emerged finally as the victor. One especially notable victory came when he fended off a coalition between some of the northern Lithuanian dukes, led by Tautvilas, his nephew who had allied himself with the Livonians by being baptized Catholic in 1250, the first of the medieval dukes to become Christian.

Mindaugas the Catholic

MINDAUGAS DECIDED TO STAVE OFF further attacks from the Livonians by being baptized Catholic himself in 1251 as well as agreeing to cede his claim to Samogitian lands in western Lithuania to the Order. The *Livonian Rhymed Chronicle* records the visit of the Master of the Livonian Order to the court of Mindaugas in 1250. The master conferred with his Sword Brothers and then rode a long distance with some of them until he reached Mindaugas's lands, where he was received as a noble lord by the queen and others. Together they all dined in a sumptuous fashion. After this warm welcome, the master said to Mindaugas, "If you become a Christian, I will give you great honor. I will win a crown for you, unless I die." The *Chronicle* goes on to say that Mindaugas, pleased with these words, promised the master some of his lands, and together the two swore oaths to bind them to the agreement.[3]

But his deal with the Livonians was not only for peace. It was for a crown. Even though he had been called king by the Livonians, he was not yet truly king.

---

3   Smith and Urban, 46–47.

But why would he need agreement from the Livonians to be crowned king? Could he not simply claim the title? In the end, the title was itself a prize dependent upon religious politics. In the thirteenth century, for any European monarch to be recognized with the title of king, he had to receive it from the Pope of Rome. Since Mindaugas was now a Catholic, that meant he wanted recognition from the pope. The *Livonian Rhymed Chronicle* recounts a second visit to Mindaugas by the Master of the Livonian Order:

> The Master then had two crowns, rich in ornament and artistry, made for King Mindaugas and his wife, [Morta]. He had already sent messengers to Bishop Henry of Prussia, who was pleased at the news. He happily rode to the Master in Riga, and without delay they all set out on the journey to Lithuania. Priests and Brothers joined the Master's party. When they arrived in that land, they baptized and consecrated the noble King Mindaugas and his wife, [Morta]. The king rejoiced and gave the Master documents, generously conferring upon him rich and fertile lands in his kingdom. When all this was done, the Master left priests and Brothers in Lithuania and ordered them to teach the people, so that they would eventually be blest. The bishop and the Master and all their subordinates then returned to their own lands, and thus the journey ended.[4]

Although Mindaugas was now a fellow Catholic, in 1252 Tautvilas attacked Mindaugas's capital of Voruta. Voruta was the legendary first capital of Lithuania, whose location, and even very existence, is not agreed upon by historians. Tautvilas was defeated and eventually fled to Galicia.

With one of Mindaugas's rivals out of the way and the Livonians placated for the moment, the Sword Brothers now supported Mindaugas's claim to be King of Lithuania, and Pope Innocent IV of Rome agreed and issued two papal bulls in response. The first instructed the Bishop of Chelmno in Poland to crown Mindaugas as king, to appoint a bishop for Lithuania, and to build a cathedral. The second made the new Lithuanian diocese directly subordinate to Rome rather than to the archbishop in Riga.

---

4   Smith and Urban, 48.

Mindaugas the King

IN THE SUMMER OF 1253, Mindaugas and Morta were crowned the first King and Queen of Lithuania. Although the exact date is not known, July 6 is celebrated as Statehood Day in Lithuania even to the present day.

The pope gained a Christian Lithuania, a hoped-for bulwark against Mongol invasions that had already made inroads into the Slavic Ruthenian lands to the southeast. The Livonians gained something of a victory by now having a Catholic on the throne of Lithuania. And Mindaugas gained his crown.

Mindaugas had expanded the territory of Lithuania to include most of the present-day country as well as lands directly to the south and east, which are now part of modern Belarus.

Some near-contemporary sources say that Mindaugas did not remain Christian but reverted back to the worship of Perkūnas and the other gods. Pope John XXII in 1324, some sixty-two years after the death of Mindaugas, said that he had returned to his pagan errors. The *Galician-Volhynian Chronicle* says that even after baptism Mindaugas sacrificed to the Lithuanian gods, conducted pagan rituals in public, and burned corpses—that is, he practiced cremation. These were not the actions of a Christian ruler. Yet Pope Clement IV in 1268, lamenting the manner in which the Lithuanian king died, wrote of him as "Mindaugas of happy memory," suggesting that he died a Catholic.[5]

Whether these claims from non-Lithuanian sources are true or not, while officially a Catholic kingdom, Lithuania did not become Christian under Mindaugas as the pope and Livonians hoped. Most of the nobles remained pagans, and the citizens were not expected to convert.

The Death of the King

IN THE 1250S MINDAUGAS SAW how the Livonian Order suffered defeats from rebellions of Prussians to the southwest, and so with the encouragement of his nephew Treniota, he broke peace with the Order and retook Samogitia on the Baltic coast. The political advantages he had gained from becoming Catholic had dissolved with the Livonian losses. The *Livonian Rhymed*

---

5   Sužiedėlis, "Mindaugas," 538–543.

Chronicle records a supposed conversation between Mindaugas and his wife Morta after his decision to ally with Treniota.

In it, Morta grieves that Mindaugas joined with Treniota, whom she calls "that ape, who has betrayed you," reminding him of how the master made them king and queen. Mindaugas replies that he has decided to abandon Christianity and return to paganism, that it's too late to rejoin with the Master of the Livonian Order. He knows he acted foolishly, but he will make his new alliance work in the end. The *Chronicle* then goes on to say that although Mindaugas had received many good things from Master Werner, he ignored them and dishonorably attacked the Crusaders along with Treniota.[6]

As the Livonian Order lost its control in the region, a coalition formed between Mindaugas's nephew Tautvilas, Tautvilas's son Constantine, and St. Alexander Nevsky, to attempt to oppose the Lithuanian king. Nothing came of the plans, however, while Treniota led his troops to victories along the Baltic coast against the Livonian Order, all the way up to Estonia.

While Treniota expanded in the west, pursuing an agenda of encouraging Baltic pagans to rise up against Christian rulers, Mindaugas focused on the Ruthenian lands to the southeast.

In 1262, Mindaugas's wife Morta died, and he decided to marry her sister, whose name history does not remember. There was, however, a problem with this marriage—she was already married to another Lithuanian noble named Daumantas. In retaliation, Daumantas allied himself with Treniota, and in the autumn of 1263 the two came upon Mindaugas in the Latvian city of Aglona, and they assassinated the king and two of his sons.[7] The *Livonian Rhymed Chronicle* says that Daumantas then intended to take the kingdom for himself, but that one of Mindaugas's sons, who had been south in Ruthenia, hurried back to Lithuania and took action against the assassins.[8]

Treniota claimed the rulership of Lithuania, though he did not have that crown from the pope. He was known as the grand duke. But he held that title for only a year before being deposed himself by Mindaugas's son Vaišvilkas, who was the one who had returned to Lithuania. The *Chronicle* records that

6   Smith and Urban, *Livonian Rhymed Chronicle*, 81–82.
7   Daumantas later went on to become an Orthodox saint. His story is told in chapter 40.
8   Smith and Urban, 88.

Vaišvilkas turned to the Livonian Master for help, since he was a fellow Christian. In response, many of the Sword Brothers were dispatched to Lithuania. Vaišvilkas meanwhile freed Christians who had been imprisoned by the pagans, taking no recompense for this act, a deed the *Chronicle* calls "noble and virtuous," a "great charity toward the Christians."[9]

No one would ever again be King of Lithuania. But Lithuania was no longer a region of tribal dukes and little fiefdoms. It was becoming truly a nation of its own.

Aftermath

ALONG WITH THE EMERGENCE OF the Lithuanian state, two stories emerge that are particularly of interest to Orthodox Christians.

One is of Daumantas, who helped Treniota to assassinate Mindaugas in retaliation for stealing his wife. After a military defeat by Vaišvilkas, Daumantas soon left Lithuania and traveled north to the city of Pskov in northwest Russia. There he became its leader and was baptized as an Orthodox Christian, even later being canonized as a saint. We will tell more of his story in chapter 40.

As for Vaišvilkas, he became the third monarch of Lithuania, ruling as grand duke for three years. He did not share Mindaugas's Catholic religion, however, nor did he remain a pagan as Treniota had been.

In 1254, he signed a treaty on behalf of Mindaugas with Daniel, the Prince of Galicia-Volhynia, transferring the lands referred to as Black Ruthenia to Lithuania, territory that is now part of modern Belarus. As part of the treaty, Daniel's son Shvarn was married to Vaišvilkas's sister. Vaišvilkas himself was baptized, but not as a Catholic. He was baptized as an Orthodox Christian, taking the baptismal name Laurušas.

As mentioned earlier, Mindaugas appointed Vaišvilkas duke of some of the lands he had gained in the treaty, but the young duke became drawn to Orthodox monastic life and founded Laurušavas Monastery on the banks of the Nemunas River near Novogrudok in his new domain and handed his rule

---

9   Smith and Urban, 87.

over to Roman, another son of Prince Daniel. He soon set off on a pilgrimage to the Holy Mountain of Athos but had to return before he got there due to wars he encountered in the Balkans.

Vaišvilkas later escaped the assassination plot that killed his father in 1264 and became grand duke himself with the death of Treniota in 1265. That same year, he and his brother-in-law Shvarn defeated an army of Poles to the west, and in 1267 he again retired to monasticism, turning over Lithuania to Shvarn.

Not long after, however, he would be assassinated in April of that same year by Leo, Shvarn's brother, in retaliation for not receiving a share of the lands himself. Vaišvilkas was buried near the Dormition Church in Volodymyr in northwestern Ukraine.

And so passed the last son of Mindaugas and the first and only Orthodox Christian Grand Duke of Lithuania. Other Lithuanian nobles became Orthodox Christians in this period, especially those who ruled the Ruthenian lands where most of the citizens were Orthodox themselves.

But there were also Orthodox Christians in Lithuania proper, such as in another early capital, Kernavė, where pagans and Orthodox mixed together among the lower classes. The presence of Christians is known from archaeological work done on the nearby Kriveikiškės burial ground, where traditional Christian burials were found, in contrast with the cremation common amongst pagans.

Soon, however, the great capital of Lithuania, itself founded to be a multicultural city, would rise from the earth.

CHAPTER 4

The Iron Wolf

O N OUR FOURTH DAY IN Lithuania, we climbed up to the windy top of Gediminas Hill to have a look at Vilnius and to stand in the place of a legend.

THE DAWN OF THE FOURTEENTH century was a time of great change and upheaval. Far to the east, a man whom Europeans called Tamerlane began a bloody rise to power as he sought to restore the glory of the Mongol Empire. In Western Europe, the French and English thrones became locked in a long and bloody series of struggles known simply as the Hundred Years' War. And on the northeastern edge of Europe, in a land of beautiful pine forests on the shores of the Baltic Sea, Grand Duke Gediminas stepped out of legend and into history.

This story begins with a hunt—not for a boar or stag but for the wisent, the powerful and dangerous European bison. For hours, Gediminas tracked his quarry through the Valley of Šventaragis at the confluence between two rivers named the Neris and the Vilnia.

The hunt took him through a sacred forest believed by some to be the burial ground of the ancient Dukes of Lithuania going back to Šventaragis himself, a late member of the legendary Palemonid Dynasty. As later legends tell, the Palemonids had left Rome during the time of the Emperor Nero, founding the civilization that would become the Grand Duchy of Lithuania.

The hunt had taken Gediminas many miles away from his capital of Trakai, through this sacred wood, until finally the great beast was cornered and slain at the top of a great hill. By the time the hunt was over, it was too late to return home. So Gediminas lay down in the ancient forest, surrounded by the graves of his ancestors, and slept at the base of the great hill. And as he slept, he dreamed.

In his dream, Gediminas saw a great wolf, covered in plates of iron armor, standing at the top of the hill. The wolf opened its jaws, raised its massive head toward the moon, and howled. The howls of the enormous beast were louder than the howls of a hundred wolves, shaking the countryside for miles around. Gediminas awoke in a sweat. He sent for his childhood friend, Lizdeika. As a pagan priest, Lizdeika would know about such matters.

Lizdeika's origins are even more shrouded in mist than Gediminas's own. According to legend, Gediminas's father had found the infant Lizdeika in an eagle's nest and raised him as his own son:

"I have dreamed a strange dream," the grand duke said to his friend, and told the priest what he had seen.

"Do not fear," said the priest, when Gediminas told him of his dream. "This iron wolf is a strong and fortified city which you will build at the top of this hill. The sound of his howl is the fame of the city, which will be spread abroad throughout the whole earth, and distant lands will quake in fear when they hear its name."

The Grand Duke Gediminas believed the dream and its interpretation, and lost no time in bringing it to fulfillment. He built a fortification on top of the hill, which now bears his name, and soon a settlement, and then a town, sprang up around the tower, which was ideally situated to command the passage of two rivers. From one of these rivers—the Vilnia—the city took its name: *Vilnius*.

As generations passed, the dream of the Iron Wolf seemed to come true. Vilnius grew in fame and glory and became the capital of the Grand Duchy of Lithuania, the center of what would become, for a time, the largest state in Europe. But this was only the beginning.[1]

---

[1]   This is Richard's telling of the story, adapted from oral versions we were told while in Lithuania, supplemented with other material found in research.

Looking out at Vilnius from those windy heights, we tried to imagine ourselves standing next to Gediminas after he woke from his dream. There on Gediminas Hill stand the remnants of an old castle, now just one red brick tower that houses a museum. Topped with a Lithuanian flag, the tower is a symbol of Lithuanian national identity.

The red roofs of Vilnius Old Town stretch out and surround the hill, littered with churches, mostly Catholic, some Orthodox. You can see Dormition Orthodox Cathedral and the Orthodox Monastery of the Holy Spirit. Nearby is a monument of three white crosses commemorating martyred Franciscan friars.

Vilnius has stood for over seven hundred years, and over time, it has been home to many cultures and religious groups. The dream of Gediminas for a diversity of peoples to all make their home in the city has largely held true.

Gediminas was born in 1275, not even a decade after all the assassinations and unrest of the earliest years of the formation of the Lithuanian state around Mindaugas. He came to power in 1316, and it is not really known who his father was. His predecessor was Grand Duke Vytenis, who ruled from 1295 to 1316.

Because of the lack of written sources from the period, there are various theories as to the relationship between Gediminas and Vytenis. Some say Gediminas was his son, some say his cousin, some say his brother. The *Livonian Rhymed Chronicle*, notable for its negative take on almost everything Lithuanian, says he was Vytenis's hostler—a servant who works in the stables—who murdered him and usurped his throne.

Whatever the case, between Vytenis and Gediminas, the borders of the Grand Duchy of Lithuania greatly expanded into what is modern Belarus, encompassing the cities of Polotsk, Vitebsk, Minsk, Brest, and the lands surrounding them.

And while the political history of Gediminas is central to the early history of Lithuania, perhaps his most enduring and pervasive legacy is the legend of the Iron Wolf itself. It is the founding legend of Vilnius and an icon of Lithuanian identity.

One might say, "Well, this is a pagan story about pagans." And that is true. Gediminas lived and died a pagan, and even the interpretation of the dream was supplied by a pagan priest. As we said earlier, though, true paganism is long gone in Lithuanian history. It is not a practiced religion any more. So that means that this legend cannot carry within it the demonic force of pagan worship.

Instead, what is left is transmitted without the pagan content. The Iron Wolf has become a symbol of Lithuanian history and identity. As the Lithuanians' neighbors across the Baltic Sea, the Christianized Norse, would include images from their own legends of Sigurd and Fáfnir even on the outer doors of churches, Christian Lithuanians also keep and honor their legends, imbuing them with new meaning and telling the stories with a Christian maturity. What is in the past is in the past, but it can also be brought from the past into the present with a new form and with new possibility.

IN THE COURSE OF OUR tale, we have not yet emerged from pagan Lithuania. It is not Christian, not yet. The tale of Grand Duke Gediminas gave rise to another, even more enduring tale, a tale of eternal significance. But first we will learn the tale of the beginnings of an Orthodox diocese in the Grand Duchy of Lithuania.

CHAPTER 5

The Metropolis of Lithuania

IT IS NOT OFTEN REMEMBERED now, but there was once an Orthodox Metropolis of Lithuania that was part of the Ecumenical Patriarchate of Constantinople. It did not last even sixty years, and its existence was due mainly to the power struggles between the Grand Dukes of Lithuania and Moscow, as well as the incursions of the Mongol Horde in the lands of modern Ukraine.

As we said earlier, the Grand Duchy of Lithuania was still expanding in the medieval period and now included lands populated by Ruthenians, that is, Orthodox Christian Slavs. This expansion was helped by the weakening of the Ruthenian nobility due to the Mongol invasions. Although the grand dukes themselves were still mostly pagans in the fourteenth century, they ruled over many Orthodox Christians, and some Lithuanian nobles had been baptized in the Orthodox Church.

The grand dukes did not insist that their citizens be pagans, and because the Orthodox Church was so important in their lands, alongside the program of the grand dukes for the recognition of a unified Lithuanian state it was only natural that they would seek to have their own ecclesiastical province, independent of the metropolitans in Kyiv, Vladimir, and Moscow. This would bolster not only the Lithuanian state but also help to deflect influence from the Roman Catholic Church in Lithuania, which by this point did not have much of a presence there.

Theophilus

SO IT WAS SOMETIME BETWEEN 1315 and 1317, as Gediminas was coming to power, that Ecumenical Patriarch John XIII ordained a Ruthenian named Theophilus as the Metropolitan of Lithuania, with his seat in Novogrudok, where Vaišvilkas had built his monastery decades before, and two diocesan bishops dependent upon him in Polotsk and Turov. Around this same time, a Metropolis of Galicia was created in western Ukraine but was often left vacant with no bishop.

In 1325 St. Peter, the Metropolitan of Kyiv, moved his headquarters west from the city of Vladimir to Moscow, owing to the weakening of the region by Mongol invasions. When he died the following year, Gediminas put forward Metropolitan Theophilus of Lithuania as a candidate for the Kyivan See, hoping to unite the two under his influence.

Meanwhile, the Grand Duchy of Moscow also put forward its own candidate, but the Ecumenical Patriarchate rejected both and in 1328 installed Theognostos, a Greek from Constantinople, as Metropolitan of Kyiv. Theognostos made his headquarters initially in Volhynia and later in Moscow. He suffered much from the Muslim Tatars in defense of the Church and was eventually canonized by the Russian Orthodox Church in the nineteenth century.

Saint Theognostos

THEOPHILUS DIED IN 1329, AND his Lithuanian See was left vacant, effectively giving Theognostos control over the Orthodox Church in the Grand Duchy of Lithuania. He argued that no bishop should be appointed to replace Theophilus, since the Grand Duchy was still too pagan. Saint Theognostos himself died in 1353.

Meanwhile, Gediminas had died in 1341, and after some years of civil war, his son Algirdas, another pagan, took his place as Grand Duke of Lithuania. He did not attempt to revive the Lithuanian metropolis at first but with the death of Theognostos sought to put his own candidate Theodoret on the united ecclesiastical throne of Kyiv.

Constantinople instead chose St. Alexios, Bishop of Vladimir, as Metropolitan of Kyiv in 1354, who had been favored for the position by St. Theognostos before his death. Theodoret then went to the then-schismatic Bulgarian church for ordination, but Algirdas soon withdrew his support in favor of a monk from Tver named Roman, who was a relative of his wife's.

Roman

WITH THE BRIEF RISE OF St. Philotheos Kokkinos to the throne of the Ecumenical Patriarchate in 1353 and 1354, then the return of Patriarch Kallistos in 1355, an agreement was made between all parties to appoint Roman as Metropolitan of Lithuania, uniting the Lithuanian metropolis with the Galician metropolis and creating a new Metropolis of Lithuania-Volhynia, with the see at Novogrudok. Meanwhile, in 1360 Algirdas took Kyiv and incorporated it into the Grand Duchy of Lithuania.

The Ecumenical Patriarchate did not immediately clear up ambiguity between the authority of the new metropolis and the Kyivan metropolis headed by St. Alexios and with its headquarters in Moscow. And so a struggle between the two lasted until Roman's death in 1362. With his death, St. Alexios became the sole metropolitan in the Ruthenian lands controlled by the Grand Duchies of Lithuania and Moscow, and he administered the vacant Lithuanian metropolis until 1371.

Dissolution

AT THIS TIME, THE LITHUANIAN See was demoted to the status of a bishopric and made dependent on the Kyivan metropolis. Despite the new canonical responsibility, the Orthodox of the Grand Duchy of Moscow made no attempt to evangelize their Lithuanian neighbors by sending missionaries.

Kyiv itself, which was the city in the metropolitan's title, had been much reduced in population due to the Mongols. So the lands of the Grand Duchy of Lithuania remained a mix of pagans, with Orthodox populations to the southeast in its Ruthenian lands largely neglected by the Church responsible for their evangelization. Nevertheless, Algirdas, while insulted by the demotion of the Lithuanian See, did not promote Orthodox mission work among his people since he did not wish to alienate his still largely pagan nobility.

Oddly enough, in December 1375, St. Philotheos consecrated a Bulgarian monk named Cyprian with the title Metropolitan of Kyiv, Russia and all Lithuania, even while St. Alexios was alive and serving as the Metropolitan of Kyiv. Saint Alexios died the following February, and Cyprian was left as the sole Orthodox metropolitan in the region. He was canonized in the fifteenth century.

One more attempt was made in 1414 to appoint a metropolitan of Lithuania by Grand Duke Vytautas, but ultimately this venture went unrecognized in the Orthodox world.

Legacy

WHAT ARE WE TO MAKE of all this? Is it all just ecclesiastical and civil politics with their normal tug-of-war for power and position? In an earthly sense, yes, this is true.

But did you notice how many saints were involved in all this? Among them is a holy confessor like St. Theognostos, who suffered at the hands of the Tatars. Or St. Philotheos Kokkinos, who would go on to be a significant liturgical commentator and reformer as well as the canonizer of St. Gregory Palamas. And Ss. Peter and Alexios and Cyprian.

This is often how the Holy Spirit works in the world. While the world sees the "real story" as being about the politics, this is only the earthly frame within which the true story of Christ's work is being done. These saints became of eternal significance for the Orthodox Church, and all of them in one way or another touched the story of Lithuania and helped to shape its history, bringing salvation to souls. All Orthodox Christians therefore have them as part of our own story.

BUT NOW, THERE IS ONE more story to share with you from this earliest period of our tale. Rising out of all this complication and confusion are three shining stars whose lights forever shine from Lithuania and throughout the world.

CHAPTER 6

The Three Martyrs of Vilnius

T HE GRAND DUKE GEDIMINAS HAD seven sons.
The dream of the Iron Wolf and the prophecy of Lizdeika seemed to have come true during Gediminas's lifetime. Gediminas extended his rule south and east, conquering Kyiv and carrying his banners to the borders of the Golden Horde in the east and south almost to the very shores of the Black Sea. His main enemies, two kingdoms of Roman Catholic Crusader knights known as the Teutonic and Livonian Orders, posed little threat to the new empire he had forged, and Gediminas remained a staunch pagan until his death.

At his death, he divided his realm among his sons, leaving his capital, Vilnius, in the possession of his son Jaunutis. This choice puzzled many and angered his other sons, especially the assertive Algirdas. After all, Jaunutis was not a natural warrior or an able ruler, nor was he the eldest.

But he was the eldest son of Gediminas's second wife, an Orthodox Christian duchess named Jaunė. And Jaunė was a force to be reckoned with. The role of the "queen mother" had always exerted great authority among the pagan Lithuanians, and Gediminas seemed to hope that the son of an Orthodox duchess might be more accepted by the citizens of the growing Grand Duchy; since Gediminas's conquests of the south and east, Orthodox Christians outnumbered pagans in Lithuanian lands at a rate of two to one.

And so Algirdas and the other brothers bided their time, expanding their own territories and successfully making war against the Livonian Order. Then, around 1344, Jaunė died. Algirdas and his brothers descended upon Vilnius. Jaunutis was imprisoned—though he did manage to escape to his brother-in-law, Simeon of Moscow, where he spent most of the rest of his life unsuccessfully trying to find someone willing to give him an army in order to retake his throne.

Algirdas was grand duke now, and he would preside over an empire that stretched from the Baltic to the Black Sea, and from Brest to within fifty miles of the city of Moscow. The Grand Duchy of Lithuania was now the largest state in all Europe.

Algirdas himself was married to an Orthodox Christian princess by the name of Maria of Vitebsk, and at her request a church, dedicated to St. Paraskevi, was built in Vilnius on the site of an old pagan temple once dedicated to Ragutis, the old Lithuanian god of beer and mead. She also brought with her to Lithuania an Orthodox priest named Nestor. The Church of St. Paraskevi was the first Christian church to be built in Vilnius and, indeed, the first church in all of Lithuania. As long as Maria lived, Algirdas continued his father and brother's policy of tolerating Orthodox Christianity alongside paganism so long as the Christians did not proselytize.

But two years later, Maria died. Algirdas fell under the influence of the pagan priests who had advised his father and, in time, began to attempt to root out Lithuanians who had converted to Orthodox Christianity. Among these new converts were two young noblemen by the name of Nežilas and Kumetis, who had been baptized at the Church of St. Paraskevi and taken the names Anthony and John.

Anthony and John were, we are told, careful not to flaunt their Christianity, but they would neither keep the same feasts as the pagans nor cut their hair in the same manner as the pagans, believing that both of these actions would involve them in the worship of demons.

The grand duke and his priests became increasingly suspicious of the two brothers, until one day a test was proposed: The two brothers should be summoned to a great feast during the Orthodox Nativity Fast, and there they should be offered the richest servings of the finest meat and wine. The brothers came to the feast but refused to break their fast, and the grand duke had them clapped in irons and imprisoned in his dungeon.

They spent the next year fasting in truth, barely kept alive on bread and water. The darkness, hunger, and isolation proved too much for John. He agreed to do whatever the prince asked. Triumphant, Algirdas had the brothers hauled before him, once again offering them a rich meal during a time of fasting. John capitulated and was allowed to go free—but Anthony refused to betray Christ and was returned to the dungeon.

John soon learned, however, that to deny Christ was worse than any torture he might have faced in the grand duke's dungeons. He was a pariah, rejected as a turncoat by Christians and pagans alike, and worst of all, he had lost the fellowship and friendship of his brother. Secretly, via the priest Nestor, he asked his brother to forgive him. Anthony's reply was firm: "When you openly confess Christ, then we will be reconciled."

Desperate, John—who by now had been reinstated to his old position in the grand duke's service—approached Algirdas in the sauna, confiding in him, begging his mercy, and telling him of his secret desire to be reconciled with the Church and with his brother.

Algirdas's response was cool and collected. "Do you think I care," he asked, "what a man believes in the privacy of his own heart and home? Worship the gods of our people. Worship your Crucified One. I care not. But when you are in public, as a member of my court and a citizen of this city, you must do as we do. You must eat what we eat."

And then, there in the middle of the bathhouse, something extraordinary happened: John found his courage. Standing up in the middle of Algirdas's courtiers and retainers John loudly proclaimed, "I am a Christian!" He was immediately beaten with canes and then thrown into the dungeon, back with his brother, and a few days later the two of them partook of the Holy Mysteries together in joy.

Meanwhile, crowds gathered at the prison to hear the preaching of the two brothers, and many were converted to faith in Jesus Christ. The place meant to contain the gospel had become the platform for its spread.

After this, Anthony was executed by hanging on an oak tree revered by the pagans. In that moment, the tree that had been sacred to the old gods became sacred instead to the Christians of Vilnius, imaging the wood of the Cross of Christ even as Anthony in his martyrdom became an icon of his Savior. Anthony was martyred on April 14, 1347.

The city of Vilnius was electrified by the martyrdom, and by the news of John's renewed resolve. The pagan priests hoped that John would falter once again, seeing the death of his brother and the torments that awaited him. But every day, the crowds around the prison grew larger. And every day, John's resolve grew stronger. Finally, they strangled him and hanged his dead body on the same oak tree. Saint John's martyrdom took place ten days after his brother's, on April 24.

The martyrdom of the two brothers did not have the effect the pagan priests intended: Instead of cowing Vilnius's little Christian community, it strengthened their resolve. Among those inspired by the sufferings of the two brothers was a kinsman of theirs, Krulis by name, who had been given the name Eustathius in Holy Baptism. Eustathius was well known amongst Algirdas's court for his good looks, valor, and courage in the hunt and in battle. But his physical courage was matched by his strength of character. When once again it was the Nativity Fast, Eustathius—like his kinsmen, and like Daniel and the Three Holy Children of old—refused to pollute himself by eating the delicacies of the king's table.

At this point, Algirdas had had enough. He ordered the young noble to be beaten with iron rods, ice water poured in his mouth, his ankle bones broken, and the hair and skin ripped from his head. Finally, they cut off his nose and ears. Eustathius endured all of these terrible torments with so much joy and courage that even his tormentors were astonished at the power that was given to him by his God.

Finally, on the thirteenth day of December 1347, the martyr Eustathius finished his struggle. He was strangled, his body hung on the same oak tree as his two kinsmen.

For three days, the Christians were not allowed to come and take his body down. During that time, a pillar of smoke miraculously enveloped the body, preventing wild beasts and carrion fowl from harming it. Later, a church dedicated to the Holy Trinity would be built on that very hill, its altar table built on the stump of the same oak on which the martyrs had died. The relics of the three holy martyrs were soon found to be incorrupt, and their veneration soon spread as far as Constantinople and even to the great Russian ascetic Sergius of Radonezh, who requested particles of their relics for his veneration.

Their relics have been hidden and moved many times during the wars and conflicts of intervening centuries, but they currently lie incorrupt in the center of the Monastery Church of the Holy Spirit in Vilnius, a source of blessing and intercession for the city, and for all of Lithuania.

As for Algirdas, his persecution of the Christians soon ebbed, and he even married another Orthodox wife. Some even say that Algirdas finished his life in the Orthodox Church, receiving baptism and the monastic tonsure shortly before his death. It is said that his name is still commemorated among the departed monks of the Kyiv Caves Lavra.

Father Andrew: For years, I had dreamed of making the pilgrimage to Vilnius to stand at the reliquary of the Three Martyrs, to ask for their intercessions. And then, there we were in the great baroque Orthodox Church of the Monastery of the Holy Spirit. It rises up high, suffused with sunlight, the pale pastel walls glowing with ornate sculptures adorning every curve and height. At the east end is an almost shockingly saturated green-painted iconostasis, framing time-darkened icons whose images hold deep shadows.

In the center of the church is a dark red wooden reliquary, large enough to hold the full bodies of all three martyrs, the holy brothers Anthony and John with their cousin Eustathius—in Lithuanian, Antanas, Jonas, and Eustachijus (or Eustatijus). The bodies show forth a quiet miracle, still ongoing since 1347. They are incorrupt, preserved by God from fading into dust, their bodies still belonging to the saints, still showing forth the hope of resurrection.

Raised pagan worshippers of the fire- and thunder-god Perkūnas, these men suffered nearly seven hundred years ago for their love for Jesus Christ. The Faith had been brought to them by a princess, but it was not for her that they were baptized. They were baptized into Christ, redeemed and saved by His love for them. They are the protomartyrs of Lithuania. With their martyrdom, the name of Christ was forever sealed in that country.

Not long after, the worship of Perkūnas and the other gods finally began the descent into oblivion. Where the Baltic sun cross had been a pagan emblem, it too became a legend transformed by the love of Christ. The martyrs' blood had marked the land forever for Christ. And we magnify them:

Tested in the fire of torture like gold in a crucible, ye were radiantly tried, O ever-memorable martyrs, and have been shown to be more precious than gold in your nature; for, showing forth the all-radiant beauty of your souls, ye truly offered yourselves to the Master as most precious vessels, not having worshiped fire. Wherefore, pray to the Lord for us all, that He grant remission of sins unto those who honor your memory with love.

Refusing to worship fire, and being subjected to fire and torments, O ever memorable ones, ye received heavenly dew, divine rest and everlasting joy; and having utterly consumed the princes of darkness by your endurance of pain, O all-wise martyrs, ye have made the faithful steadfast in true piety.

O valiant and honored athletes who spurned earthly honors and glory, mightily and manfully did ye endure torments for the sake of the Faith, giving yourselves over to death for the Master, the Life of all. Wherefore, with a pillar of cloud from heaven did Christ all-gloriously illumine you. Standing before Him with the angels, pray ye that our souls be saved.

Having caused branches of the Orthodox Faith to spring forth from a barren root, O all-blessed ones, ye were shown to be namesakes of the protomartyr; for ye were not daunted by the wrath of the evil and impious prince, who commanded you to renounce Christ. Wherefore, having received crowns of victory, and standing with the angels before the throne of the Master, O all-blessed ones, pray for us who in Orthodox manner honor your holy memory.[1]

I was greatly blessed to concelebrate the Divine Liturgy at the Monastery of the Holy Spirit with His Eminence, Metropolitan Innocent of Vilnius and Lithuania, to stand next to the martyrs, worshipping alongside them at the altar of Christ. And at the end of the service, Metropolitan Innocent gave into my hands relics of each of the three martyrs.

HOLY MARTYRS ANTHONY, EUSTATHIUS, AND John, pray for Lithuania. Pray for the Church in Lithuania. Pray for us. Pray for my family. Pray for me.

---

1   *April Menaion*, Service to the Three Martyrs of Vilnius, celebrated April 14.

PART II

The Scepter and the Spear

The Conversion of Lithuania (1387–1410)

CHAPTER 7

Pagans Between Rome and Constantinople

N EARLY SEVEN HUNDRED YEARS AGO, the Three Martyrs of Vilnius were martyred by pagan priests at the behest of the Grand Duke Algirdas, their bodies hung on a sacred oak. In time, that same oak would be felled to build a church and an altar to the Most Holy Trinity.

Six and a half centuries later, no true pagan temples remain in this land of ancient forests, little hills, and green valleys, while churches dedicated to the worship of the Holy Trinity can be found in every city, town, and village. Even in the wake of the crippling secularism and religious persecution of twentieth-century Europe, the vast majority of Lithuanian people identify as Christian—specifically, Roman Catholic.

In some respects this should not be surprising—after all, every nation in Europe has a "conversion story." But Lithuania was the last to convert, and the story of how the Baltic sun cross came to bear the image of the crucified Christ is not a simple one. It is the story of civil wars, quarreling brothers, marriage alliances, Crusaders, and a land ruled by pagans caught between Rome and Constantinople.

One of the things that makes this story difficult to tell is the fact that modern national borders and nation-states map somewhat poorly to their medieval equivalents. For instance, the modern nation-state of Lithuania covers a territory of 25,200 square miles. By contrast, the Grand Duchy of Lithuania in the time of Algirdas was several times larger, stretching from the Baltic Sea in the north and west to the city of Poltava near the Black Sea in the south (in modern-day Ukraine), and within fifty miles of Moscow in the east.

Famously, in an exchange with the Teutonic Order, Algirdas boasted that the entire Rus' should belong to the Grand Duchy of Lithuania. In this second part of our tale, when we speak of the "Grand Duchy of Lithuania" and later the "Polish-Lithuanian state," we're talking about a territory that included much of the present-day Baltic states, as well as Belarus, Ukraine, parts of modern-day Russia, and then Poland.

In this story, we've been referring to the people who inhabited some of these lands as *Ruthenians*. This name is an exonym—that is, a name from outside the region—derived from Latin *Ruteni*, applied to Eastern Slavs starting in the eleventh century and probably ultimately deriving from the Slavic *Rus'*. Correct or not, the name stuck, especially in historical sources, and we find it used consistently throughout the Middle Ages to refer to some of the people of the Grand Duchy of Lithuania, which itself comprised two groups—Lithuanians and Ruthenians. Ruthenians formed the majority of the population, but Lithuanians were the greater part of the nobility.

Both Orthodox Christians and Roman Catholics made missionary efforts in Ruthenian lands throughout the early Middle Ages. It should especially not be forgotten that Ruthenian lands included the Kyivan Rus'—themselves only baptized as late as the year 988. Most Orthodox Christians are probably familiar with this story, but it is so important to the history of the Christianization of the Ruthenian lands within the Grand Duchy that it bears repeating.

The Conversion of the Rus'

SOME THREE HUNDRED YEARS BEFORE the time of Gediminas, the Great Prince Vladimir (or Volodymyr) of Kyiv rose. The grandson of the famous and powerful Princess St. Olga, Vladimir had a pagan father and a Christian mother. While still a teenager, he was forced by his fratricidal brother Prince Yaropolk to flee to Norway, where his kinsman Haakon Sigurdson gave him an army of Norse warriors.

At the age of nineteen, Vladimir returned home for vengeance. After a brief war, he defeated his brother Yaropolk, took the cities of Kyiv and Novgorod

the Great, and was proclaimed sole ruler of the Rus'. But Vladimir's new kingdom was troubled by religious strife. The small Orthodox Christian communities in Kyiv—the fruit of the labors of St. Olga—were persecuted, and even
the pagans under Vladimir's rule revolted against his attempts to alter and
reform their religion. Vladimir needed to unite his people under a single faith.

What happens next is recounted in a work of medieval history known variously as the *Tale of Bygone Years*, the *Rus' Primary Chronicle, Nestor's Chronicle* (after the monk who wrote it), or simply the *Primary Chronicle*. It was first
compiled in Kyiv in AD 1113 and is an important record of how the East Slavs—
the people of the Ruthenian lands—understood their own story in the context of the wider Greek, Roman, and Christian world.

The entry for AD 987 tells how the Great Prince Vladimir set out to choose
a religion for his people.[1] Vladimir gathered his vassals and elders among the
Rus' and told them how the Bulgars (Muslim Turkic nomads) urged him to
accept their religion, then the Germans (who were Roman Catholics) presented theirs, then the Jews did the same. Finally, the Greeks (who were
Orthodox Christian) came to him with critiques for all the other faiths, as
well as an account of the history of the world, expressed in words Vladimir
found eloquent and pleasing, telling how the path of resurrection was found
in Orthodox Christianity but that (so the *Chronicle* says) damnation awaited
those who accepted other religions instead.

The vassals then suggested that Vladimir send ten emissaries to experience these religious traditions for themselves. The emissaries set forth and
visited the Bulgars, the Germans, then the Greeks, investigating each religion
to see what its worship was like. The only one of these groups whose worship
is described in detail is the Orthodox, with glorious beauty shown in the
Church of Hagia Sophia in Constantinople, including the patriarch, many of
the clergy, choirs, and the burning of incense. The emperor himself welcomed
the Rus' emissaries, and after the services were over he explained the Orthodox Faith to them in the middle of the Hagia Sophia.

The emissaries were sent home with many gifts, and then they delivered
their famous report to Vladimir:

---

1   Cross and Sherbowitz-Wetzor, *Russian Primary Chronicle*, 110–119.

Vladimir then announced the return of the envoys who had been sent out, and suggested that their report be heard. He thus commanded them to speak out before his vassals. The envoys reported: "When we journeyed among the Bulgars, we beheld how they worship in their temple, called a mosque, while they stand ungirt. The Bulgarian bows, sits down, looks hither and thither like one possessed, and there is no happiness among them, but instead only sorrow and a dreadful stench. Their religion is not good. Then we went among the Germans, and saw them performing many ceremonies in their temples; but we beheld no glory there. Then we went on to Greece, and the Greeks led us to the edifices where they worship their God, and we knew not whether we were in heaven or on earth. For on earth there is no such splendor or such beauty, and we are at a loss how to describe it. We know only that God dwells there among men, and their service is fairer than the ceremonies of other nations. For we cannot forget that beauty. Every man, after tasting something sweet, is afterward unwilling to accept that which is bitter, and therefore we cannot dwell longer here." Then the vassals spoke and said, "If the Greek faith were evil, it would not have been adopted by your grandmother Olga, who was wiser than all other men."[2]

As the *Primary Chronicle* records, Vladimir's path to the baptismal font was by no means straightforward: He went to war with the Eastern Roman Empire, experienced miraculous healing, married a Byzantine princess, and finally received baptism at the Church of St. Basil in Kherson, the site of an ancient Greek colony in Crimea, by the shores of the Black Sea.

It is also worth noting here the legendary character of this story. The Rurikid Dynasty to which St. Vladimir belonged was part of a set of tribes called the Varangians, who beginning in this same century provided an elite corps of guards serving the emperor in Constantinople. Rus' warriors had been in the emperor's service since at least AD 874, however, so Orthodox liturgical worship would have been well known to St. Vladimir's family for more than a century before he sent out his emissaries. It was not new to them, despite the interpretation one might derive from the *Primary Chronicle*. That said, the

---

2   Cross and Sherbowitz-Wetzor, 111.

Primary Chronicle is not making empirical historical claims but rather telling the story of the rise of the Rus' as an Orthodox Christian people.

Once he was baptized, St. Vladimir returned to his people and the great baptism of the Rus' began, accompanied by an exorcism of the land itself.[3] Arriving in Kyiv, Vladimir commanded that all the idols the Rus' had worshiped should be thrown down, cut in pieces, and burned. Perun[4] in particular was to be tied to the tail of a horse and dragged to the nearby Dnieper River. Twelve men beat the idol with sticks in an effort to insult and ridicule the demon who inhabited the idol. Many of the people, as yet unbaptized and seeing this affront to their god, began to weep. Nonetheless, the idol was eventually pushed over a waterfall and fell into the river.

Saint Vladimir then sent heralds throughout Kyiv to direct that all the people should come to the river to be baptized and would risk his disfavor if they refused. The *Primary Chronicle* then says that the people received this command with joy and enthusiasm, since, as they said, Vladimir and his men would not have accepted baptism into this religion if it were not good. The whole multitude thus came to the river and were baptized by the priests who had accompanied Vladimir back from Kherson.

It is then written that the devil himself lamented: "Woe is me! how am I driven out hence! For I thought to have my dwelling place here, since the apostolic teachings do not abide in this land. Nor did this people know God, but I rejoiced in the service they rendered unto me. But now I am vanquished by the ignorant, not by apostles and martyrs, and my reign in these regions is at an end." After everyone was baptized, St. Vladimir then looked up to heaven and said, "O God, who hast created heaven and earth, look down, I beseech thee, on this thy new people, and grant them, O Lord, to know thee as the true God, even as the other Christian nations have known thee. Confirm in them the true and unalterable faith, and aid me, O Lord, against the hostile adversary, so that, hoping in thee and in thy might, I may overcome his malice."[5]

The people of his capital baptized, St. Vladimir then began to have churches built all throughout his lands and to have priests ordained for them. In every

---

3   Cross and Sherbowitz-Wetzor, 116.
4   Some scholars regard the Slavic Perun as equivalent to the Baltic Perkūnas.
5   Cross and Sherbowitz-Wetzor, 117.

city and town, the Rus' were called to Holy Baptism. He also instituted learning, for children in particular, selecting them from the best families, that they might especially know the words of the Scriptures. A church dedicated to St. Basil the Great was founded directly on the hill where the idol of Perun had once stood. The place where idolatrous sacrifices had once been offered now was sacred to the worship of the Holy Trinity.

Although in modern times we may hear of the baptism of the Kyivan Rus' as the birth of the Russian Orthodox Church, it's important for the story of the Grand Duchy of Lithuania to remember that it took place in Ruthenian lands, centered around Kyiv, the capital of modern Ukraine. This story did not happen in Russia. And in the later medieval period, the story of the Orthodox Rus' was happening in the Grand Duchy of Lithuania.

Thus, by the time of Algirdas in the fourteenth century, the pagan Grand Dukes of Lithuania ruled over a vast kingdom composed mostly of Orthodox Christians, some four centuries after the death of the Great Prince St. Vladimir. These pagan grand dukes often took Orthodox wives (a useful alliance with the Orthodox princes of Kyiv and elsewhere), and those wives brought Orthodox priests with them.

A Spear in the West

ANOTHER SIGNIFICANT SIGN TOWARD THE Christianization of Lithuania was happening around the same time as the baptism of St. Vladimir. In Western Europe, the tenth-century Holy Roman Emperor Otto I—called "the Great"—had warred with the Slavic tribes on the border of his Empire, a conflict his son, Otto II—called "the Red"—inherited. Otto II ascended the throne just a few years before Prince Vladimir entered the baptismal font, and he found an ally in Bolesław I "the Brave" of Poland, the second Roman Catholic Polish monarch and the first to be crowned king. To cement this friendship, Otto II sent Bolesław a replica of the Spear of St. Maurice.

Saint Maurice, the African commander of the famous Theban Legion, was martyred in AD 287 in what is now modern-day Switzerland. Starting at least with Otto I, St. Maurice was considered the patron saint of the Holy Roman emperors, and he had come to be closely associated with a relic known as the Holy Lance of Vienna. The Holy Lance of Vienna was a spear, believed to have belonged to St. Maurice or St. Constantine the Great, in which was embedded (so the legends say) one of the nails used at the Crucifixion of Our Lord Jesus Christ.

Many legends surround this object, but by the time of Otto II it had become one of the official insignia of the Holy Roman emperors, a symbol of their authority and divine right. By giving a replica of this weapon to Bolesław, Otto was sending a clear message to the Polish king about his status as a Christian monarch and the role he was expected to play in converting the pagan Slavs. As we will see, this lance eventually plays a small but crucial role in how the story of the Lithuanian conversion was told—although perhaps not in a way that Otto would have expected.

CHAPTER 8

Baltic Crusaders

IN THE EARLY DAYS OF the Grand Duchy of Lithuania, a significant number—at times, a majority—of its citizens were Orthodox Christians. This was thanks to early contacts with the Kyivan Rus' as well as the eastern and southern expansion of the Grand Duchy, which eventually encompassed most of what today is the modern state of Ukraine. In those early days, Orthodox Christians outnumbered both pagans and Roman Catholics, but they were (with a few notable exceptions) common folk, ruled over by pagan grand dukes and their aristocracy.

Eventually this would all change with the baptism of Algirdas's son Jogaila into the Roman Catholic Church. That event marked two important moments in the life of the Grand Duchy: First, Jogaila made Roman Catholicism the official religion of the Lithuanian state. Second, he effected a dynastic union with the Kingdom of Poland and took the name Władysław II, King of Poland. This turns out to have been one of the most important events in the history of the two states—indeed, in the history of Europe. But it was not the first time Lithuania had had a king holding the scepter of the grand duke.

The Livonian Brotherhood of the Sword

IN CHAPTER 3, WE LEARNED the story of the first and only King of Lithuania—Mindaugas. In 1253, nearly a hundred years before Grand Duke Gediminas (who had the dream of the Iron Wolf) rose to power, Mindaugas united the warring Lithuanian tribes and presented a unified front against their external enemies.

He opposed the Tatars—a fierce, nomadic people of Muslim Turkic origin—and their incursions from the Crimea while also making a brief peace with the Livonian Order. The Livonian Order was the first of two Roman Catholic crusading orders that would have a major impact on Lithuanian history, functioning as the pressure that forged the warring Lithuanian tribes into a nation.

The history of the Livonian Order begins within the first decade of the thirteenth century, when Pope Innocent III sanctioned a Crusade against the tribes of Baltic pagans and Orthodox Christians living in what we now know as the Baltic states. This Crusade was ostensibly called to protect clergy and missionaries along the important Baltic trade routes, in particular the Bishopric of Riga. The Semigallians and Samogitians fiercely resisted these efforts at forceful conversion.

One Bishop of Riga, a German named Berthold of Hanover, was even killed in battle with the Livonians. The Sword Brothers themselves recounted how Berthold began to build Riga in such a way that indicated he planned to stay and make it his home. He was said to be a virtuous man who faithfully led the Christians, and then, in a "quest of glory, the Estonians came against them." The bishop comforted his followers:

> Good heroes, remember that Jesus Christ spilled His holy blood for us on the cross. The heathen's power is never so great that we may not attack them before they descend upon us. We are here for the sake of God in Heaven, who never abandoned his friends in the heat of battle. Those Christians who die will shortly receive eternal life. Let my soul be your guarantee of this exchange. I will stay by you, both in life and death.[1]

Encouraged by his words, all armed themselves and went to battle against the Estonians on the beach near Riga, boldly charging toward them. The bishop rode at the forefront on a horse. Eleven hundred died, including the bishop himself.

In his speech to his troops, Bishop Berthold repeated a common promise made to Crusaders: that anyone who died on the field of battle against the infidel would receive the forgiveness of their sins and eternal life.

---

1   Smith and Urban, *Livonian Rhymed Chronicle*, 8–9.

Bishop Berthold was succeeded by a man named Albert. With the blessing of Pope Innocent III as the new Bishop of Riga (also called the Prince-Bishop of Livonia, since Livonia was ruled as an ecclesiastical state) he established the Livonian Brotherhood of the Sword as his own personal standing army. Here is the story the Sword Brothers tell of their origins, spoken by the pope:

> Because of the nature of the region, you shall also have authority to found a crusading order on the model of the Templars, who are known as the knights of God overseas and elsewhere. Give them one-third of the people and land to rule as their own. They shall stand under my protection and that of all future Popes.[2]

The Crusade was ultimately successful, and the new lands—modern-day Estonia and Latvia—were declared a new province of the Holy Roman Empire known as Terra Mariana—"Mary's Land." According to the sponsors of the Crusade, the Virgin Mary had chosen the Baltic lands to be her own kingdom, conquered by the swords of Crusaders.

The Livonian Brotherhood of the Sword was made up of warrior-monks, on the model (as the *Rhymed Chronicle* suggests) of the Knights Templar. It is odd, as an Orthodox Christian, to imagine monks carrying weapons of war, but it had proven to be a popular and effective model for the Latin Crusades in the Middle East.

There, what had started as essentially small security forces offering protection and hospitality to Christian pilgrims in the Middle East became powerful standing armies with their own governments, territories, and even banks. As subsequent history would show, this particular mixture of religious zealotry, wealth, and military power was often unleashed as a destructive force on the people these warrior-monks had sworn to convert and protect.

The Teutonic Order

ONE SUCH MILITARY ORDER—THE ORDER of Brothers of the German House of Saint Mary in Jerusalem, also known as the Teutonic Knights—would

---

2   Smith and Urban, 9.

prove to be even more important to the history of Lithuania than the Livonian Brotherhood. As the full name of their Order implies, the Teutonic Order had its origins in Jerusalem and the Crusader city of Acre during the early thirteenth century.

However, thanks to Hermann von Salza, the well-connected Grand Master of the Order, they were soon charged with guarding the border of the Kingdom of Hungary against the Turkic Cumans, in what is now central Romania. Here, the Teutonic Order perfected what was to be their favorite military tactic—constructing a line of impregnable fortresses from which they would conduct lightning raids, always retreating back to their castles before their enemy could mount serious resistance. This proved to be extremely effective against the Cumans.

In just a few years the Teutonic Order would repeat these same tactics on the shores of the Baltic; for by 1225, the Order had overstayed its welcome in Hungary. At the behest of Polish dukes, they relocated to Pomerelia, near the modern city of Gdańsk. Grand Master Hermann von Salza absorbed a small, preexisting military order known as the Order of Dobrzyń, the "Prussian Cavaliers of Christ," and began the project of subduing the pagan Baltic tribes of Old Prussia. These Baltic wars became the training grounds for new initiates into the Teutonic Order, preparing them for battle in the Crusader states, where the Order still had strongholds.

The so-called "conversion" of Prussia played out over fifty very bloody years. The Teutonic Order inched slowly forward, forcing the Prussians, Lithuanians, and Samogitians to be baptized at the point of the sword. Those who did not accept baptism were deported or executed. For their own part, the pagan Prussians showed no mercy to those members of the Order they managed to capture, offering them as sacrifices to their gods. Perhaps the most memorable of these deaths is that of Brother Gerhard von Rude.

In 1320, Marshall of the Order Heinrich von Plotzkau led forty Teutonic Knights on a raid from Klaipėda Castle (Klaipėda, on the Baltic coast, being part of the Teutonic territory of Prussia at this point). The raid was successful, but as they were returning home, laden with the spoils of their pillaging, they were ambushed by a force of Samogitians. Twenty-nine of the knights were slain, and Heinrich was taken captive. *The Chronicle of*

Prussia, the Teutonic Order's primary set of records, tells the story of what happened next:

> When the heathens had killed everyone they captured Brother Gerhard von Rude . . . put him in chains and cruelly put him to death in this way: they dressed him in the armour of three men and set him on a horse which was tied to four stakes, according to their custom, and they put so much wood around it that they could barely see horse or man, and then they set fire to the wood and burned God's elect knight to death in the resulting furnace. This was done as an offering to the heathen gods for their victory.[3]

After their devastating defeat at the hands of Samogitians and Semigallians at the Battle of Saulė in 1236, the Livonian Brotherhood of the Sword was subsumed by the Teutonic Order, thereafter operating as a semiautonomous branch known as the Livonian Order. The Crusader states of the Baltic were now united. After their northern march was checked by St. Alexander Nevsky at the Battle on the Ice in 1242, they turned their attention to the southeast and set their sights on the Grand Duchy of Lithuania.

However noble their initial aims of protecting pilgrims and comforting the sick, by the fourteenth century the Teutonic Order had grown into a distorted parody of itself. Its grand masters made war on Christians and pagans indiscriminately, acting to further the territory and privileges of the Order rather than to further the gospel.

The Order's own chroniclers followed Bernard of Clairvaux in justifying the Brothers' bloodshed in the name of spiritual warfare. In the end, their efforts to convert the Prussians, Samogitians, and Lithuanians were never really successful—at least not in the ways that they intended. All of these people would eventually convert to Christianity, more in spite of the Teutonic Order than because of it. Even after their forced conversion, the Prussians would spend centuries revolting against the Order until the time of the Protestant Reformation, when the Order was finally ousted.

---

3   von Jeroschin, *Chronicle of Prussia*, 272.

CHAPTER 9

Christianization

THE PRESSURE EXERTED ON THE Grand Duchy of Lithuania by the Teutonic and Livonian Orders is a key piece of context for understanding the Lithuanian conversion in 1387. Algirdas, whose pagan priests had executed the Three Holy Martyrs of Vilnius, had married two different Orthodox wives, both of whom had borne him offspring.

In 1377, Algirdas's son Jogaila succeeded him as grand duke. The kingdom he inherited looked very different than it had in his grandfather Gediminas's time: It was a vast, sprawling territory—almost two different countries. The power of the Gediminid Dynasty was centered in Lithuania proper in the northwest, with the vast Ruthenian territories of the former Kyivan Rus' in the south and east. It was a land of Orthodox Christians in the east and Roman Catholics in the west, ruled over mostly by pagans. But what would Jogaila, the son of an Orthodox mother and a pagan father, become?

Jogaila was an ambitious man of naturally abstemious tendencies. Historian Daniel Stone tells us that, "He drank no alcohol and ate lightly except at occasional banquets. Hunting was his favorite activity and he also liked music, especially by Ruthenian fiddlers."[1] And the kingdom he inherited seemed doomed to be torn apart by civil war.

His uncle and junior coruler Duke Kęstutis, based out of the city of Trakai, was responsible, during the time of Algirdas, for defending the realm against

---

1   Stone, *The Polish-Lithuanian State*, 8.

the Teutonic and Livonian Orders. Under increasing pressure from the Crusader kingdoms, he began opening negotiations with the pope to convert to Christianity (thus, he thought, giving the Crusader orders no further quarrel with him) in exchange for a crown.

The intermediary for these negotiations was the Polish King Casimir III. Before a deal could be done, he took advantage of the opportunity in 1349 unexpectedly to attack the Grand Duchy in its Ruthenian lands, ruining Kęstutis's plan.

In 1361, Kęstutis was captured at the age of sixty in a skirmish after defeating two Teutonic knights in battle. Later, with the help of his brother Algirdas and a servant, he escaped imprisonment in one of the Order's castles by boring a hole through the three-meter-thick walls of Marienburg (Malbork) Castle (still the largest castle in the world). Kęstutis was no one to trifle with.

After the death of Algirdas in 1377, Jogaila decided to buy himself some time by signing a secret treaty with the Teutonic and Livonian Orders, in which he agreed not to interfere while they waged war on his uncle Kęstutis and cousins. This is one of the most controversial moments of Jogaila's life. Historians have pointed out that there was a fifty-year gap between the uncle and nephew, and that Jogaila was open to Christianity (unlike Kęstutis, a dedicated pagan) and needed his western front secure so that he could focus on his war with the Grand Duchy of Moscow.

Kęstutis found out about the secret agreement. While Jogaila was away, he marched on Vilnius and took it, then had Jogaila captured as he returned to the city. The octogenarian Kęstutis then resumed his war on his old enemies, the Teutonic Order. While he was away fighting, the citizens of Vilnius freed Jogaila, and uncle and nephew marched to face each other in battle.

But the battle never happened. The kinsmen agreed to negotiate the night before the battle, and Kęstutis and his son Vytautas rode to Jogaila's castle at Kreva in modern Belarus under a flag of truce. But it was a trap—they were taken prisoner, and five days later Kęstutis was found dead, strangled in his cell. His son Vytautas, truly the image of his father, escaped to fight another day, making his way under cover of night dressed as a woman.

Kęstutis would prove to be the last of Lithuania's great pagan dukes, and he is something of a folk hero to this day. His deeds have been the subject of symphonic overtures and short stories, and there are monuments to him even as far away as Russia.

Vytautas fought on, escaping from the clutches of his cousin into the waiting arms of the Teutonic Order. Over the next two years Vytautas led a perilous existence, mired in constant treaty negotiations between Jogaila and the Order. During this time, Vytautas—the son of Lithuania's last pagan duke and a famously beautiful pagan priestess—received Roman Catholic baptism and the name Wigand.

Upon reconciling with Jogaila, however, Vytautas abandoned the Order and returned to Lithuania. It appears that during this time, Vytautas—who seems to have had sympathy and admiration for Orthodox Christianity and would later marry his only daughter off to the Grand Prince of Moscow—converted, at least for a time, to the Orthodox Church.

It's difficult to speculate what the young duke's motivations might have been for converting. Cynically, we might say he was hedging his bets. There was a large Orthodox majority in Lithuanian lands at this time, and as an Orthodox ruler Vytautas would be able to build alliances with the powerful grand princes of Moscow, who had just broken the power of the Mongol Golden Horde in the region and were now on the rise.

A more charitable reading—borne out somewhat by Vytautas's later efforts to bring East and West together as grand duke—is that he really found something beautiful and compelling in the Orthodox Faith. But the very idea that medieval people compartmentalized their choices between "politics" and "religion" in this manner is probably anachronistic. After all, people are complicated and usually have more than one reason for doing things—reasons not always known even to themselves at the time.

In any case, Vytautas did not remain Orthodox for long. His cousin, Jogaila, was about to make a decision that would forever change the course of Lithuanian history—he was about to get married.

The Union of Krewo

IN 1387, GRAND DUKE JOGAILA faced a difficult choice: The Teutonic Order was offering him a treaty that would, among other things, mean his conversion to Roman Catholicism. Converting to Roman Catholicism at the hands of the most hated enemies of Lithuania might get the Order off his back, but it would likely mean a revolt among his own people. His mother, the Orthodox Christian Princess Uliana of Tver, encouraged him to marry Sophia, the daughter of St. Dimitry of the Don. This would have required Jogaila to convert to Orthodox Christianity—but the crusading orders saw the Orthodox as heretics little better than pagans, and this move would have meant a protracted conflict with the Teutonic Order.

Jogaila found a third way. The Polish crown was currently undergoing its own dynastic crisis, and he saw a way out of both of their difficulties. The Polish King Louis I of Hungary had died without sons, and his elder daughter Mary was rejected by the Polish nobility because they did not wish to continue union with Hungary, which led to civil war. The younger daughter, Jadwiga, was eventually crowned with the title King of Poland (not Queen) in Krakow in 1384 at just eleven years old, the title emphasizing her right to rule.

She was briefly betrothed to the Habsburg Duke of Austria, but he was intercepted by Polish nobles who rejected him. So she still needed a husband, and Poland was not yet at peace. Some of the Polish nobles looked to Lithuania.

Thus, on August 14, 1385, at the Lithuanian grand duke's residence of Kreva (in Polish, *Krewo*) in modern-day Belarus, Jogaila signed the Union of Krewo:

Although there have been many emperors, kings, and various princes who have striven, aspired, and desired to contract perpetual relationships with this same Grand Duke of Lithuania, almighty God has preserved any such deed until the present day for thine own very royal majesty. Therefore, may thy majesty, most serene princess, for this most salvific plan, acknowledge that same, lord and Grand Duke, as your son, and consent that he be joined into lawful matrimony with thine own most beloved daughter, the most illustrious princess Jadwiga, queen of Poland. For we do believe that divine glory, the salvation of souls, honour for the people, and growth of the Kingdom shall ensue from this.

However, before the matter mentioned here comes to fruition, Jogaila, Grand Duke, shall first, together with all his brethren who have not yet been baptized, and likewise with his relatives, the nobles, and land-owners great and small who reside in his lands, earnestly seek and desire to accept the Catholic faith of the Holy Roman Church. And although many an emperor and sundry princes laboured toward this end, they attained very little, notwithstanding their strenuous endeavours. Nevertheless, God almighty has reserved this honour for thine own royal majesty. . . .

Done in Krewo, Monday, on the eve of the Assumption of the glorious blessed virgin Mary, in the year of our Lord 1385.[2]

It was essentially an elaborate prenuptial agreement by which he agreed to settle some of Poland's diplomatic difficulties by converting to Roman Catholicism, making Roman Catholicism the official religion for the Lithuanian nobility, and attaching the Grand Duchy to the Polish state—all in exchange for marrying the young monarch Jadwiga of Poland and taking the Polish crown. Jadwiga was just twelve years old. The two married the following February 15, 1386, and Jogaila held the scepters of both King of Poland and Grand Duke of Lithuania.

THE UNION OF KREWO IS a watershed moment in Lithuanian history. Although Jogaila (now Władysław II Jagiełło, King of Poland) was baptized Roman Catholic (as were his brothers and his cousin), he did not attempt to convert his people by the sword as the Teutonic Order had done. Jogaila personally translated the Lord's Prayer and the Apostles' Creed into Lithuanian, and a number of enthusiastic (some said overly hasty) baptisms were held. What was more, the Polish and Lithuanian nations were now joined in a personal union that would eventually become known as the Polish-Lithuanian Commonwealth, a powerful state that endured into the twilight years of the eighteenth century.

But Jogaila's problems were far from over. Vytautas, never one to sit on his hands, almost immediately initiated a civil war with his cousin, one that ultimately saw him installed in Vilnius as Grand Duke of Lithuania under Jogaila's overlordship. With his ascent to grand duke, he became known to Lithuanian history as *Vytautas Didysis*—Vytautas the Great.

If Jogaila thought that his quarrels with the Teutonic Order would end with his conversion to Roman Catholicism, however, he couldn't have been more wrong. We will discuss more about that later. For now our pilgrimage brings us to a castle.

---

2   Korecki and Steele, *Union of Krewo*.

CHAPTER 10

Trakai

REMEMBER KĘSTUTIS, JOGAILA'S SWASHBUCKLING UNCLE who unhorsed Teutonic knights and escaped from Europe's most secure castle at the ripe old age of sixty? He was the Duke of Trakai, and Trakai would continue to have a special importance for his son Vytautas after his death. It was here that his project of trying to reunite East and West would come the closest to being accomplished, resulting in one of the most multicultural cities of medieval Europe.

Trakai itself was first established by the Grand Duke Gediminas, before he founded Vilnius. A place of deep natural beauty, Trakai is almost hidden, a peninsula of land surrounded by three deep glacial lakes. Gediminas and his son Kęstutis built a series of castles in the area, the most famous of which is the Trakai Island Castle.

Trakai Island Castle

DURING OUR PILGRIMAGE WE VISITED Trakai and its island castle, one of the most popular tourist destinations in the country. And although it is restored and beautiful today, it was only a few decades ago that it was in ruins.

Construction began on the island castle in the fourteenth century as part of Kęstutis's overall plan to harden Trakai's fortifications against attacks from the Teutonic Order. After his assassination, his son Vytautas continued the project, even (during his brief truce with the Order) enlisting the Teutonic

Order's stonemasons and engineers to help him finish the fortifications. It continued to serve as an important military outpost right up until the Battle of Grunwald, which we will discuss soon.

In the sixteenth century, no longer of military importance, the castle was damaged and not rebuilt, eventually becoming the object of romantic poetry and painting by the nineteenth century. It was not rebuilt until the decades of the 1950s and 1960s, when the Soviet occupiers permitted its restoration as a symbol of resistance against German invaders.

Try to imagine for a moment the beauty of the castle. It is a castle of orange and red bricks nestled among evergreens, with pointed Gothic towers adorning its corners and its keep. The island is in the middle of Lake Galvė, which is deep blue and still and smooth as glass. Sailboats and bevies of swans glide across the deep azure waters, the silence and tranquility of the moment broken only by the chatter of tourists and an old man playing a concertina for tips on the bridge outside of the castle.

As we walked through the castle, all three of us pilgrims agreed that we were "living our best medieval life." Father Andrew couldn't believe he was finally there, Richard was ready to "Errol Flynn" the drawbridge, and Evangelia gathered images for story writing.

IT TOOK VYTAUTAS A WHILE after his civil war with his cousin before he was able to get Trakai back. When he did, it became his favorite residence. After the Battle of Grunwald, when the waning power of the Teutonic Order meant that Trakai was no longer needed as a center of military power, the castle was remade into a residence for the grand duke. King Jogaila frequently visited his cousin there, and adorned the castle with art and rich furnishings.

Speaking of art—you might remember how in chapter 3 we mentioned that there was only ever one Orthodox grand duke, whose name was Vaišvilkas. As it happens, that's only mostly true. As we mentioned earlier, Vytautas converted, at least very briefly, to Orthodox Christianity. Underlying this fact is the complicated question of the schism between Roman Catholicism and the Orthodox Church in this land on the borders of East and West.

Vytautas's parents were pagans, but Jogaila's mother and even his last wife were Orthodox Christians. At various times, they had close relationships with the Orthodox Christian Metropolitans of Kyiv and All Rus', and even corresponded with the Eastern Roman emperors—the Byzantines. With the Mongols and Tatars at their door and the power of the Grand Princes of Moscow on the rise, Jogaila and Vytautas were better positioned than most of the princes of Latin Europe to appreciate the advantages of reuniting the two churches. We will discuss what they did about that in another chapter.

This openness extended not only to their political and religious policies but also to their projects of culture building and beautification. For his part, Jogaila introduced the beauty of Eastern iconography and architecture to Poland, lending Polish Christianity a unique blend of Eastern and Western aesthetics that endures to this day. Vytautas included Byzantine-style frescoes and icons both in his personal residence at the Trakai Island Castle as well as in the historic Trakai Cathedral.

Our Lady of Trakai

IN 1409, VYTAUTAS THE GREAT built a new church in Trakai. The Church of the Visitation of the Blessed Virgin Mary currently holds the rank of basilica in the Roman Catholic Church. The feast to which it is dedicated is itself a unique confluence of East and West.

The feast was first brought to the West in the thirteenth or fourteenth century by Franciscan monks who had been present in an Orthodox church at the Feast of the Placing of the Honorable Robe of the Most Holy Mother of God at Blachernae. This Byzantine feast, which has for its Gospel reading the passage in which Mary visits Elizabeth, the occasion of the Magnificat (Luke 1:39–56), was the inspiration for the Latin feast that was originally held on the same date—July 2.

The Visitation of the Blessed Virgin Mary was added to the Roman calendar by Pope Urban VI in 1389, in hopes that the Mother of God would by her intercessions bring to an end what is sometimes called the Great Western Schism—a time when there were two and even three rival papacies in Western Europe. That schism was brought to an official end at the Council of Constance in 1414–18, a council that Vytautas and Jogaila attended.

In this light, the dedication of Vytautas's church to the Visitation may be seen as a deliberate statement about his hopes of restoring church unity, not just within the Roman Catholic Church but between East and West. These hopes were nowhere better represented than in an icon housed in that church, a wonder-working icon of the Theotokos known as Our Lady of Trakai.

WHEN VYTAUTAS BUILT THE CHURCH of the Visitation of the Blessed Virgin Mary in Trakai, he himself donated a splendid icon of the Theotokos to serve as the altarpiece: *Trakai Marija,* Our Lady of Trakai. It is said that this icon had been a gift to Vytautas from the Eastern Roman Emperor Manuel Paleologos II on the occasion of his baptism—it is not told which baptism it was, for Vytautas was baptized on three separate occasions.

It may be that it was a gift to commemorate what would turn out to be his brief reception into the Orthodox Faith. The back of the icon bears an inscription commemorating the gift but also bears the original name of the icon: *Theotokos Nikopeia*—"Theotokos the Victorious." Some say it was this very icon that was carried into battle by Emperor John II Comnenus against the Persians in the twelfth century.

Soon after its installation in the church in Trakai, the Mother of God began to work many miracles through her holy icon. It thus became the first and oldest of the several wonder-working images of the Theotokos that grace the land of Lithuania.

In 1603, a plague swept through Lithuania. In hopes of ending the plague, the people of Trakai carried the holy icon on foot from Trakai to Vilnius, singing and asking for the Virgin's intercessions as they went. To mark the miraculous end of the plague through her prayers, this pilgrimage is still held annually to this day.

In 1629, Bishop Eustachijus Valavicius wrote that "God has favored us with many miraculous portraits in Lithuania of Our Lady, but the many miracles at the Shrine of Our Lady of Trakai brought many people closer to each other and to their God."[1] In 1643, for instance, a small boy drowned in Lake

---

1   Markus, "History of Our Lady of Trakai."

Galvė, and the parents brought the child's body to the altar of the church and set him before the icon of the Theotokos. Through her prayers the boy returned to life.

Over the centuries, many collections of the miracles attributed to the Theotokos through this holy icon have been written and published. Each year on September 8, the Nativity of the Theotokos, pilgrims gather to make the eighteen-mile journey on foot from the Church of the Visitation in Trakai to the Gate of Dawn in Vilnius.

Roman Catholics, Orthodox Christians, and even some Muslims venerate Our Lady of Trakai, Lithuania's first and oldest wonder-working icon. Through this icon, she serves as the protectress not only of Trakai and Lithuania but of any who in faith ask for her help.

Karaites and Tatars

WE HAVE MAINLY DEALT WITH the intersection (and sometimes clash) of pagan, Roman Catholic, and Orthodox Christian cultures. But these weren't the only cultures in Lithuania in the late medieval period. Trakai specifically was known, even in the Middle Ages, as a truly multicultural city, one in which pagans, Roman Catholics, and Orthodox Christians might find themselves alongside two other important ethnic groups—Karaite Jews and Crimean Tatars.

Before we can tell you who these people are and how they came to be living in Trakai, we need to understand a little about how medieval cities worked. For that, we need to talk about Magdeburg.

The *Magdeburger Recht*, or Magdeburg Rights or Magdeburg Laws, were a set of what are sometimes called "town privileges" first instituted in the Holy Roman Empire by Emperor Otto I. These laws were important for a few reasons. First of all, they created a system, including courts of appeal, by which cities could function as self-governing entities. They protected the trade rights of local trade guilds as well as the rights to trade, property ownership, and something like due process for ethnic and religious minorities such as the Jews. Under the Magdeburg Laws, for instance, Jews could not be compelled to inform on themselves or others if accused of a crime.

These laws were responsible for the development of the great medieval cities of northwestern Europe during this period. Trakai, which was Grand Duke Vytautas's de facto capital, was the first Lithuanian city to be granted a charter under the Magdeburg Laws. Under that charter, the Karaite Jews and the Crimean Tatars were given their own quarters in the city and protection under the law.

As we walked the streets of Trakai, we entered its historic Karaite quarter, the place of "those who read," which is the meaning of *Karajlar* (Heb. *Karaim*), their name in their own language. Strolling through their neighborhood, our guide Fr. Gintaras explained to us who the Karaites were and why they're so important to the history of Trakai.

Karaite Jews are a sect of Judaism defined by a rigorous adherence to the Hebrew Scriptures as the supreme and final authority for Jewish law and theology. This approach is in contrast to most forms of rabbinical Judaism, which recognize some form of oral tradition or "Oral Torah," codified in the Talmud and subsequent works, as binding. The Karaites thus do not use the Talmud.

In fact, the Karaite approach to the Hebrew Scriptures bears a striking similarity to the much later Protestant doctrine of Sola Scriptura, a fact that did not go unnoticed by German reformers some seven hundred years after the Karaite movement was founded. Although officially originating in the early ninth century in Baghdad under the Abbasid Caliphate, there are those who trace the roots of the movement all the way back to the Sadducees of the Second Temple period.

By the fifteenth century, there were Karaites in the Crimea, that northern peninsula jutting out into the Black Sea. The Crimean Karaites were Turkic-speaking converts to Karaite Judaism, and according to their own legends, they were relocated to Lithuania as a reward for helping Vytautas the Great in a successful campaign against the Mongol Golden Horde.

In fact, there is ample evidence to suggest they were already in Lithuania, particularly in Trakai and Vilnius, before the time of Vytautas, but that certainly doesn't rule out the possibility that they helped Vytautas in his campaign. What is known is that Vytautas valued both the Karaites and the related Crimean ethnic and religious group, the Tatars. He valued them so much, in fact, that he guaranteed their protection under the law, and exempted them from taxes even the Christian nobility had to pay.

THE TATARS OF CRIMEA WERE a Turkic-speaking ethnic group originating in the northeastern Gobi Desert in the fifth century, but by the fifteenth century they were an amalgam of most of the various tribes and people groups that had inhabited the Crimea during the previous centuries—Tauri, Scythians, Sarmatians, Alans, Greeks, Goths, Bulgars, Khazars, Pechenegs, Cumans, Italians, and Circassians.

They were part of both the Mongol Empire and its successor state, the Golden Horde, the latter of which struggled with both the Grand Duchy of Lithuania and the Princes of Muscovy and Novgorod over the lands that are today Belarus and Ukraine. This region, sometimes referred to as the "wild east" of Europe during the fifteenth and sixteenth centuries, would see various waves of Tatar settlement—first pagan Tatars, seeking refuge from Muslim persecution, and then later Sunni Muslim Tatars who settled in the region.

The Tatars were a fierce, pusillanimous people, according to medieval historians such as Michalo Lituanus (Michael the Lithuanian), the Lithuanian envoy to the Khanate of Crimea from 1537–1539, who wrote about them in a book called *De moribus tartarorum, lituanorum et moscorum,* "On the Customs of the Tatars, Lithuanians and Muscovites."

After his campaigns against the Golden Horde, Vytautas the Great relocated a group of Tatar prisoners of war, along with their wives, children, and livestock to the area around Trakai. Some of these were given to his cousin, Jogaila, who had them christened as Roman Catholics. Others were allowed to keep their Sunni Muslim faith and gladly settled around Trakai and other Lithuanian cities, more than happy to avoid the wars of the steppes and the European "wild east."

Along with Karaite Jews, they became Vytautas's personal bodyguards. The practice of hiring a foreign bodyguard is an ancient one. Another notable historical example is the Varangian Guard of the Eastern Roman Emperors, Germanic warriors guarding the Byzantine monarchs. The basic idea is simple: Since these are foreigners, they don't owe anything to anyone except the ruler who brought them there, and have nothing to gain by turning on him and betraying him.

The Tatars and Karaites were famed for their loyalty to Vytautas. In Trakai to this day, the houses on *Karaimų gatvė* (Karaite Street) have three windows facing the street. According to Karaite tradition, the windows stand for God, country, and the Grand Duke Vytautas. Today, the Karaite quarter of Trakai boasts one of the few remaining Karaite *kenesa*, or synagogues, in the world.

Richard: Military prowess wasn't the Karaite and Tatars' only contribution to Lithuanian culture: They also gave it some of its most distinctive foods! I have to say, when it comes to cuisine, the Lithuanians are my kind of people. But one of my favorite foods we ate while we were there isn't originally Lithuanian at all—it was brought there by the Tatars and Karaites. I am speaking, of course, of *kibinai* (Lithuanian) or *kybynlar* (Karaite). As our guide Fr. Gintaras pointed out, among all Jews, this dish is something only the Karaites eat, because of their unique understanding of kosher laws, which kybynlar would otherwise violate.

So what is kibinai? It's a kind of meat pasty. Whether or not the Karaites or Tatars came up with it first, the *kibin* or *kibinas* (as it is called in Lithuanian) has become synonymous for Lithuanians with the Karaite community and the city of Trakai.

There were many other dishes, including a kind of traditional chicken soup, which the Karaites were known for. On Fridays, the day before the Jewish Sabbath when no cooking was allowed, the streets of Trakai would fill with the smells of the Karaites cooking. The Lithuanian Karaite poet and clergyman Simonas Firkovičius composed a song about the sensation of walking down this street on a Friday evening:

> To fly to Trakai like a bird
> My heart wishes it so,
> When my nose is tickled by
> The smells of Friday.
>
> On the island there is a castle,
> The fortress of Vytautas,

The noodle tweaks its moustache,
The smells of Friday.

Son of Karaim, follow
The tradition of your ancestors.
Let the smells of Friday
Make you stronger.[2]

Many of the civilizations of Central and Eastern Europe have a very similar dish to kibinai. In fact, I grew up among many Chinese and Taiwanese relatives, and one of my favorite foods was (and remains) the *gyoza*, a very similar concept (though the dough is of a very different consistency, and it is usually served in a sauce). All of this has led me to a single conclusion: The ultimate measure of a civilization, and the sum total of human art and culture, is its ability to put meat inside bread.

---

2   Firkovičius, "Ijisi baraśkiniń."

CHAPTER 11

The Battle of Grunwald

IN THE PREVIOUS CHAPTERS, YOU read about the long-running conflict between the Lithuanians and the Teutonic and Livonian Orders. With the Union of Krewo, Jogaila united the Polish and Lithuanian crowns and set the course for Lithuania to adopt Roman Catholicism as its official religion. He did so at least partly hoping that a conversion to Roman Catholicism would take Lithuania off the board as a target for the Orders' crusading activities.

It did not. They denounced Jogaila's baptism and those of his subjects as phony, called his marriage to the Polish queen illegitimate, and to make a long story short, the newly baptized Jogaila and Vytautas once again found themselves at war with Roman Catholic Crusaders.

The trigger this time was an uprising in Samogitia (Lith. *Žemaitija*), the western coastlands of Lithuania, which at the time had been ceded to the Teutonic Order. Poland and Lithuania took the Samogitians' side, and rival powers in the region (including the Hungarians and Bohemians) took sides. At one point, Vytautas was even offered the Lithuanian crown in return for betraying his cousin.

His resolve held firm, however, and Vytautas and Jogaila combined their forces, preparing for a joint march on the Castle of Marienburg, the capital of the Teutonic Order, located in northern Poland, from which Kęstutis had escaped in 1361. The Teutonic Order prepared to meet them near a place called the "green wood"—Grunwald, in Lithuanian, *Žalgiris*.

THE GRAND MASTER OF THE Teutonic Order began the battle by sending a pair of messengers to Vytautas and Jogaila with a gift of two swords, along with a message intended to egg the cousins on to battle:

> Your Majesty! The Grand Master Ulryk sends you and your brother . . . through us, the deputies standing here, two swords for help so that you, with him and his army, may delay less and may fight more boldly than you have shown, and also that you will not continue hiding and staying in the forest and groves, and will not postpone the battle. And if you believe that you have too little space to form your ranks, the Prussian master Ulryk, to entice you to battle, will withdraw from the plain which he took for his army, as far as you want, or you may instead choose any field of battle so that you do not postpone the battle any longer.[1]

Jogaila responded: "We accept the swords you send us, and in the name of Christ, before whom all stiff-necked pride must bow, we shall do battle."[2]

As we shall see, the grand master's pride would come back to bite him, and the whole Battle of Grunwald would become a famous allegory for the victory of humility over pride. The Bohemian reformer Jan Hus wrote to King Jogaila in 1411 to congratulate him on his victory in the battle:

> Where, then, are the two swords of the enemies? They were indeed cut down with those swords with which they tried to terrify the humble! Behold, they sent you two swords, the swords of violence and of pride, and have lost many thousands of them, having been utterly defeated.[3]

The "Grunwald Swords," as they were called, became part of the Polish crown jewels and important Polish and Lithuanian symbols of resistance against tyranny. They would later be used in this way by anti-Nazi and anti-Soviet resistance fighters during the twentieth century. Today, a monument to King Jogaila—King Władysław II Jagiełło, as he is known to the Poles—stands in

---

1   Mikos, *Polish Literature.*
2   Davies, *God's Playground*, 98.
3   Hus, *The Letters of Jan Hus.*

New York City's Central Park. Jogaila has the two swords of Grunwald raised aloft, a symbol of defiance against the tyrants of the ages.

The Story of the Battle

USING TACTICS LEARNED FROM HIS enemies the Mongols, Vytautas used a feigned retreat to draw off part of the Teutonic Order's forces, while Jogaila and the Polish army engaged with Grand Master Ulrich von Jungingen, who personally led sixteen banners—a full third of the Crusader force—against the Polish right flank. Just as it seemed the Teutonic Knights might win the day, Vytautas returned to the battlefield, attacking von Jungingen from the rear. Surrounded, von Jungingen attempted to hack his way through the Lithuanian lines, but the grand master was pierced through the neck by a lance and instantly slain.

The Battle of Grunwald was the beginning of the end of the Teutonic and Livonian Orders. Although they'd have more conflicts with the Polish-Lithuanian Union in the years to come, their territory shrinks from this point onward. By 1454, the Teutonic Order had been ousted from Poland.

Many tales have been told about the Battle of Grunwald. For Poles and Lithuanians, it is a moment of great national pride. For German nationalists of the twentieth century, it was an example of how cowardly Slavs had betrayed and backstabbed the glorious Teutonic Order. But perhaps no retelling of the battle has been as important, or as artistically significant, as Jan Matejko's 1878 painting.

This painting, called simply *The Battle of Grunwald*, is a masterpiece of mythopoeia and shows how battles such as these are far more than mere historical events: They are powerful stories that shape the identities of those who live many centuries after they took place.

The painting is huge—ten feet high and nearly seventeen feet long. It depicts all of the most important events of the battle compressed into a single, violent, glorious moment. At the center of the whole piece is the Grand Duke Vytautas. He is portrayed in this painting as a wild, liminal figure, his clothing and battle gear half belonging to the "civilized west" (from the perspective of Matejko, who was Polish) and half to the "wild east" of Europe.

The small cross on the ducal crown of the neophyte duke contrasts strongly with the massive cross of the Teutonic banner behind his head, which is tilted and falling to the ground. Vytautas himself sits wildly in his saddle, holding his shield and sword aloft, his eyes blazing as though in a battle frenzy, reminiscent of his father, the last of Lithuania's great pagan warriors.

To the grand duke's right (our left as we look at the painting), we see the Teutonic Grand Master Ulrich von Jungingen. His horse is rearing, his sword and empty hand attempting to ward off one blow even as a lance is leveled at his neck. Here, Matejko brings together chronicle and legend.

A close look at the painting reveals that the lance with which the grand master is about to be slain is the lance of St. Maurice. More specifically, it is the copy of that lance that the emperor Otto II gave to Bolesław the Brave, the symbol of his mission to convert the Eastern Slavs. But the lance is not wielded by a Christian figure. It is wielded by a half-naked Lithuanian, or perhaps Samogitian, pagan. Above it all, Stanislaus, the Polish and Roman Catholic saint whose patronage included justice, moral order, and the chastisement of wicked rulers, watches with care, lending aid to the Polish and Lithuanian forces.

The message of this painting could not be clearer: The Teutonic Order, by attacking and oppressing the pagan Prussians, Lithuanians, and Samogitians rather than seeking their salvation, had failed in their Christian duty to the point that they now found themselves in battle with baptized Christian rulers. For this, they had to answer not just to the people they oppressed but to the saints and emperors whose mission they had betrayed.

Father Andrew: The story of history, including the story of Lithuania, includes many battles. As we study the story and try to grapple with its currents, it can be easy to become cynical. After all, the good guys often lose and the bad guys often win. And how do we even know who the good guys and bad guys are? History is, they say, written by the winners. Perhaps my good guys were actually the bad guys. Perhaps my chosen heroes of history were actually complex figures who had motivations with which I cannot sympathize.

Sometimes, the stories of a nation's past are turned to the purposes of ideological nationalism. Or sometimes ideology can turn religion into a weapon.

This phenomenon is perhaps no more sharply illustrated than with the tales of the northern Crusaders, who in the name of Christ thrust spears and swords into both pagans and Christians. They had lost the plot.

Even the names by which we call things, names arising out of various times, places, and contexts, can stir up ideology and violence: These Orthodox Christian people in the southern and eastern parts of the Grand Duchy of Lithuania—are they Rus', Ruthenians, Russians, Ukrainians, Belarusians? How one answers that question in our time can be the source of anger and even hatred.

But if there is anything that should be clear to us as Christians, it is this: History is complicated and should not be turned to ideological purposes. It should not be used to destroy, to crush the distinctiveness and personality of another person or another people.

The Crusaders lost the plot. They started out as guardians for pilgrims but transformed into an army with imperialistic impulses. As we try to make sense of the shifting borders of nation-states or even of ecclesiastical territories, we can also lose the plot.

In the history of Lithuania, East and West synthesize, and we see Christians in their better moments take whatever is near them and use it for the real gospel, the gospel of Jesus Christ, the gospel of peace. We also see those who take the trappings of the gospel and turn it into alienation, even into death. But if we keep our eyes fixed on Christ and on the works of His saints, on whatever is good, pure, honest, and holy, then we are in that great story, the story of God Himself.

History in the traditional sense is the story of a people. If we are Christian people, then how we read, tell, and understand history should always point to Christ.

Lithuania in Photos and Maps

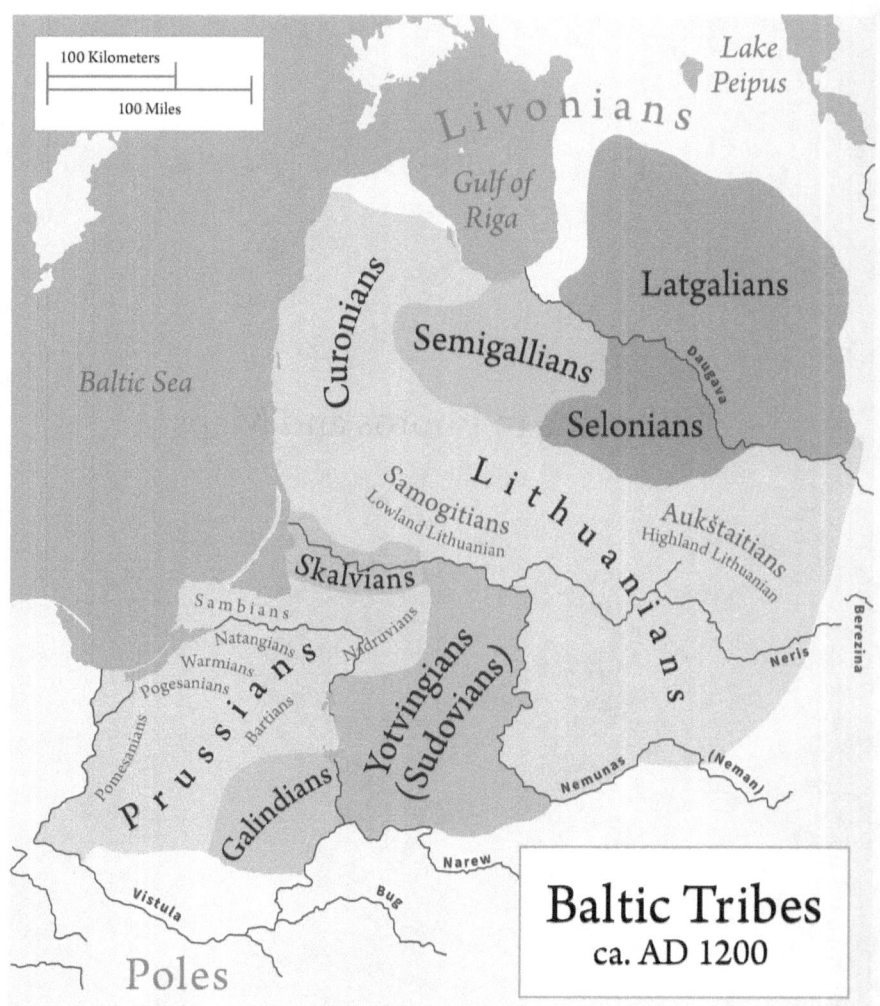

100 Kilometers

100 Miles

Lake
Peipus

L i v o n i a n s

Gulf of
Riga

Baltic Sea

Curonians

Semigallians

Latgalians

Daugava

Selonians

L i t h u a n i a n s

Samogitians
Lowland Lithuanian

Aukštaitians
Highland Lithuanian

Skalvians

Sambians

Nadruvians

Natangians

Warmians

Pogesanians

P r u s s i a n s

Bartians

Yotvingians
(Sudovians)

Neris

Berezina

Pomesanians

Galindians

Nemunas

(Neman)

Narew

Vistula

Bug

Poles

Baltic Tribes
ca. AD 1200

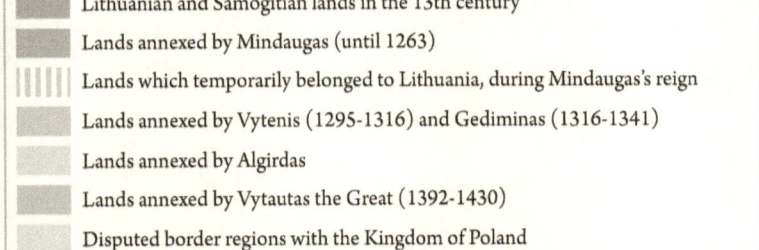

Baltic Sea

Tallinn/
Reval

Velikiy Novgorod

Livonia

Pskov

**Lands of Velikiy
Novgorod**

Riga

Tver

Šiauliai

Polatsk

Medvėgalis

Moscow ☆

Kaunas

Kernavė

Vitebsk

Smolensk

**Grand Duchy
of Moscow**

Königsberg

Vilnius

Trakai

Medininkai

**Teutonic
Order**

Lida

Kreva

Minsk

Bryansk

Hrodna

Novogrudok

Brest

Chernigov

Lublin

Lutsk

Kiev/Kyiv

Krakow

Kingdom of Poland

Poltava

Košice

Bratslav

**Kingdom of
Hungary**

Suceava
☆

*Crimean Khanate
(from the 15th century)*

Moldavia

Black Sea

Lithuanian State
in the
13th-15th Centuries

Lithuanian and Samogitian lands in the 13th century

Lands annexed by Mindaugas (until 1263)

Lands which temporarily belonged to Lithuania, during Mindaugas's reign

Lands annexed by Vytenis (1295-1316) and Gediminas (1316-1341)

Lands annexed by Algirdas

Lands annexed by Vytautas the Great (1392-1430)

Disputed border regions with the Kingdom of Poland

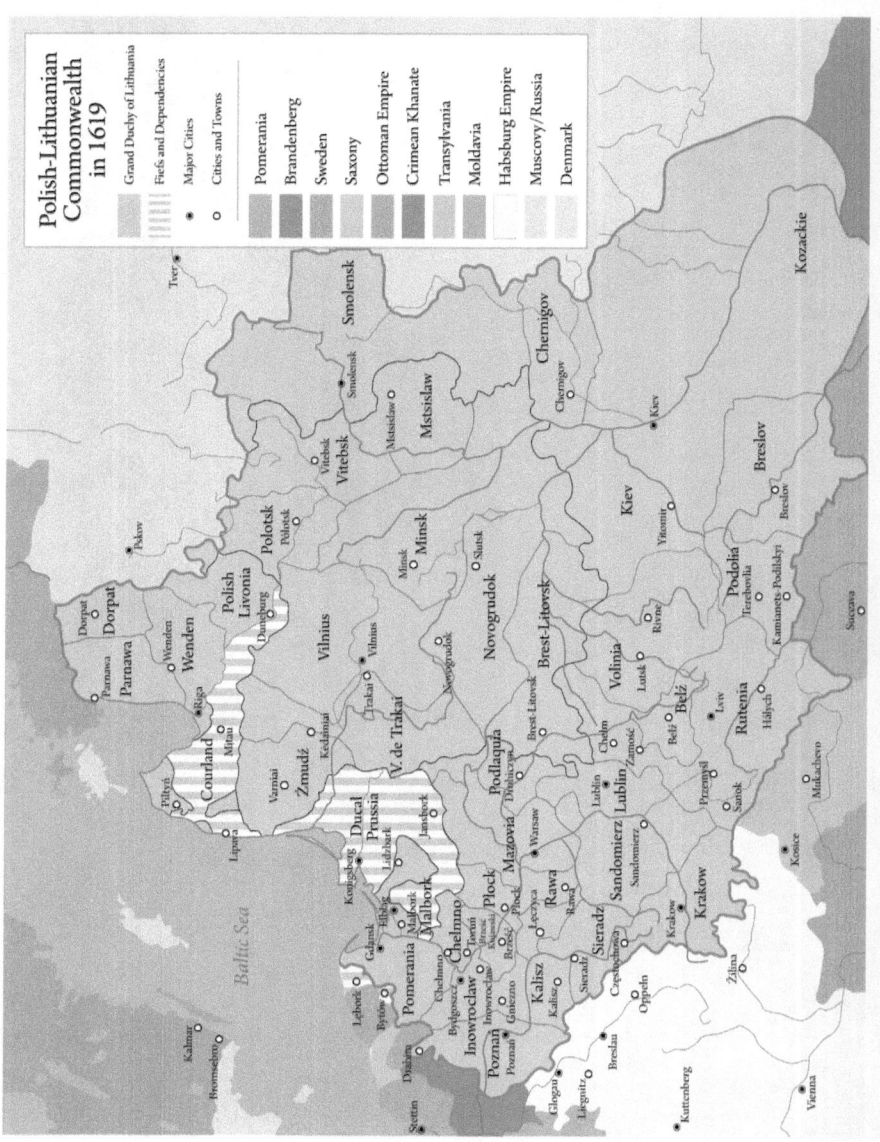

Polish-Lithuanian Commonwealth in 1619

Grand Duchy of Lithuania

Fiefs and Dependencies

● Major Cities

○ Cities and Towns

Pomerania

Brandenberg

Sweden

Saxony

Ottoman Empire

Crimean Khanate

Transylvania

Moldavia

Habsburg Empire

Muscovy/Russia

Denmark

Tver

Pskov

Smolensk
Smolensk

Vitebsk
Vitebsk

Mtsislav
Mtsislaw

Chernigov
Chernigow

Kiev

Breslov
Breslov

Polotsk
Połotsk

Minsk
Minsk

Slutsk

Kiev
Kiev

Zhytomir

Podolia
Kamieniec-Podilskyi
Iterebovlia

Suczaea

Kozackie

Dorpat
Dorpat

Parnawa
Parnawa

Wenden
Wenden

Polish Livonia

Dünaburg

Vilnius
Vilnius

Novogrudok
Novogrudok

Brest-Litovsk
Brest-Litovsk

Volhnia
Lutsk

Rivne

Belż
Belz

Ruthenia
Hålych

Matkachevo

Riga

Mitau

Courland

Lipau

Varniai

Żmudź
Zmudź

Kedainiai

Trakai
Vilnus

V. de Trakai

Novogrudok

Chełm
Zamość

Przemysl

Lviv

Sanok

Koszice

Baltic Sea

Kalmar

Bornholm

Szetin

Danzak

Bytóm

Leborč

Elbabnan

Bydgoszcz
Inowrocław
Inowrocław

Gnezno
Gnezno

Poznań
Poznań

Glogou
Lieguitz
Breslau

Königsberg

Elbing

Malbork
Malbork

Frombork

Ducal Prussia

Chełmno
Chełmno

Toruń
Toruń

Brześć
Brześć

Kcrzyca

Płock
Płock

Płock

Rawa
Rawa

Ravac

Mazovia

Warsaw

Jambork

Podlaquia
Drahinym

Lublin
Lublin

Sandomierz
Sandomierz

Sandomierz

Kalisz
Kalisz

Kalisz

Sieradz
Sieradz

Sieradz

Częstochowa

Ogrodin

Krakow
Krakow

Krakow

Zelina

Kattenberg

Vienna

User:Mathiasrex, based on layers of User:Halibutt, CC BY 3.0 <https://creativecommons.org/licenses/by/3.0>, via Wikimedia Commons

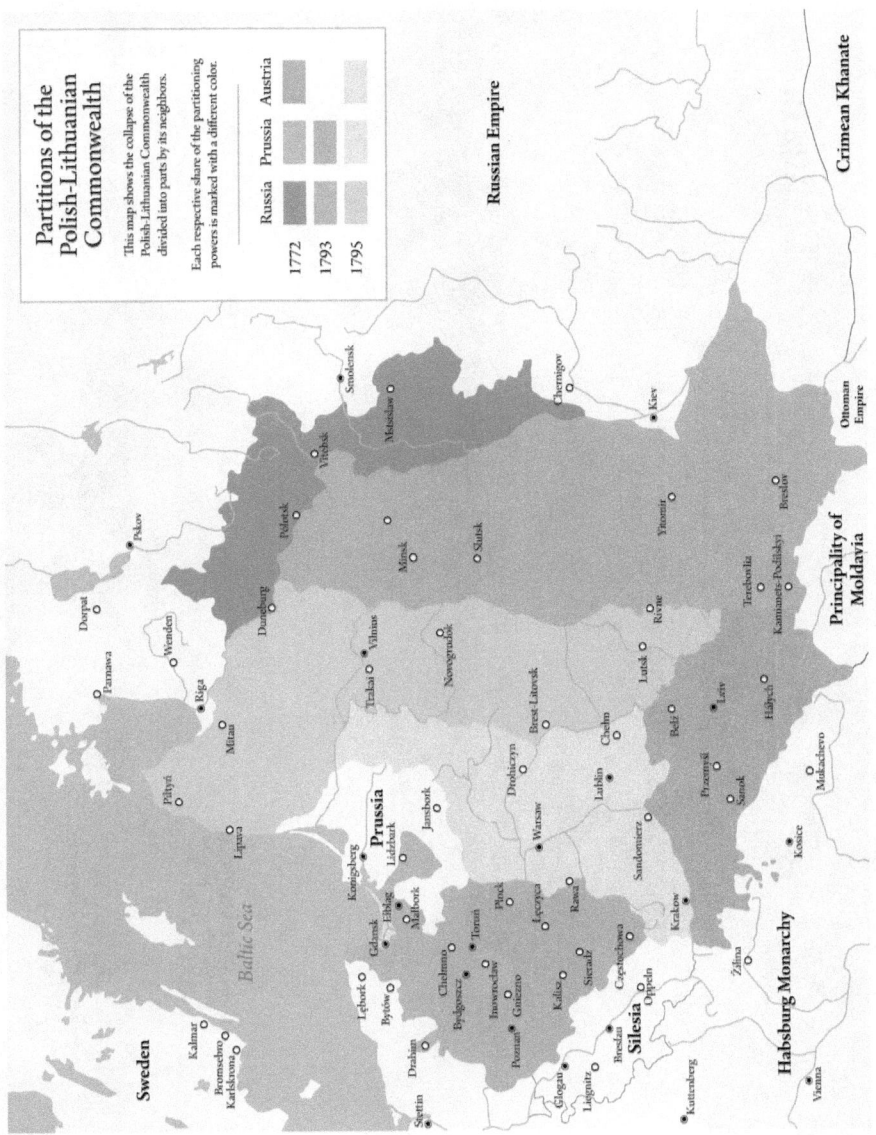

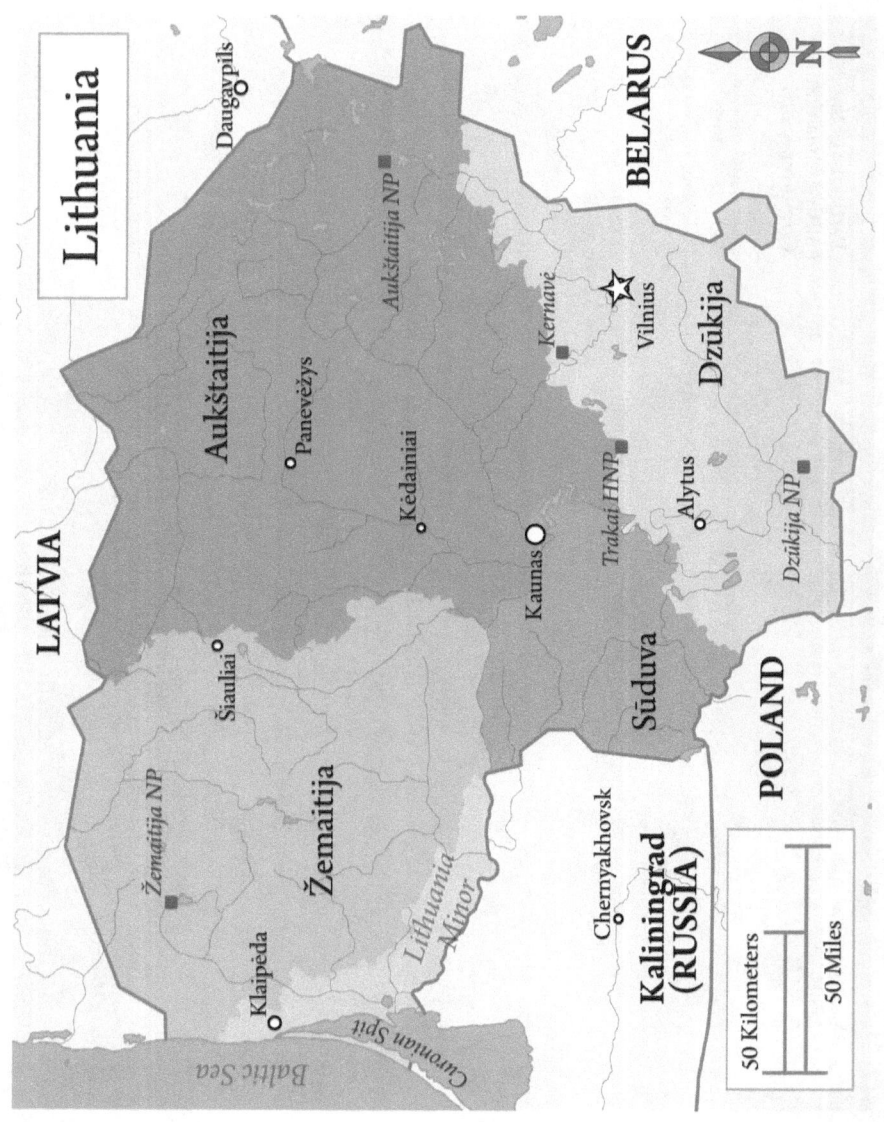

Photos from the Pilgrimage

Joy of All Who Sorrow Church, Druskininkai

Karaite Kenesa, Trakai

Father Andrew concelebrating the Divine Liturgy, Monastery of the Holy Spirit, Vilnius

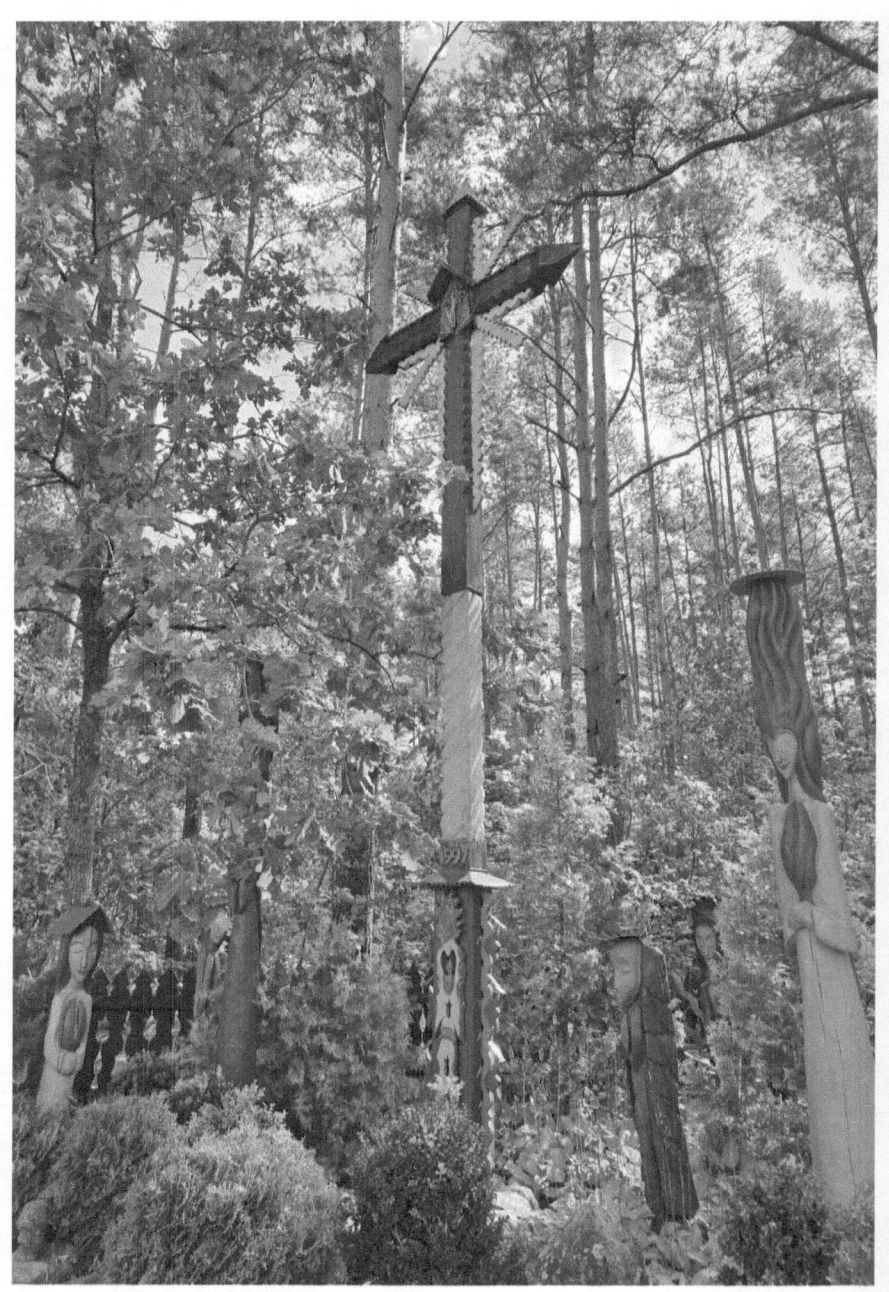

Carvings in a forest near Merkinė

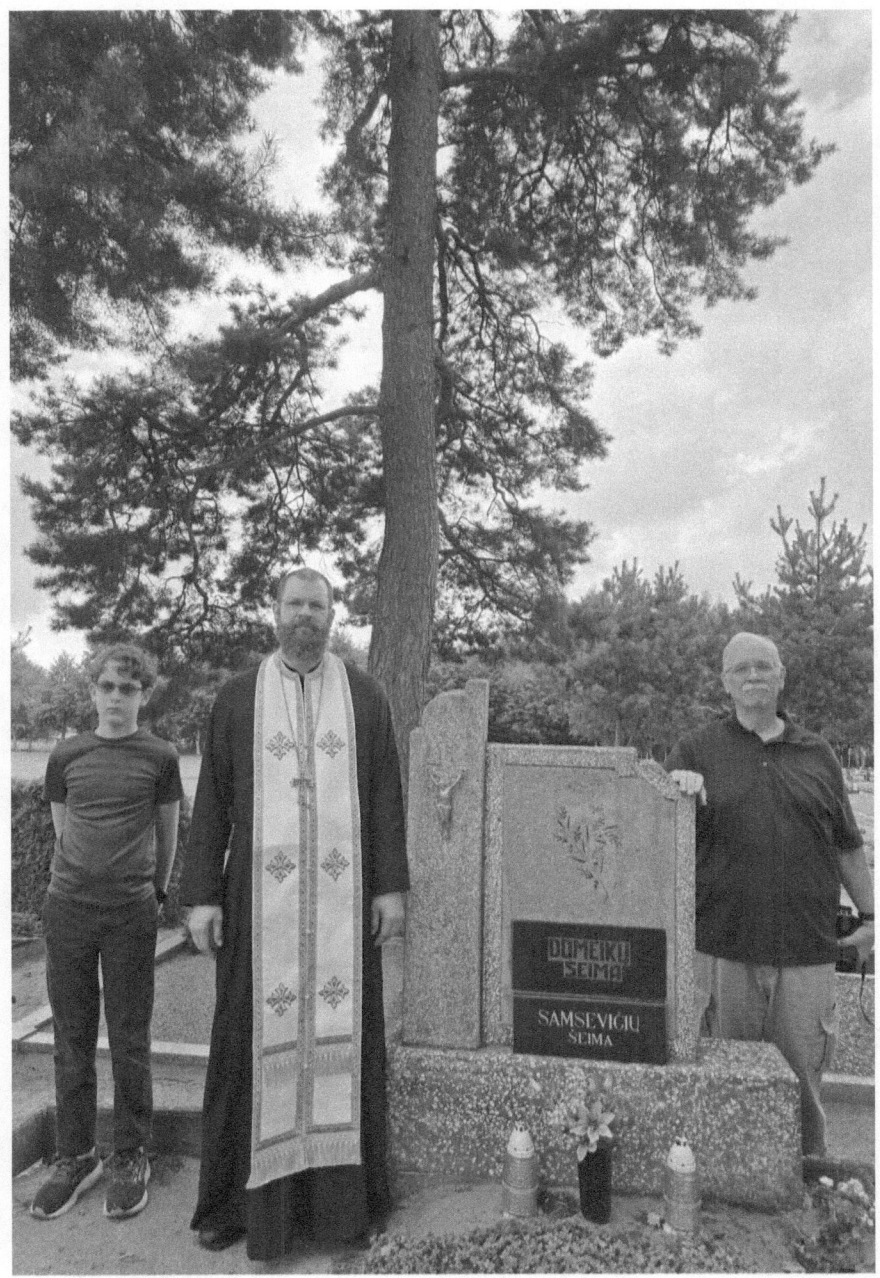

Father Andrew with his father Bill and son Raphael at Domeika grave,
Kudirkos Naumiestis

Father Andrew, his father Bill, and son Raphael meeting cousins in Dobele, Latvia

Father Andrew, his father Bill, and son Raphael with the Sungaila family, Trakai

Bill Damick being interviewed in Catholic Church of the Holy Cross, Kudirkos Naumiestis, the historic Domeika family parish

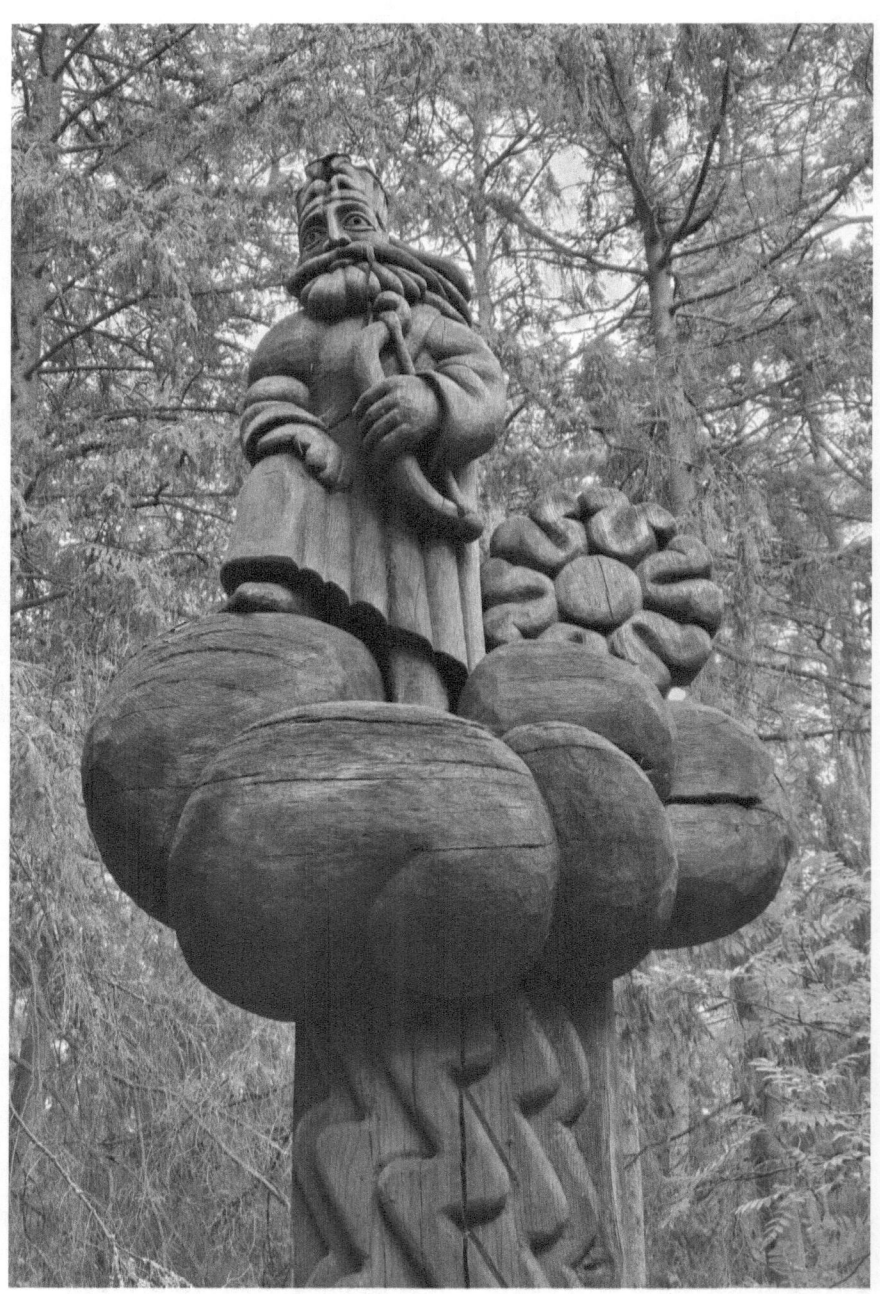

Carving of thunder-god Perkūnas, Curonian Spit

Carvings of St. George slaying the dragon, Curonian Spit

Trakai Island Castle

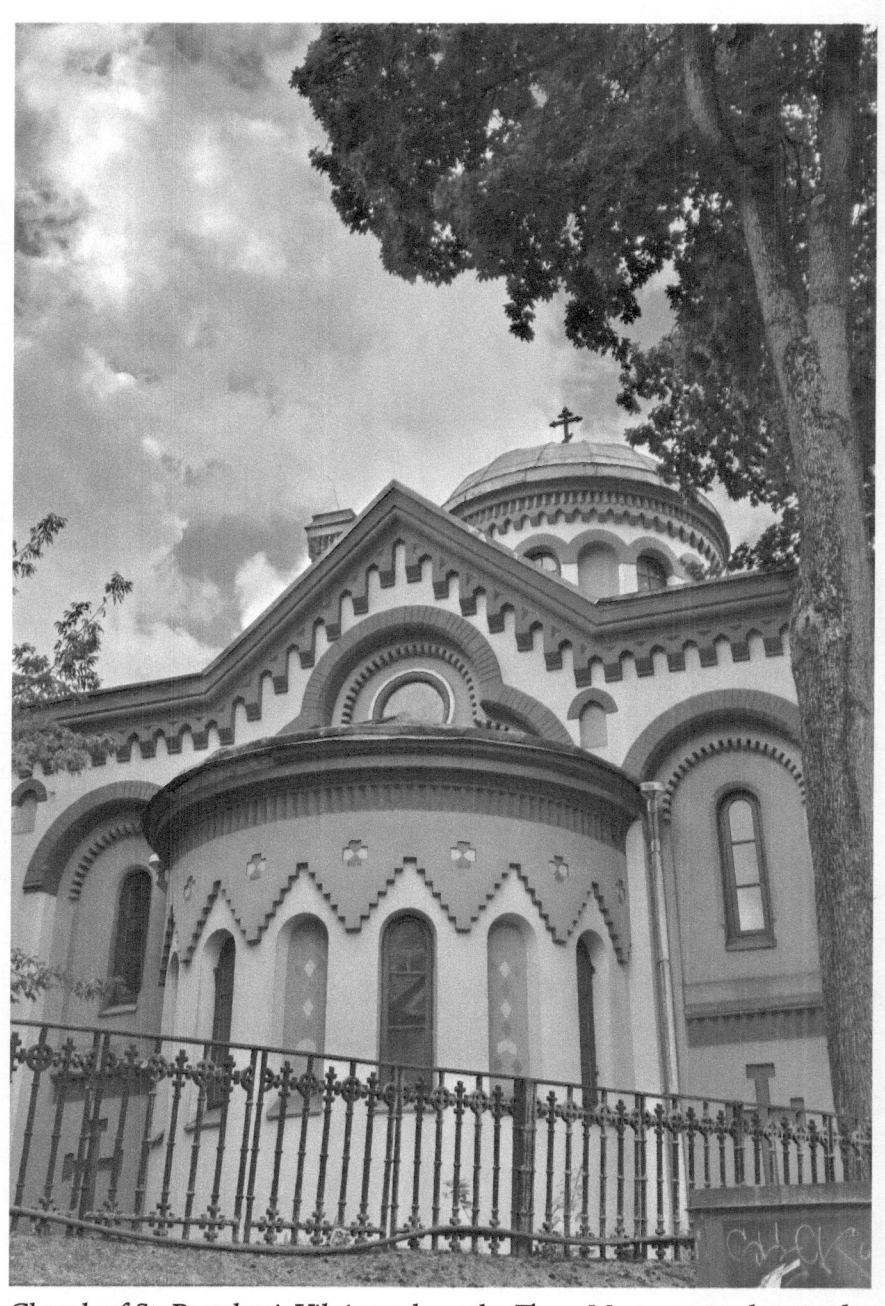

Church of St. Paraskevi, Vilnius, where the Three Martyrs were baptized

Pažaislis Monastery, Kaunas

Church of Our Lady of the Sign, Vilnius

The Hill of Crosses, Jurgaičiai

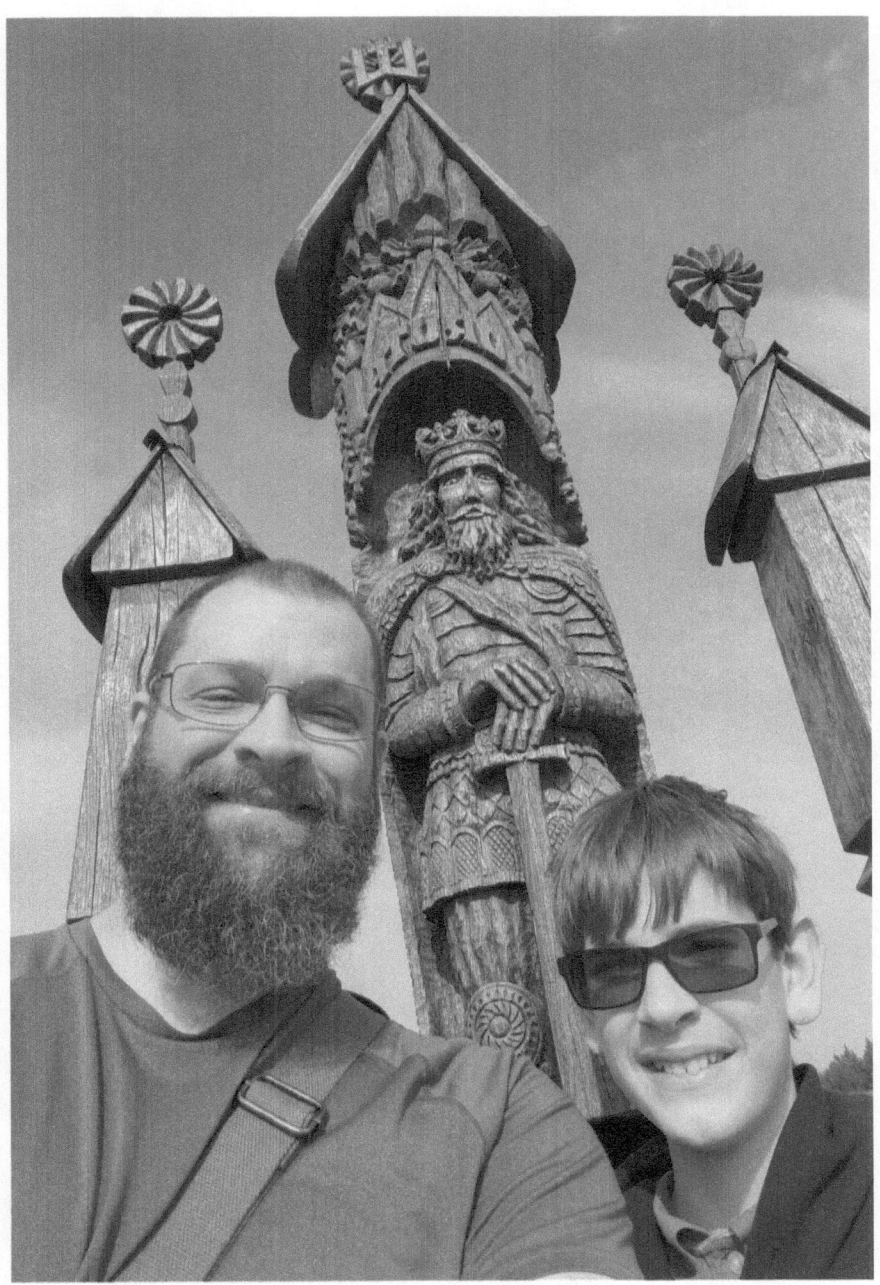

Father Andrew and his son Elias, with a carving of Mindaugas at the traditional site of Voruta

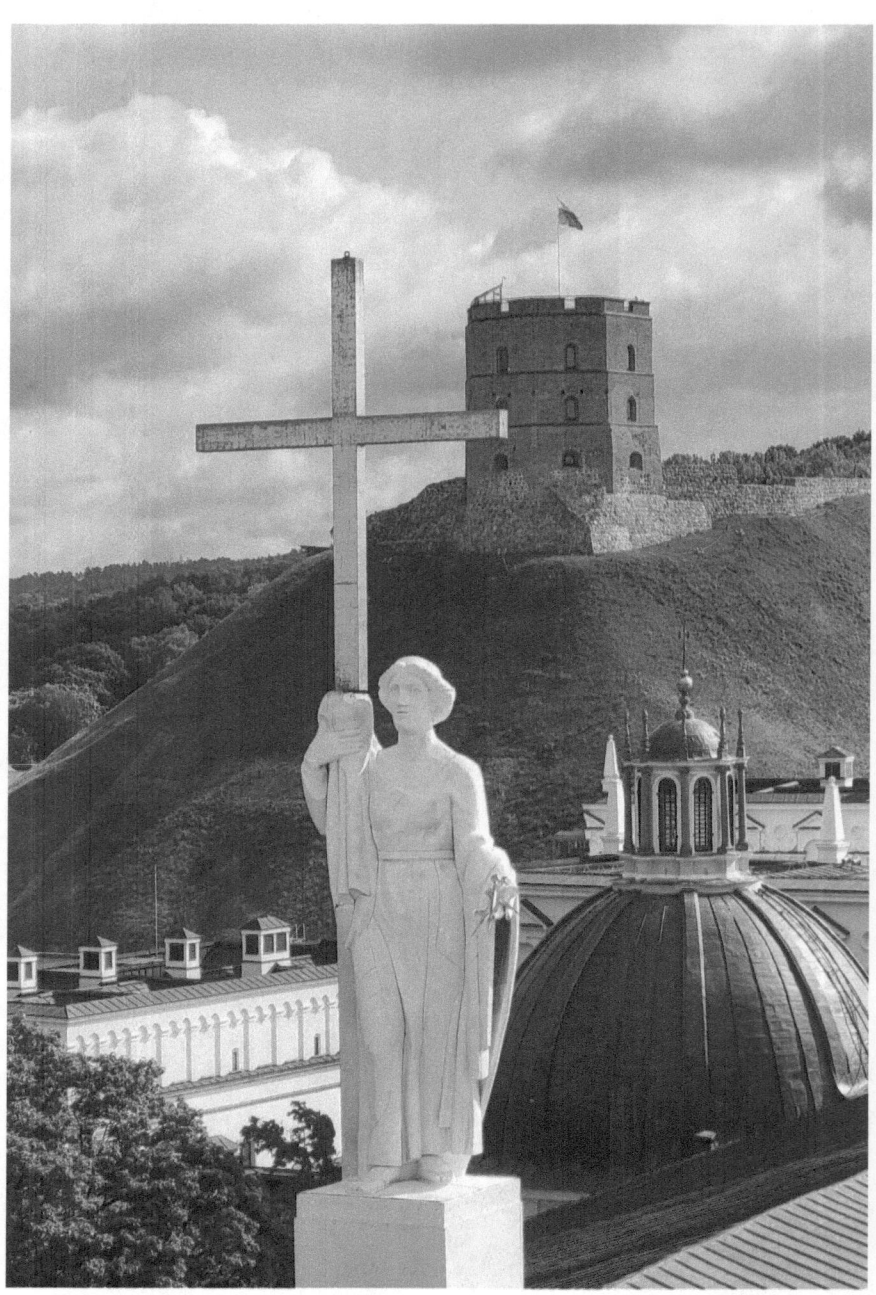

Saint Helena on the roof of the National Cathedral, with Gediminas Tower in the background

Carving of the Mother of God of Sorrows, Hill of Crosses, Jurgaičiai

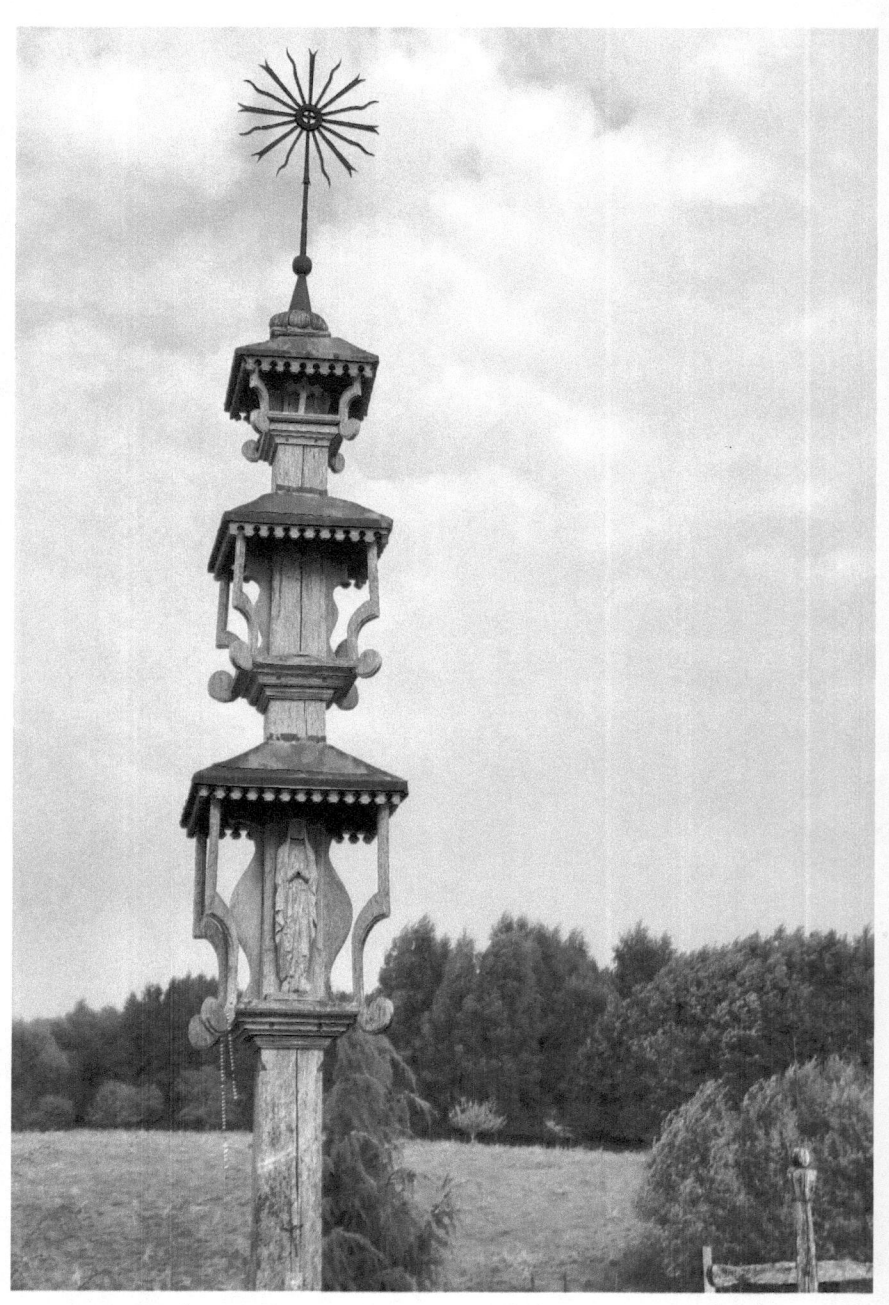

Koplytstulpis (chapel column), Hill of Crosses, Jurgaičiai

Richard at the Hill of Crosses, Jurgaičiai

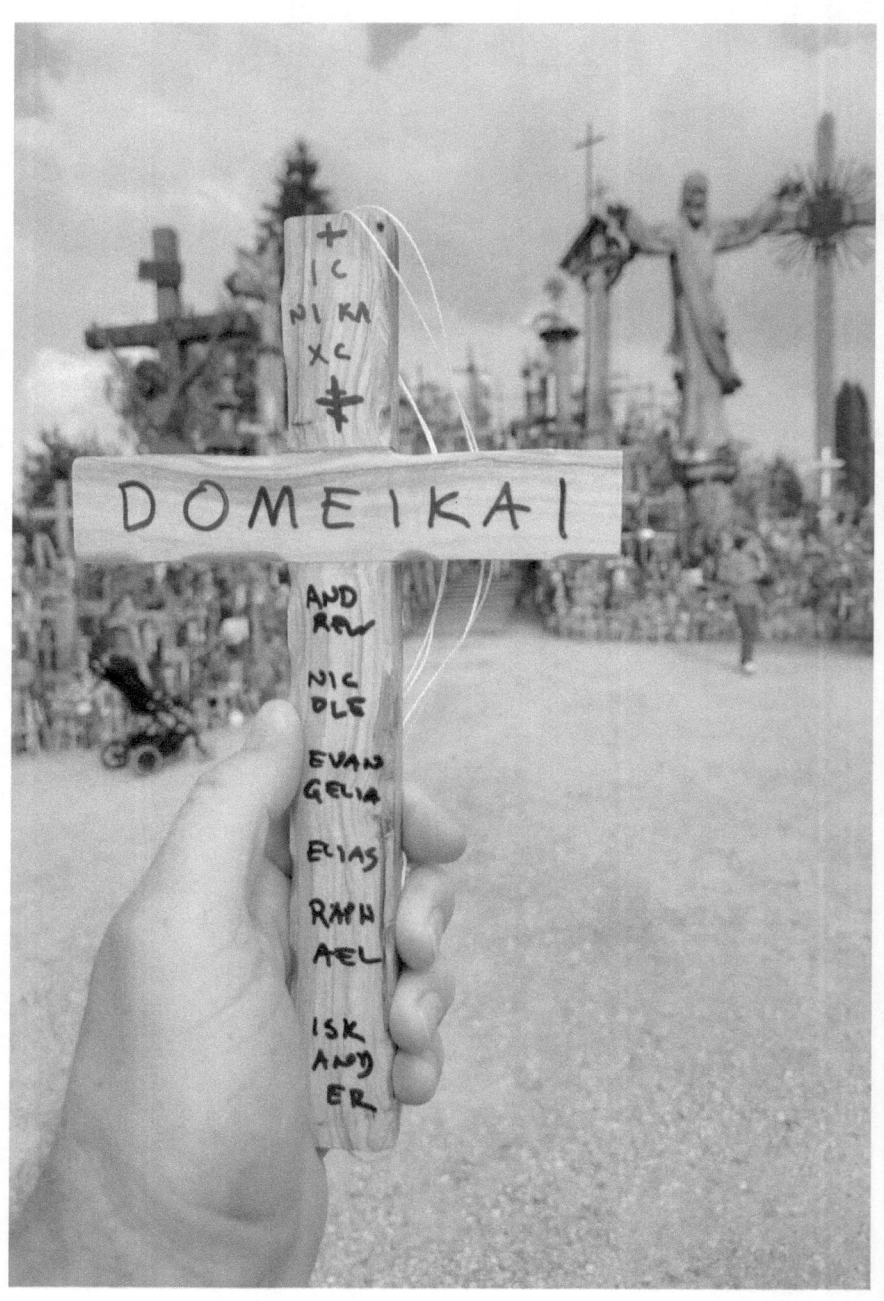

A cross for the Domeika family, Hill of Crosses, Jurgaičiai

Carved cross, Vajeliai village

Church of Ss. Michael and Constantine ("Romanovsky"), Vilnius

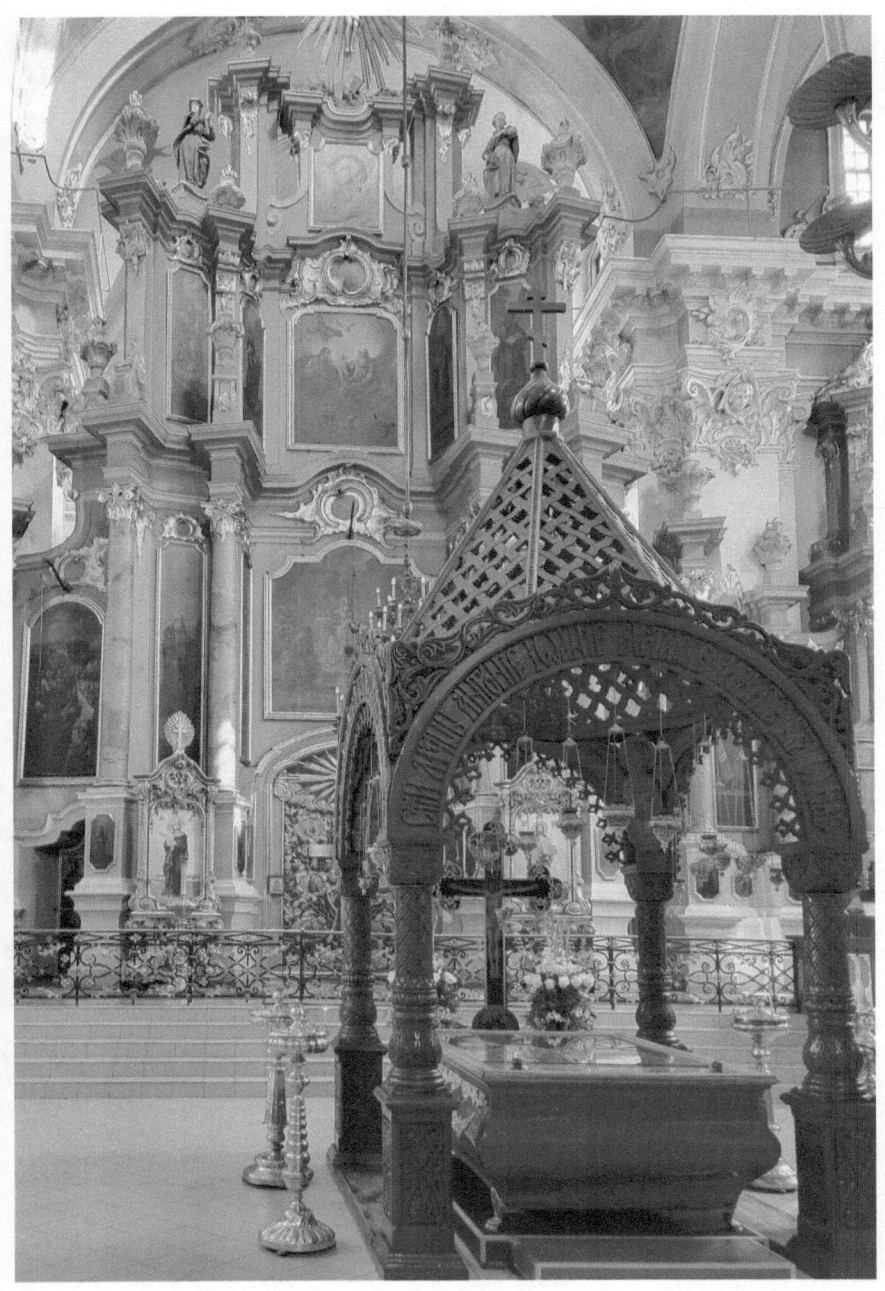

Reliquary of the Three Martyrs of Vilnius, Monastery of the Holy Spirit

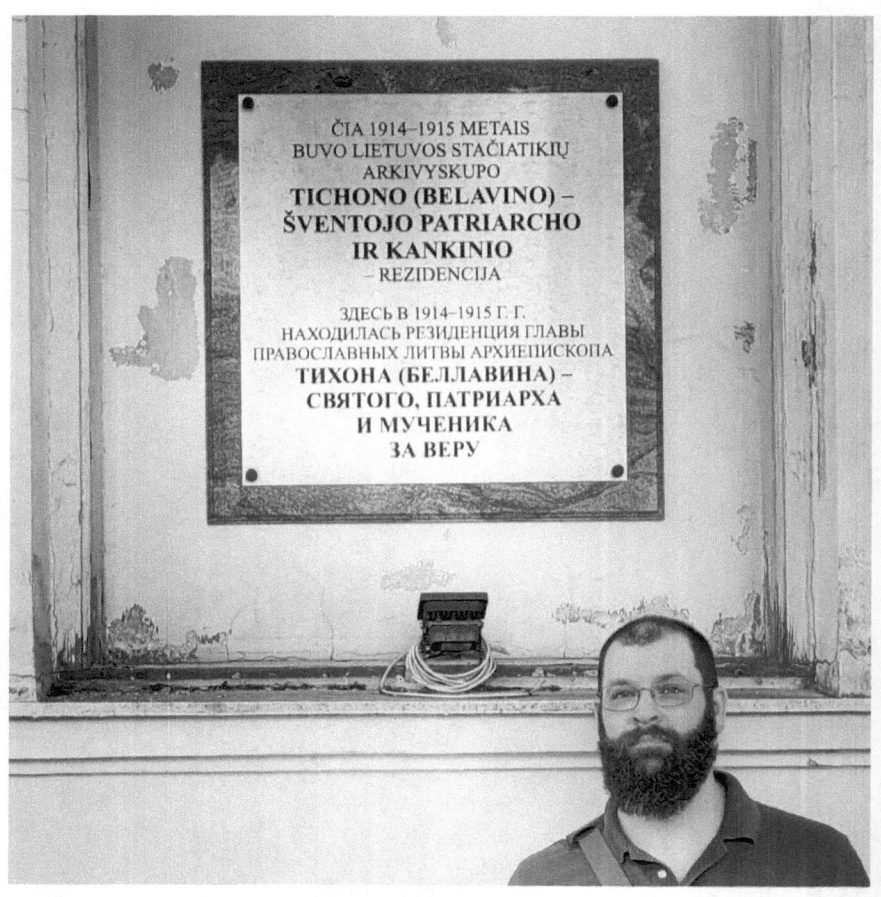

Commemorative plaque at the residence of St. Tikhon in Vilnius

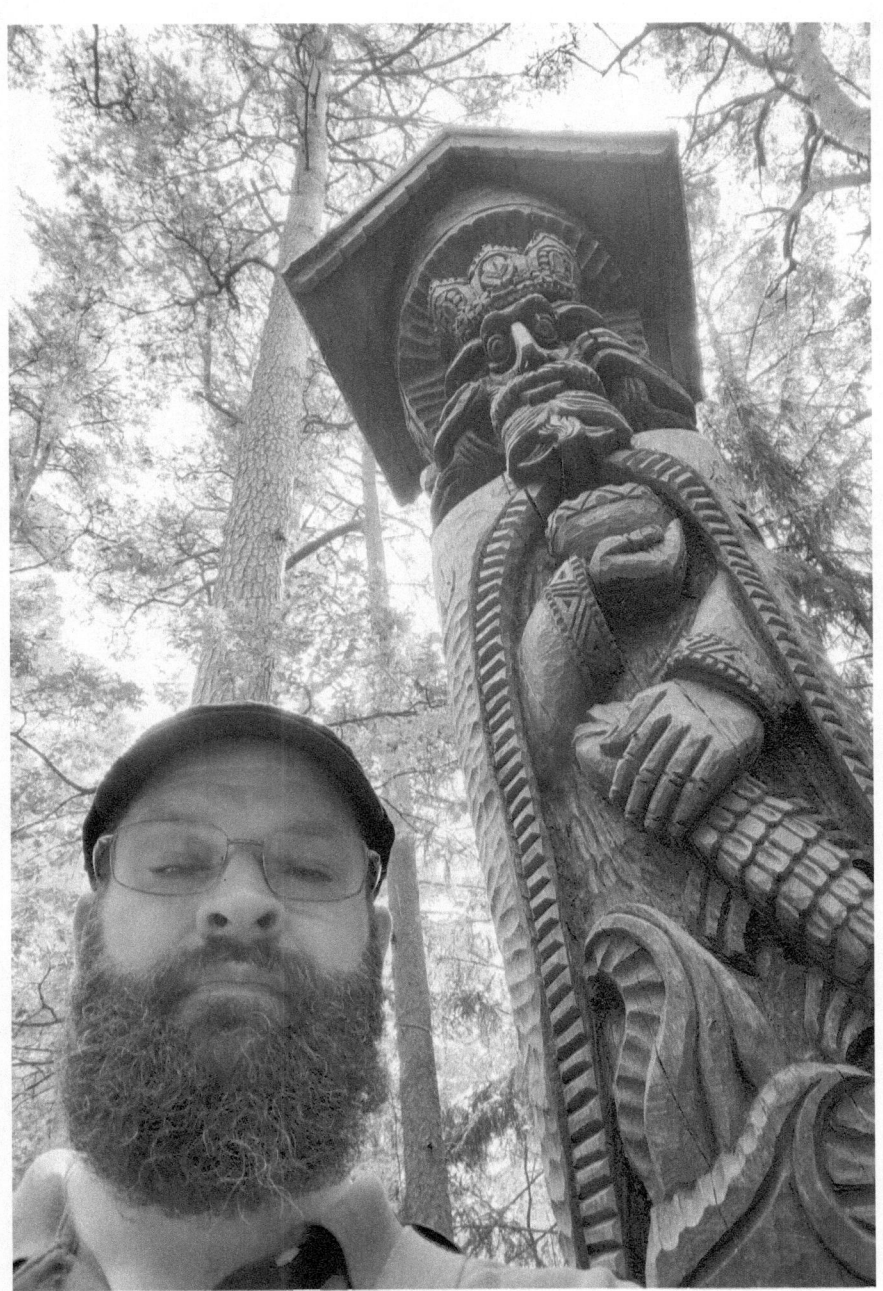

Carving of Nerijus the sea-god, Curonian Spit

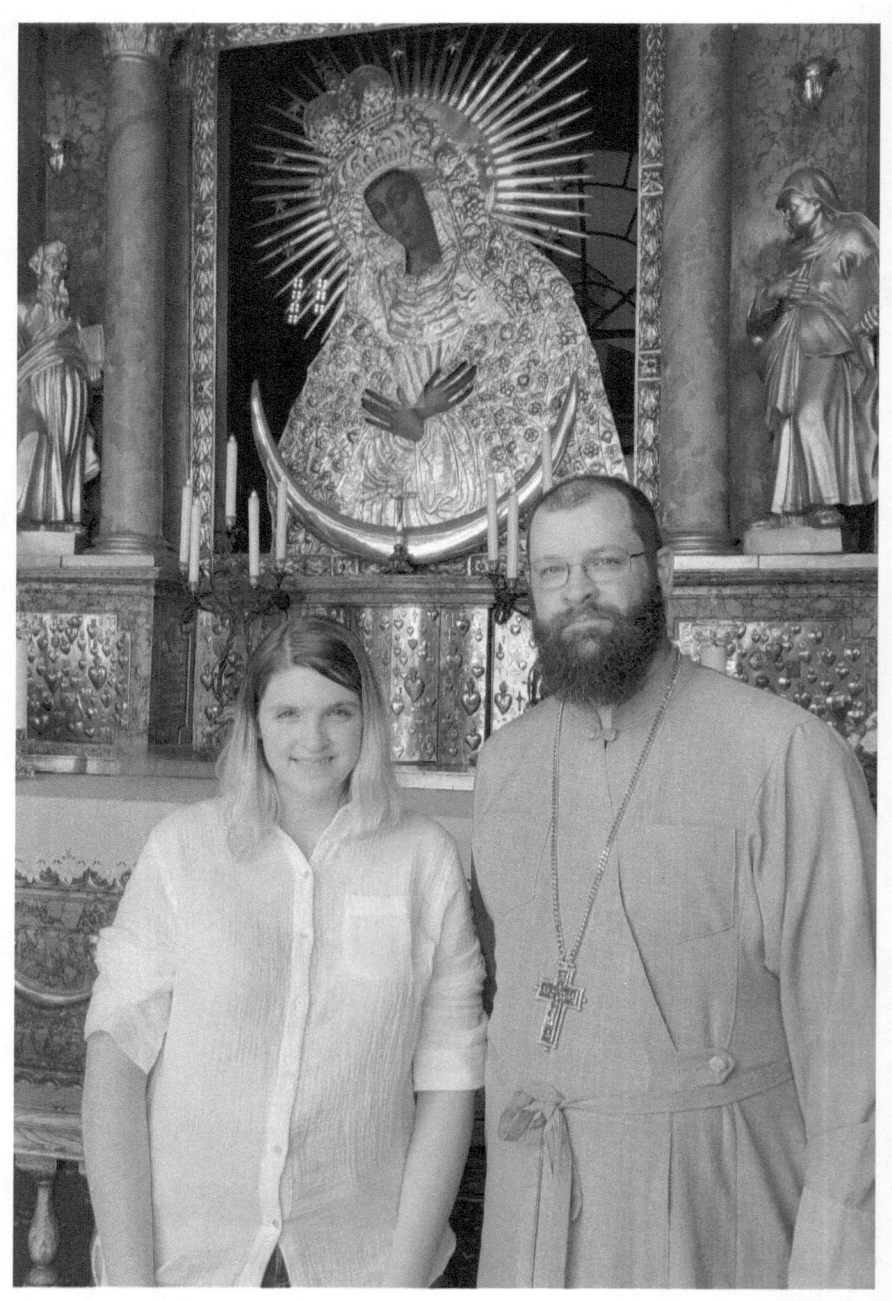

Father Andrew and his daughter Evangelia, Chapel of Our Lady of the Gate of Dawn

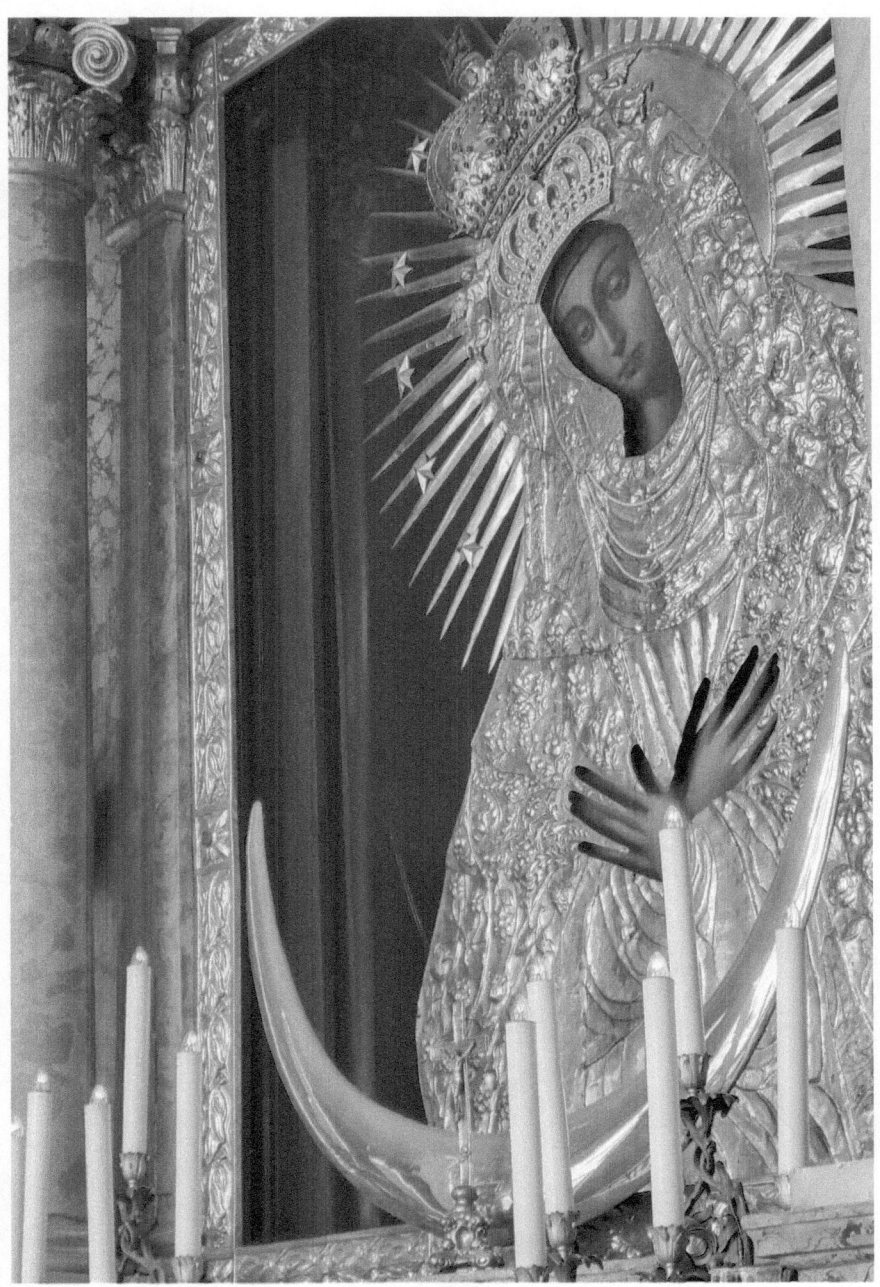

Our Lady of the Gate of Dawn

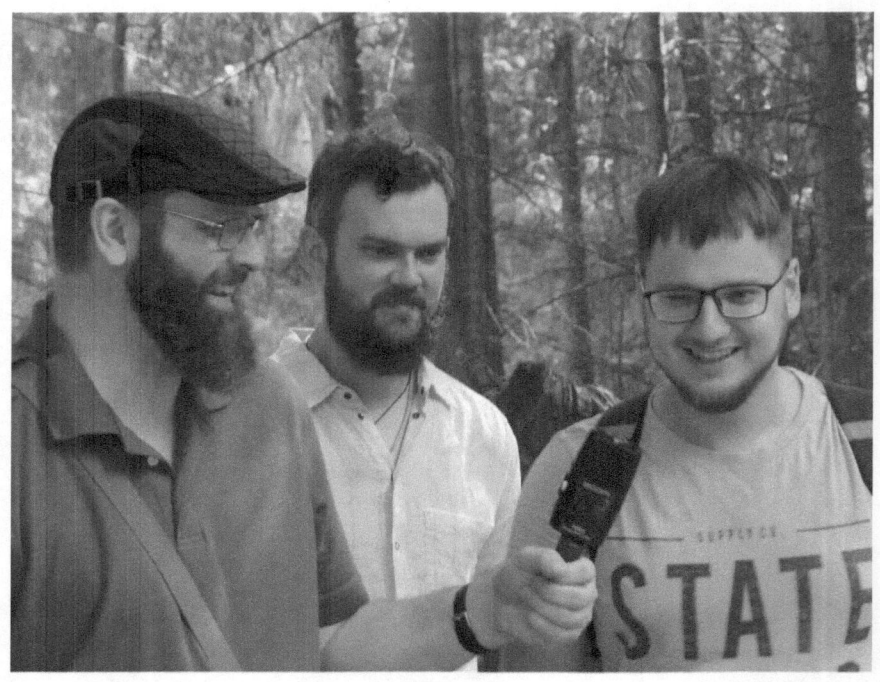

Interviewing Fr. Gintaras, Curonian Spit

The Eagle and the Knight

The Polish-Lithuanian State (1386–1795)

CHAPTER 12

From Union to Commonwealth

WITH THE CROWNING IN 1386 of Jogaila, Grand Duke of Lithuania, as King of Poland, as well as his conversion from paganism to Christianity in the Roman Catholic Church, Poland and Lithuania remained two separate sovereign states but shared one monarchy. Roman Catholicism was officially established as the state religion in both countries.

When Jogaila became King of Poland, he installed his brother Skirgaila, another son of Algirdas, as his regent in the Grand Duchy of Lithuania, who ruled in his name until 1392. This arrangement with two rulers had a precedent in the Grand Duchy a generation before. Although Algirdas had the title of grand duke, Algirdas and Kęstutis had ruled Lithuania effectively as a diarchy, with Algirdas ruling the east and Kęstutis, with the title of Duke of Trakai, governing the west.

Jogaila's choice of Skirgaila was unpopular, however, and their cousin Vytautas, the son of Algirdas's brother Kęstutis, saw an opportunity. Thus, Jogaila and his cousin Vytautas fought against each other in the years immediately following Christianization in 1389, nearly tearing the nascent political union back into two as control of Lithuania hung in the balance.

Lithuania became engulfed in two civil wars between these two branches of the Gediminid Dynasty, from 1381–84 and then again from 1389–92, with attempted coups and counter-coups, as well as alternating alliances with the Teutonic Crusader knights. Finally, though, it became clear that neither side could utterly defeat the other. So peace was made, for the sake of Lithuania.

DURING THIS PERIOD, THE RELATIONSHIP between Orthodox Christians and Catholics in the Grand Duchy of Lithuania continued to develop. Although the two nations in the union were now both officially Catholic, Jogaila recognized the historical importance and presence of Orthodox Christians in his realm. To bolster the integrity of the two religious communities, in 1389 Jogaila outlawed intermarriage between them. Yet he also favored Catholicism in the process by forcing Orthodox Christians already in mixed marriages to become Catholic.

With the signing of the Ostrov Peace Agreement in 1392, Vytautas became Jogaila's regent as Grand Duke of Lithuania. So even though there was in theory one monarch with both titles, effectively, Jogaila was king in the west and held the title of supreme prince in Lithuania, and Vytautas was grand duke in the east.

Jogaila's control of Poland came into jeopardy, however, with the 1399 death of his queen Jadwiga and the child she was birthing. The Polish nobles were already weary of Jogaila's attention being so much on Lithuania—had they elected a foreign king for Poland who had no time for Poland?

Now his Polish queen was gone along with their child. With no obvious heir for Jogaila in Poland, this provided a political opening that resulted in more autonomy for Vytautas as grand duke, who would be consulted by the Polish nobles in the event of Jogaila's death without a son.

As we saw in the last chapter, with a more peaceful and now interdependent relationship between the two cousins, Jogaila and Vytautas allied against the Crusaders and fought together at the Battle of Grunwald, called the Battle of Žalgiris in Lithuanian, delivering the final defeat to the Knights of the Teutonic Order in 1410.

The next twenty years under Vytautas until his death in 1430 were a golden age for the Grand Duchy. It is for this time of peace and prosperity that he is remembered as Vytautas the Great.

THE ORIGINAL TEXT OF THE Union of Krewo signed in August 1385 sealed not only Jogaila's marriage with the young Polish monarch Jadwiga but also stipulated that the two states would be joined and merged in perpetuity into a single, newly Christian state. Yet for nearly two hundred years, the solidification of this union remained in question, not only because of the ambitions of various rulers but also because of how the rulers of each of these states were chosen—Poland had a king elected by the nobles, yet Lithuania had an ancestral duke whose son theoretically inherited the Duchy.

The height of Vytautas's power came when for a few years he jointly administered even the Grand Duchy of Moscow when its duke Vasily I died, who had been married to Vytautas's daughter Sophia. Throughout his whole career, Vytautas sought more autonomy for Lithuania in the midst of its new union with Poland.

Plans were even being made in 1429 for Vytautas to be crowned King of Lithuania, yet fate dealt him a final ironic twist. Before he could receive his crown, Vytautas died at his island castle in Trakai in October of 1430. Jogaila died four years later.

During Vytautas's reign in Lithuania, certain wealthy merchant families rose to prominence in his government, including the Radvilas and Goštautas clans. Lithuania was beginning to modernize, replacing dynastic princelings with regional governors answering directly to the grand duke.

At the same time, another grand duchy began to rise rapidly in the east, with its seat of power in Moscow. Lithuania had fought with Moscow off and on for nearly a century by this point, but with the annexation of Novgorod by the Muscovite dukes, Lithuania became more reliant on military aid from Poland, drawing the two closer together.

FINALLY, IN 1569 THE UNION of Lublin was signed, and the two states that had been held together in a personal union in one kingdom with two sovereigns were combined into a single state—the Commonwealth of Two Nations (*Abiejų Tautų Respublika*), or as it is usually known in English, the Polish-Lithuanian Commonwealth.

The King of Poland and Grand Duke of Lithuania Sigismund II Augustus, the great-grandson of Jogaila, now ruled a single state with a common parliament, common currency, and common foreign policy. Yet within this state were many languages, many cultures, many religions, and many points of view.

After Sigismund's death in 1572, the nobles of the Commonwealth made changes to the constitution and established the monarchy as a fully elected monarchy rather than a hereditary one—the office of king and grand duke would be voted on by the nobles. And there were a lot of them.

This system gave immense power to these nobles, who, when it came time to choose their first fully elected monarch, did something you might not expect. They elected a Frenchman—Henry de Valois, the 21-year-old fourth son of King Henry II of France and his infamous queen Catherine de Medici. Over forty thousand nobles turned up for this election, and in the end, they made a deal with their new king that he had to sign in order to be crowned:

> All the conditions given by our envoys and confirmed in our name, we shall fulfill them all, and we promise all of them with our word, and whatever else the Sovereign States of both nations gave us at the Coronation, we will assume, and we shall accept, swear, confirm, and hold fast for the future. We should fulfill them, and we promise, under our faith and our oath, we promise, we confirm with our word, in perpetuity. And if we (may God forbid) will have transgressed against the laws, liberties, articles, conditions, or there are any we will not have fulfilled: then the citizens of the Commonwealth of both nations, from obedience and faithfulness to us, we thereby set free.[1]

Henry was crowned in Krakow in February 1574. The king's French culture and the culture of the Commonwealth were held together in an uneasy tension, with Henry not favoring the so-called "Golden Liberty" that gave the nobles broad control over the state. The tension was soon resolved when Henry abandoned his new throne four months after taking it, upon hearing of the death of his older brother in France—which made him king of that country.

A year later, the Polish nobles declared the throne of Poland vacant and elected Anna, the sister of the late Sigismund II, to be queen, giving rule effectively to her husband Stephen, elected as co-regent and given the title of king. It was a messy beginning to the new Commonwealth, but now there was a single state of Poland-Lithuania—multireligious, multiethnic, multicultural, and multilingual.

---

1   *Literae confirmationis articulorum.*

THE COMMONWEALTH OF TWO NATIONS forged in the sixteenth century included territory that belongs to modern Lithuania, Poland, Ukraine, Moldova, Belarus, small parts of Russia, Latvia, and Estonia.

Its population at the Union of Lublin in 1569 was about 8 million people— roughly 4.5 million Poles, 750,000 Lithuanians, 700,000 Jews, and 2 million Ruthenians. It was then the largest country in Europe, reaching almost 400,000 square miles at its most expansive—about the size of the US states of Texas and New Mexico combined.

The relationship between Polish and Lithuanian cultures during this period was complicated, to say the least, especially with the Union now allowing Polish nobles to own land inside the Grand Duchy of Lithuania. What happened, however, was a gradual Polonization of Lithuanian nobility and culture. Lithuanian became a language of the lower classes, mainly in the countryside. Many Lithuanian families respelled their names using Polish customs, and Polish became the language not only of government but of trade, church, and military.

Many non-Polish nobles desired entry into the Polish *szlachta*, the privileged elite who elected the king, and gradually many Lithuanian families adopted Polish heraldic coats of arms. Increasingly, a common identity was forged between Poland and Lithuania, reflected on its own national heraldry by the combination of the eagle of the Kingdom of Poland and the Vytis—the white knight of the Grand Duchy of Lithuania.

The famed Winged Hussars, the crack light cavalry of the Commonwealth, were considered the glory not only of Poland but also of Lithuania, and their victory against the Swedes at the Siege of Jasna Góra in 1655, defending the monastery that housed the famed icon of Our Lady of Częstochowa, was a matter of national pride throughout the Commonwealth.

That said, even while the upper classes of Lithuania came to be Polonized and even referred to themselves as "Polish" and their country—which included the Grand Duchy—as "Poland," there was still a maintenance of Lithuanian identity, and a number of distinct laws and customs remained within the region of the Grand Duchy. Many Ruthenian nobles in the southern part of the Grand Duchy—land that was transferred directly to the Polish crown—also became attracted to Polish culture while nevertheless retaining especially their Orthodox identity.

CHAPTER 13

East, West, and the Union of Brest

IT IS WITHIN THIS CONTEXT of the Polish-Lithuanian Commonwealth that another story arises, a story of church schism and recombination, the story of the Union of Brest. At the end of the sixteenth century, the Orthodox churches of the Commonwealth of Two Nations, especially centered within the Grand Duchy of Lithuania, broke from the Orthodox Church and pledged their loyalty to the Pope of Rome.

To understand this story, it is necessary to go back in time a little, back to the beginning of the Polish-Lithuanian state, before the Commonwealth, back to those cousins Jogaila and Vytautas. By their time, the Orthodox Church and the Roman Catholic Church had been out of communion for centuries. Within their lands, alongside the pagans were both Orthodox and Catholic Christians, communities whose Christian history was also centuries old.

Seeing the two types of Christianity all around them and participating in various ways in both, the royal Lithuanian cousins—both converts from paganism—must have had the disunity of their new religion frequently on their minds.

They shared enthusiasm for both traditions. What could be done to bring Christians closer together? As new converts, could they have imagined how deeply ingrained were the divisions between Catholics and Orthodox? Perhaps not, but that ignorance may have allowed them a certain freedom when it came to attempting to combine the two traditions.

We recall how, while both rulers were Catholic (with a brief interlude in the Orthodox Church for Vytautas), they brought Orthodox art and culture into their domains. In 1390, Jogaila and his queen Jadwiga founded the Holy Cross Monastery near Krakow, which was conceived as a Benedictine community that celebrated the Roman liturgical tradition in the Church Slavonic language.

When Jogaila was baptized in 1386, the pope at the time, Urban VI, wrote to him with congratulations, offering (at Jogaila's request) absolution for Christian warriors killed fighting the Turks and the Tatars. He also emphasized that Jogaila should work to bring the Orthodox within his lands into the Roman Catholic Church.

This problem of disunity must have occupied Jogaila's mind. In the closing years of the fourteenth century, while the Ottomans were advancing on Christian lands around Bulgaria and elsewhere, the Catholic Jogaila wrote to the Orthodox St. Cyprian of Kyiv and suggested to him the idea of hosting an ecumenical council in the Ruthenian lands of the Grand Duchy, aimed at bringing East and West back into communion. His suggestion seems to have been passed on to the Ecumenical Patriarch Anthony IV, who in January 1397 sent Jogaila a letter:

> You write concerning the union of churches and we ourselves also wish for and agree to this. But this cannot be done at the present time, for there is war with the unbelievers and the routes are closed off [. . .] we strongly urge that Your Nobility should join with the most noble king of Hungary in the spring season and that you should come forth on behalf of the Christians both with your army and your resources, for the destruction of the unbelievers. And then [. . .] with ease will there be the union of the churches.[1]

Patriarch Anthony died four months later, and the proposed council never was held. As medieval historian Darius Baronas notes:

> Jogaila was, in a sense, ahead of his time when compared with many of his Roman Catholic contemporaries. This resulted from his (relative) freedom

---

1   Quoted in Darius Baronas, "King Ladislas II Jogaila of Poland," 249.

to subscribe to a view which saw an ecumenical council as a suitable way to solve the problem. He, and probably Vytautas too, subscribed to this idea long before the chancellor of Paris University, Jean Gerson, produced his scholarly tract in 1409 on reaching church union by means of a general council. . . . For the Roman Catholic hierarchy, it was clear for all to see that all the Greeks had to do was simply to confess to the Roman creed of faith and acknowledge the supremacy of the pope. Unsurprisingly, an absolute majority of the Greek Orthodox clergy held quite different views in this matter and saw an ecumenical council as the only way to restore the unity of all Christian believers.[2]

It was only after the West underwent its own Great Schism from 1378–1417, when there were as many as three popes simultaneously, that Rome became more open to the idea of actual dialogue with the Orthodox rather than bald expectations of submission. The friendship of St. Cyprian with Jogaila and the like-mindedness of Vytautas both contributed to this sense of openness between East and West and were personal characteristics that made them distinct from most other European Catholic rulers.

That said, there seems to have been collaboration between Jogaila and Sigismund of Luxembourg, who around 1411 likely coauthored three letters to the Byzantine emperor Manuel II proposing an alliance against the Ottoman Turks and also collaboration in bringing about Christian reunion between East and West.

In 1414, Vytautas's granddaughter Anne (daughter of Grand Duke Vasily of Moscow) married the future Byzantine emperor John VIII. This marriage gave both Jogaila and Vytautas a claim to be relatives of the Byzantine imperium, and thus they were men whose opinions ought to be taken seriously.

The involvement of Jogaila and Vytautas in attempts at church union came to its peak when the interests of both were represented at the Council of Constance, which among other things dealt with the Teutonic encroachments on their lands. Union of course was not on the table at that council, but Lithuanian interests were represented there.

---

2   Baronas, 240–241.

Further, in the aftermath there was an audience with Pope Martin V, where Gregory Tsemblak, an Orthodox pretender to the Metropolitan of Kyiv, gave a speech on the Orthodox views on church union. These factors brought to the attention of Catholic clergy and rulers a stronger sense of the presence of their Orthodox neighbors to the East. It is little wonder—the newly forged union of Poland and Lithuania formed most of the European border of that meeting between East and West.

Vytautas and Jogaila died in 1430 and 1434 respectively, with civil war once again in their wake. Their successors were largely less enthusiastic or sincere about rapprochement between Orthodox and Catholics, and Vytautas's successor Švitrigaila (a Catholic who otherwise seemed to have been favorable toward reunion) even had the pro-union Orthodox Metropolitan Gerasim burnt at the stake.

Švitrigaila's successor Sigismund Kęstutaitis turned a rather cold shoulder to reunion, giving little welcome, for instance, to Metropolitan Isidore of Kyiv. Isidore returned to the region from the Council of Florence in 1439 having become a Catholic cardinal and declaring that the Great Schism was over after the capitulation of most of the Orthodox to Rome in exchange for military help against the Ottomans. Isidore was ultimately deposed from his see for his part in the council.

Sigismund was himself murdered in 1440, and regions belonging to the Grand Duchy rose up in revolt, weakening it and setting the stage for closer union with Poland to face off against military threats from the Grand Duchy of Moscow. Grand Duke Alexander made some more attempts at reunion around the turn of the fifteenth and sixteenth centuries, but by then Constantinople had fallen to the Ottoman Turks and the Grand Duchy was turning more and more to its Polish partner for help. The creative tension between Christian East and West that had been sustained for centuries in Lithuania could not hold.

The Unia

SO THAT BRINGS US BACK to the Commonwealth of Two Nations, which was formally created in 1569 with the Union of Lublin, and to a series of events that happened not even thirty years later.

At this time, the Orthodox of the Commonwealth belonged to the Ecumenical Patriarchate, but with the death of the last Byzantine emperor in 1453 and the loss of Constantinople to the Ottomans, the Patriarchate's influence on the international stage was significantly reduced. Internally within the Commonwealth, the condition of the Orthodox Church in the eastern lands was not good, as noted by historian Anastacia Wooden:

> At the end of the sixteenth century the Orthodox Church in the Grand Duchy of Lithuania was in a state of institutional, moral, and cultural decline, characterized by the lack of even basic education of clergy, corruption and moral decay among hierarchy and clergy, decline of monastic life, and general demoralization among the Orthodox, exacerbated by the pressure from Polish culture as well as lack of consistent political equality with the Catholic Church.[3]

Further, the authority of Orthodox bishops was now checked by two major factors. We have already discussed the rise of the influence of the Catholic kings of Poland and Grand Dukes of Lithuania, who often involved themselves in church matters—for good or ill. Because they were Catholic, they of course tended to favor Roman Catholicism within the Commonwealth—even while Orthodox Christians actually outnumbered other religious groups within the Grand Duchy.

The second major factor was the formation of lay brotherhoods of Orthodox Christians, composed of wealthy nobility, merchants, and intellectuals, with the earliest known brotherhood chartered in 1463 in Kyiv. These brotherhoods controlled religious education, publishing, and other aspects of parish life, including ownership of church property, and they were centered mostly in Ruthenian cities such as Kyiv, Minsk, Lutsk, Lviv, and Vitebsk, but also in Vilnius itself.

The brotherhoods were stavropegial, meaning that they did not answer to the local Orthodox bishops but rather directly to the Ecumenical Patriarch. When they felt that the local clergy were corrupt or incompetent, they would use their wealth and influence to exercise control over them.

---

3   Wooden, "Brief History," 53.

In 1588 and 1589, Ecumenical Patriarch Jeremias II set out on a fundrais-ing voyage in Eastern Europe, especially in the lands of the Commonwealth. During his travels, he granted the title of patriarch to St. Job, Metropolitan of Moscow, as the head of the Russian Orthodox Church, whose independence was formally recognized in 1593. This strengthened the Russian Church, whose rise in the region was connected with the political rise of the Grand Duchy of Moscow.

The Metropolitan of Kyiv, situated within the Polish-Lithuanian Com-monwealth, remained independent of Moscow during this period, and during his voyage, Patriarch Jeremias deposed Onesiphorus Divochka, then the Kyiv metropolitan, and consecrated Michael Rohoza in Vilnius in his place in August 1589, with the consent of Sigismund III, the King of Poland and Grand Duke of Lithuania. Michael was a Ruthenian noble who had studied at the new Jesuit University in Vilnius, founded in 1579, and became a monk at a monastery in Minsk.

In 1590, Metropolitan Michael inaugurated a program of reform designed to lessen the influence of laity on the Church, and he met opposition by the powerful stavropegial brotherhoods. Frustrated by his inability to make the desired changes, Michael called together the bishops of his region to discuss solutions in a series of synods from 1590 to 1595.

A prominent leader among the brotherhoods, the Ruthenian nobleman Konstantin Vasyl Ostrogsky—in Lithuanian, Konstantinas Ostragiškis— proposed that these synods ought to include the participation of bishops from the Constantinople and Moscow hierarchies. Konstantin, born 1526, was the ruler of Ostrog, where Orthodox culture flourished, boasting the Ostrog Academy, founded in 1576, and the first complete Bible in Church Slavonic— the Ostrog Bible.

Konstantin's insistence on including other Orthodox bishops was ignored. The gathered Ruthenian hierarchs were not seeking to change the faith of the Ruthenian Orthodox Church, but they did want more control over their churches—men like Konstantin stood in their way.

On the one hand, Metropolitan Michael had seen the vigorous work of the Jesuits in the wake of the Council of Trent with the Counter-Reformation, which purged the Roman Catholic Church of much of its medieval corruption.

Part of that work involved a dedication to proselytization among Protestants and the Orthodox. But he also saw that Roman Catholic bishops were far more powerful than their Orthodox counterparts within the Commonwealth.

On the other hand, Michael and his bishops could not look to Moscow for help, since Moscow was a direct military threat to the Commonwealth, and the Ruthenians could be seen as traitors to the Commonwealth. Further, Moscow's new patriarch was an ecclesiastical rival to the new Metropolitan of Kyiv.

Thus, Metropolitan Michael and his bishops turned to Rome. They drew up thirty-three articles of union, signed finally by all nine Ruthenian bishops in the city of Brest on June 12, 1595, located in what is now Belarus, about 240 miles south of Vilnius.

The articles stipulated that the Ruthenian Church would retain its liturgical traditions, its current hierarchy, and all its customs, including married clergy. They would be willing to accept the New Calendar, but only if the Paschal calculation remained untouched.

Further, they would not be expected to recite the Latin *filioque* addition to the Creed, only Ruthenians and Greeks could be appointed as bishops, all church property would be under the control of the bishops, and they could not be Latinized. The bishops would also be given seats in the Senate of the Commonwealth just like the Latin bishops. The brotherhoods would be confirmed but would be expected to be obedient to the local bishops. They also requested that the king prevent Orthodox hierarchs from the East from entering the Commonwealth to interfere with the union. In exchange, the Ruthenian bishops recognized the supremacy of the Pope of Rome:

> All these things we the undersigned, desiring holy concord for the praise of God's Name and for the peace of the Holy Church of Christ, we have given these articles which we consider necessary for our Church and for which we require agreement in advance and guarantees from the Holy Father the Pope and from the King's Grace, our merciful lord, for greater security, we have committed our Instructions to our Reverend brothers in God, father Hypatius Potij, the Protothrone, Bishop Volodymyr of Brest', and Father Cyril Terletsky, Exarch and Bishop of Lutsk and Ostrih, so that in our name and in

their own name they should ask the Most Holy Father the Pope, and also the King's Grace, our merciful lord, to confirm and guarantee beforehand all the articles which we have here given in writing, so that assured as to the faith, the Mysteries, and our ceremonies, we might come to this holy accord with the Roman Church without any violation of our conscience and the flock of Christ committed unto us and likewise that others who are still hesitating, seeing that we retain everything inviolate, might more quickly come after us to this holy union.

Given in the Year of God 1595, the month of June, the first day according to the Old Calendar.[4]

These articles had been negotiated in strict secrecy. Word got out, however, and in August of that year Konstantin Ostrogsky, along with many of the Ruthenian nobles, the brotherhoods, and the Cossacks, as well as many Orthodox priests and deacons, launched a public campaign against the Union. The Patriarchal Exarch, representing Constantinople, called on the people to resist the Union and install a parallel hierarchy to ensure the continuation of Orthodoxy in the Commonwealth. Two of the bishops withdrew their support from the Union amid the outcry against it.

The articles were nevertheless brought to Rome, where they were approved by Pope Clement VII in December. The following year, in October 1596, the Union of Brest[5] was proclaimed and fully accepted by both sides.

It was and often still is called the *Unia*—whence comes the historical term *Uniate* for those who signed on to the Unia and who belong to its communities. In our time, *Uniate* is often regarded as a derogatory term, but it was used by both sides of the conflict for centuries and has only recently been regarded as negative. In the early seventeenth century, there was also the term *Disuniate* (Lith. *Dizunitas*), which was used derogatively to refer to those who resisted the Unia, meaning (from the point of view of the Unia) that they were the real schismatics.

---

4   *Reunion Treaty of Brest.*
5   The Unia is also sometimes called the *Union of Brest-Litovsk*, but that is an anachronism, as the city of Brest—now in Belarus—did not acquire that longer name for almost two hundred more years, and it does not use it now.

WHILE THE UNIA WAS RESISTED, especially by the brotherhoods, resistance was uneven. Parish priests, for instance, generally continued to commemorate their own bishops even if they were Uniate bishops; they still regarded them as their bishops. Monasteries, however, tended to resist. As historian Sophia Senyk writes:

> Except for a small group of persons committed to the Union and an equally small group actively opposed to it, most people were probably indifferent, if at all aware of it. The bishops remained in their sees, the priests in their parishes. In parish churches and in monasteries prayers continued to be offered for their pious founders. The liturgical rites remained unchanged. People made pilgrimages to the same icons as before.[6]

Nevertheless, coercion was used to enforce the Unia. Churches would be locked until clergy accepted it, and there was civil persecution of citizens who remained Orthodox.

Konstantin Ostrogsky died in 1608, but resistance continued, centered especially in the Kyiv Caves Lavra and among the Cossacks. In 1620, a restored Orthodox hierarchy, answering to Constantinople, was appointed through their efforts, with the consecration of Job Boretsky by Patriarch Theophanes III of Jerusalem. With competing hierarchies now present, violence sometimes accompanied the transfer of church properties.

The height of strife between the two sides was probably in November 1623 in Vitebsk, when an Orthodox mob—the Disuniates—possibly along with some Lithuanian Protestants, attacked and murdered the Uniate Archbishop of Polotsk, Josaphat Kuncevich, who had studied with the Jesuits in Vilnius.

He was held to be responsible for the imprisonment of Orthodox clergy and also the burning of Orthodox laity after they celebrated a prayer service of thanksgiving—actions that drew the criticism of his contemporary, the Catholic nobleman Lew Sapieha. He denied the allegations, but he was known for using harsh methods, and his words often left real violence in their wake.

---

6   Quoted in Wooden, "Brief History," 45.

The attack was in response to the order to arrest the last Orthodox priest in Vitebsk, who had secretly been holding services. Contemporary accounts of the events say that bells began ringing all over the city, and numerous people, including men, women, and children, gathered together to rise up against Josaphat. One account says that when he was approached by the mob, Josaphat stood up and said:

> You people of Vitebsk want to put me to death. You make ambushes for me everywhere, in the streets, on the bridges, on the highways and in the marketplace. I am here among you as your shepherd and you ought to know that I should be happy to give my life for you. I am ready to die for the holy Unia, for the supremacy of Saint Peter and of his successor the Supreme Pontiff.[7]

He was attacked, beaten, and his dead body was dragged throughout the streets of Vitebsk before finally being thrown into the Divna River.

He was canonized in 1867 by the Roman Catholic Church, a controversial act because he was regarded by his Orthodox contemporaries as a cruel persecutor. So to this day, among Greek Catholics he is "Saint Josaphat," a "martyr for unity," but to many Orthodox he is "Josaphat the Malevolent." His story, like the story of the Unia in general, remains a lightning rod for controversy.

Relations eventually became more peaceful, but within two hundred years of the proclamation of the Unia in 1596 the institutions of Orthodox Christianity were almost entirely wiped from the lands of the Polish-Lithuanian Commonwealth. In what is now Belarus, for instance, by the late eighteenth century, where almost the entire population had been Orthodox only 6 percent remained so, while three quarters of the population belonged to the Unia.

---

7   *Memorial of Saint Josaphat.*

CHAPTER 14

A Faithful Cry in the Dark: St. Athanasius of Brest

F OR ORTHODOX CHRISTIANS, PERHAPS THE most significant story
that rises out of the tale of the Unia is about an abbot in the city of Brest
named Athanasius Filipovičius (or Filipovich). He was born in Brest in 1597,
the year after the Unia went into effect, to a noble Ruthenian-Lithuanian family belonging to the szlachta. He studied in the Jesuit university in Vilnius and
had a gift for languages, learning Latin, Greek, Polish, and Ruthenian.

Initially, he made his living as a tutor for the family of the Chancellor of
the Commonwealth, but in 1627, at the age of thirty, he was tonsured a monk
at the Orthodox Monastery of the Holy Spirit in Vilnius, one of the centers of
resistance to the Unia in Lithuania. He later joined the monastery in Dubovsk,
where he was ordained to the priesthood.

He was known especially for his love of his fellow monastics and for the
poor. During his life, he was granted a vision of the Mother of God, who
directed him in finding donors to rebuild the church at his monastery.

In 1640, he was elected the abbot of the Monastery of St. Simeon in Brest.
In that city, where the Unia had been signed forty-five years before, the Jesuits
were especially active in working to bring the local Orthodox into the Unia,
and the city authorities also discriminated against the Orthodox.

Athanasius encouraged them to remain faithful to the Orthodox Church,
and at one point he went before the legislature of the Commonwealth in
Warsaw to protest their treatment, speaking boldly before the king and
the assembled szlachta, criticizing the Unia and saying that the Mother of

102

God warned that the Lord was displeased with the plight of the Orthodox in Brest.

For this, he was thrown into prison as mentally ill. He escaped from the prison on the Feast of Theophany in January, walking through the streets wearing little clothing. He went into the Roman Catholic churches in Warsaw and warned them that God was going to punish them. The police arrived and had him flogged and kicked, then thrown into a ditch. He was hauled before a judge, who declared him stripped of his office of abbot and even of the priesthood, sentences St. Peter (Petro) Mohyla, the Orthodox Metropolitan of Kyiv, initially confirmed but later quietly ignored when Athanasius was allowed to return to his monastery as its abbot.

The persecutions against the Orthodox in Brest continued, with Jesuits even instigating riots to prevent Orthodox services from being held. Athanasius went back to Warsaw to plead before the king but was again thrown into prison, this time on the charge of conspiring against the Commonwealth with the Grand Duchy of Moscow, which he had visited to raise funds for his monastery.

While in prison, he wrote a series of letters to the king against the Unia, demanding that the king honor the Commonwealth policy of religious tolerance. The king released him to Metropolitan St. Peter on the condition that he stay in Kyiv and not return to Brest. He thus stayed at the Kyiv Caves monastery until St. Peter's death in 1647, then headed back to Brest.

In 1648, during an uprising of Cossacks against the Commonwealth Athanasius was charged with conspiring with them by smuggling gunpowder through his monastery. The authorities searched the monastery, and finding no gunpowder, they instead charged him with profaning the Roman Catholic Church and the Unia. He was only too glad to speak out against both in response, and so he was again thrown into prison, where he was offered freedom if only he would join the Unia. His response was to shout, "Anathema to the Unia!"[1]

During one of his prison stays, besides writing letters denouncing the Unia, he also wrote poetry, which was later set to music. This prison song is

---

1   Hieromonk Makarios, *The Synaxarion*, 46.

composed of heartfelt cries alternating between pain, anger, bitterness, love, and prayer:

> Grant peace to your Church, O Christ God,
> I do not know if it is possible for us to endure.
> Give help from sadness
> so that we remain whole
> and remain steadfast in the immaculate faith in these times
> When these horrible days are coming—in the end times!

> You know, O Lord,
> who will stand at your right hand.
> Conquer the traitors, first of all the Uniates,
> the prelates and the nominated bishops,
> so that they will leave us alone—
> Let them peacefully live to the end of their lives!

> Stun all opponents and their councils,
> so that deeds of anger will not continue
> Between the Greeks and the Romans
> Where your chosen people are!

> The time of separation from the damned has come:
> The shabby ones shall not eat bread with those who were called.
> When the unworthy one will be thrown into darkness
> And will suffer for eternity.

> Here is the anger of the Antichrist! Uniate,
> Liar and profit-seeker, horned brother of lies!
> Stop your anger,
> Do not continue in your cruelty!

> Hell is prepared for you
> Your pride and your evil thoughts will be burned.
> Stay away from this flame
> And believe not what the devil says.

For you the Greek Church laments
And suffers persecution in many places.
Stop this anger,
Cease evil-doing.

Do you really think that you matter to the Romans?
A Roman can live without a Ruthenian.
Return to the Holy Church of yours
The Eastern Church.

The Immaculate One and the saints will help you,
Through their dear prayers
in the glory directed to God,
One in the Holy Trinity.

Be a son of Orthodoxy, O Uniate,
As long as we live, there is an option of repentance, dear brother!
Christ is calling you,
the Immaculate One is waiting.

She prays for you with bitter weeping,
the Mother of the Son who was Crucified, saying:
"For now the human has grace
but later he will lose it."

We all praise Christ and our Creator
For His merciful Mother has been given to us,
For His words and signs
are inerrant unto the ages. Amen.[2]

These words are difficult to read, and of course they could never be used as a liturgical hymn or in catechism. But they show us that even saints can have a broad range of emotions, from the heights to the depths. Yet they always return to Christ.

---

2   "Diary of Afanasy Filippovich," 108. Translated by Fr. Gintaras.

ON SEPTEMBER 5, 1648, ATHANASIUS was taken from the prison to the forests near Brest and tortured there with hot coals while he watched his grave being dug. Again he was told to renounce Orthodox Christianity, but he remained adamant.

Finally, the soldier who had been assigned to execute him, seeing how steadfast he was knelt down before him to ask for forgiveness, then drew his gun and shot him twice in the head. Somehow, the bullets did not immediately kill the saint, so he was cast down into the grave and then buried alive.

Thus, the Hieromartyr Athanasius of Brest triumphed over the enemy—the devil who always seeks to divide Christians through heresy and schism.

Eight months later, with the help of a boy who had seen where the saint was martyred, monks from the monastery in Brest found his holy relics, exhumed him, and found that his body was incorrupt.

HOLY HIEROMARTYR ATHANASIUS, PRAY FOR US!

CHAPTER 15

St. Leontijus Karpovičius
and the Monastery of the Holy Spirit

T HERE ARE MANY SIGNIFICANT ORTHODOX stories connected with the Commonwealth of Two Nations. One that is especially significant is the story of the Monastery of the Holy Spirit in Vilnius, one of two remaining Orthodox monasteries in modern Lithuania. This monastery is especially important to the Orthodox pilgrim to Lithuania because there the incorrupt relics of the Three Martyrs of Lithuania are enshrined in a large reliquary in the center of the church.

This monastic community did not start out being named for the Holy Spirit, however. Originally, the brotherhood was named for the Holy Trinity, and the brotherhood that belongs to the Holy Spirit Monastery still officially bears this name. So why is the monastery now named for the Holy Spirit?

The original location for the brotherhood was at the Church of the Holy Trinity in Vilnius that was built where St. Anthony was hung from the tree at his martyrdom. It is said that its original altar was made from the oak from which the martyr hung. By the end of the fifteenth century there seems to have been a monastic brotherhood connected to the church, though perhaps not formally organized as a traditional monastery with an abbot heading a cenobitic community.

During this period, as was the case with all Orthodox churches in Lithuania, the monastery belonged to the Patriarchate of Constantinople, though it was stavropegial.

When the Unia began, Holy Trinity Church was closed, but it was not exactly the closing of a monastery as we would normally conceive of it. The monks there belonged to one of the stavropegial Orthodox brotherhoods we mentioned earlier, which had grown in membership to around five hundred people by the time of the Unia.

In the wake of the signing of the Unia in 1596, Holy Trinity Church was given to the Greek Catholics and in 1608 became part of a Uniate monastery. The Orthodox Brotherhood moved their activities across the street to a newly constructed church, completed in 1597, which they named for the Holy Spirit.

Why not keep the old name? The explanation is simple: They hoped that the Unia would eventually be abolished or at least that the Orthodox would receive Holy Trinity Church back. So that there would not be two churches next to each other that would celebrate competing feast days on the same day, they had the new church consecrated to the Holy Spirit. The new church's feast day was thus on the day after the feast of Holy Trinity Church, which is on Pentecost.

Soon, however, with all other Orthodox churches in Vilnius transferred to the Unia, the Holy Spirit Church was the only Orthodox church remaining in the city. Around this time, a number of the newly Uniate churches were destroyed in fires, so the Holy Spirit Church came to be one of the only churches in Lithuania proper still celebrating services according to Eastern traditions.

By 1610, a traditional cenobitic monastic brotherhood was resident at the Holy Spirit Church, led by its first abbot, Leontijus Karpovičius (Leonty Karpovich).

Leontijus (born with the name *Longinus*) was from a Ruthenian family in Pinsk, in what is now southwestern Belarus, which had been part of the Grand Duchy of Lithuania since the early fourteenth century. He was educated in either Ostrog or Vilnius. When he had completed his education, he worked at the print shop of the Vilnius Orthodox brotherhood. He would have been sixteen years old at the beginning of the Unia and, being associated with the brotherhood, was thus involved in its resistance.

He would have been there when Holy Trinity Church was forcibly removed from the brotherhood and they took up residence in the new Holy Spirit Church. Many of the Orthodox priests serving there at the time were exiled.

In 1609, when a number of members of the brotherhood journeyed to Warsaw to protest against the treatment of the Orthodox in Vilnius, Longinus went with them. They returned home dissatisfied with the response, and upon his return Longinus received monastic tonsure and took the name Leontijus. He was also ordained to the priesthood.

After the brotherhood published a book denouncing the Unia, the Uniates rounded up and burned all copies that could be found, and they threw Leontijus into a pit, where he remained for two years. After his release in 1612, he became the first abbot of the organized monastic brotherhood, instituting its first rule of cenobitic life.

Life as an Orthodox abbot in Vilnius was not easy in the early seventeenth century, and it was often the case that people would throw rocks at Orthodox Christians on their way to church. On one occasion, Leontijus himself was injured with a brick in an attack that included Josaphat Kuncevich. He remained meek and also preached meekness in the face of these attacks.

In 1620, Leontijus was elected by the Ecumenical Patriarchate to become a bishop among the Ruthenian Orthodox. He was ill, however, and died in October 1620, before he could be consecrated. He was just forty years old. His body was later found to be incorrupt, and he was locally venerated for centuries.

The Venerable Leontijus Karpovičius was canonized as a saint of the Orthodox Church in 2011.

HOLY FATHER LEONTIJUS, PRAY TO God for us!

CHAPTER 16

Lithuanian Easter Eggs in American Orthodoxy

M OST ORTHODOX CHRISTIANS IN AMERICA probably do not real-ize that the history of Orthodox Christianity in Lithuania has had multiple direct influences on parts of our life here. If you know the story of St. Alexis of Wilkes-Barre, you may have guessed by now that his story ulti-mately finds its origins in the Polish-Lithuanian Commonwealth. He was born in 1853 in what is now Slovakia and was then part of the Austrian Empire, but the church he served there was Greek Catholic, part of the Unia that had its origins in the late sixteenth-century Grand Duchy of Lithuania in the Commonwealth.

After the death of his wife, he came to America in 1889 to serve Uniate parishes but was stymied by his Roman Catholic Bishop John Ireland. He thus left the Greek Catholic Church and became Orthodox, leading numer-ous Ruthenian Catholic churches in America into the Orthodox Church: roughly twenty thousand people. This movement became the core of the modern Orthodox Church in America (OCA), and a number of these par-ishes eventually became part of the Russian Orthodox Church Outside Rus-sia (ROCOR).

A second wave of thirty-seven former Uniate parishes in America also came into the Orthodox Church in 1938, forming the American Carpatho-Russian Orthodox Diocese (ACROD). Thus, with these two movements of former Uniates into the Orthodox Church, the traditions of Ruthenian Orthodox Christianity, nourished in the late medieval period in the Grand Duchy of

Lithuania, became part of the fabric of American Orthodox life. American Orthodox Christians often don't know about the origins of these traditions. I want to tell you about two that are probably very familiar.

Glory to Jesus Christ!

Father Andrew: On one of our nights in Lithuania, Fr. Gintaras took us into the countryside to meet Motinėlė Justina's family and to share food and drink together in a gathering at her grandmother's home. He said to me that I should greet her parents and grandmother by saying *Garbė Jėzui Kristui.* Apparently it is a greeting well-known especially among older people in Lithuania.

When we arrived, I said this greeting to them as best as I could. They responded solemnly with *Per amžius, Amen.*

I later asked Fr. Gintaras what the exchange meant—I could tell that *Jėzui Kristui* meant "Jesus Christ," but I wanted to know the rest. As you might have guessed by now, the exchange means "Glory to Jesus Christ" and "Forever, Amen."

Orthodox Christian Americans—especially those who belong to the OCA, the Carpatho-Russian diocese, the ROCOR, or the Ukrainian churches—will of course immediately recognize their own well-beloved greeting "Glory to Jesus Christ!" (*Slava Isusu Christu*) and the response as very similar to their accustomed "Glory forever!" (*Slava naviky*).

It turns out that these greetings are from the Grand Duchy of Lithuania, stretching centuries into the past, and were commonly used by all Lithuanians up until the period of Soviet occupation starting in the 1940s. They were part of the Christian cultural inheritance of Uniates, who then brought them to America during the immigration of the late nineteenth and early twentieth centuries.

Holy Supper

Father Andrew: Another piece of beloved Orthodox culture in America is what's commonly called Holy Supper. It is a fasting meal celebrated on Christmas Eve that usually includes twelve dishes. This ritual meal, shared with family, is well-known in parishes belonging to these same traditions—OCA, ROCOR, Carpatho-Russian, and Ukrainian.

What people may not know, however, is that there is an exact parallel among Polish Catholics, who call it *Wigilia*, and it is also celebrated among Lithuanians, who call it *Kūčios*. In most Slavic languages, it's something like *Sviati Vechera*. It is celebrated in modern Ukraine and Belarus, as well. If you were to look at a map of Eastern Europe and put a pin in every city where a twelve-dish Christmas Eve fasting supper is celebrated, you would essentially produce a map of the former Polish-Lithuanian Commonwealth.

Orthodox Christians, Catholics, and Protestants celebrate it there. Traditions vary considerably, with variation from which foods are eaten to how ritualized the meal is.

After I got back from Lithuania, realizing that my own Lithuanian Catholic ancestors would have celebrated Kūčios, and knowing also that the Orthodox of Lithuania celebrate it even today, I decided that it was time to reintroduce it into my family.

We had no family tradition for this meal, so along with a lot of research to find which dishes I wanted to make and what the ritual could look like, I decided to recruit Michael, who is a Ukrainian-American belonging to our local parish and an expert on what his own family has done for generations. Michael helped me organize a Holy Supper celebration for our parish. We melded together many traditions, invited dozens of people to join us, and on Christmas Eve of 2022, we held a meaningful, prayerful Holy Supper right in our little town of Emmaus, Pennsylvania.

In Michael's family, the meal is eaten while standing. A small child is taken outside to find the first star of the evening, and when he or she spots it, the meal may begin. While the patriarch of the family presides, the matriarch and whomever she has pressed into service brings a series of twelve courses to the table. Everyone present takes a taste of each course, and various tales, anecdotes, comments, and remembrances may be spoken with each course.

When everything was prepared, we prayed God's blessings on each other for the New Year, asked mutual forgiveness, remembered our newly departed, shared our special foods, and shared the joy of the Birth of Christ. In the years that followed, we did it again and again.

Why? There's something that Holy Supper does to you. And I want that again.

THERE IS ONE MORE PIECE of Lithuanian Christian history that touches the lives of Orthodox Christians in America that we want to discuss. For this part of the book, it will be our final tale.

CHAPTER 17

The Gate of Dawn

THE BLACK MADONNA OF CZĘSTOCHOWA in Poland, the Virgin of Guadalupe in Latin America and the American Southwest, the Theotokos of Vladimir, Our Lady of Walsingham, the Golden Madonna of Essen, Our Lady of Perpetual Help . . .

Throughout the history of the Church, when cities, nations, and cultures convert to Christianity they invariably produce or acquire an icon of the Theotokos that becomes emblematic of their self-identity—the Mother of God interceding for their land and people, and helping them to see how they fit into the Christian story. For Lithuanians, be they Orthodox Christian, Roman Catholic, or Protestant, that icon is Our Lady of the Gate of Dawn—*Aušros Vartų Dievo Motina*.

As is perhaps befitting for such a wondrous gift to the people of God, the exact origins of this icon are unknown. Some say it came from Crimea, acquired by Duke Algirdas as a trophy of war and presented as a gift to his Orthodox wife. Others say it was commissioned by the Polish King Sigismund II Augustus, a descendant of Jogaila, and that his wife Barbara sat as the model for the portrait.

Recent art historians have assigned a much later date to the painting of this icon, naming it a product of the Northern Renaissance of the seventeenth century. But to see her icon for yourself is to know that they are all, in a way, wrong. Our Lady of the Gate of Dawn does not belong to a conqueror, a century, or a particular artistic movement. She belongs to the Lithuanian people, her image serene and timeless.

Copies of this icon—painted, printed, engraved in wood or metal, or even fashioned from Baltic amber—adorn the walls of homes and parish churches all throughout Lithuania: Orthodox, Roman Catholic, and sometimes even Protestant. You almost cannot find a Christian church in Lithuania that does not have a copy of it. This image is found even on gravestones.

The icon, after having been moved once or twice for safety over the past four centuries, now resides in a chapel above the Dawn Gate, all that remains of the old medieval walls of the city. There is something fitting about this: In our services, we refer to the Theotokos as "our refuge and our wall."

Why is it called the Dawn Gate? Does it face the east, the place of the rising of the sun? Curiously, it faces south. There are several theories about the name, but no one really knows.

There is something enchanting, a serendipitous grace, for the pilgrim who rounds the corner and first sees the icon, shining in the sunlight through the balcony window of the gatehouse. The pilgrim enters through a doorway to their left, climbing a flight of narrow stairs and passing through a corridor before they emerge in the small chapel above the gate. Even with the noise of the street below, it is a silent place.

The chapel, although maintained by the Roman Catholic Church, is a sacred place for Orthodox Christians of Lithuania as well. In the Orthodox Church, the feast day of this icon is the day after Christmas, when an Orthodox prayer service is conducted before the icon. In Russian, it is known as *Ostrobramskaya.*

The pilgrim will be struck by the size of the icon, some six and a half feet in length, and by the countless silver votive offerings that adorn the walls of all three sides of the chapel, each one a testament to a miracle wrought by the intercessions of the Mother of God. To her right and left are golden statues of her parents, Ss. Joachim and Anna. As you face the icon, a large window to the city is behind you, the light flooding the chapel and revealing the face of the Lord's mother.

A steady stream of pilgrims moves silently through the chapel: watching, weeping, invited by the icon to join the Theotokos in her prayers. There is no

Christ child depicted in Our Lady of the Gate of Dawn. Instead, the Mother of God has her hands folded in prayer across her breast, her head inclined, her eyelids closed. There is a tradition that says this icon depicts her at the moment of the Annunciation, right after the moment she uttered the words "Behold, the handmaiden of the Lord."

An old woman who has been to the shrine many times before starts chatting to a pilgrim next to her. It doesn't matter. Nothing can shatter the peace of that moment.

That isn't to say, of course, that this icon of our Most Pure Lady hasn't seen its fair share of tumult and unrest. At the beginning of the sixteenth century, a series of walls were built around the city of Vilnius. In keeping with the custom of the time, icons and relics were placed above the various gates to protect it against attack.

Over one of these gates, the Dawn Gate, a magnificent image of the Mother of God was placed. Although subsequent centuries would see the walls destroyed, the Dawn Gate was always left intact, and it is now all that remains of those old fortifications. The icon of the Dawn Gate quickly became associated with several miracles, and in 1671, Carmelite monks built a wooden chapel beside the gatehouse, dedicated to the icon.

During the Great Northern War at the dawn of the eighteenth century, Swedish forces briefly captured the city of Vilnius. Inspired perhaps as much by the lust of conquest as they were by Protestant iconoclasm, the Swedish soldiers mocked the icon and forbade the usual hymns and prayers offered at the chapel.

On the night of Holy Saturday, they sang jeering and blasphemous songs, and caroused outside the chapel all night. One of the soldiers even put a bullet through the icon. That night, the great iron gates of the city collapsed, killing four of the carousing Swedish guards. No further attempts were made to damage the holy icon.

The next morning, the Lithuanian army launched a successful counterattack against the gate, which enabled them to retake the city. In gratitude to the Theotokos for her intervention on behalf of the city, the Lithuanian commander offered a handsome gift of silver to adorn her icon.

Over the years, many miracles associated with Our Lady of the Gate of Dawn were recorded, and love and veneration for the Mother of God through this icon spread to surrounding lands, including to modern-day Ukraine and Belarus.

IN THE YEAR 1755, A young man named Prókhor Isídorovich Moshnín made the three-hundred-mile pilgrimage from Kursk to Kyiv to seek the counsel of the great eldress St. Dosithea of Kyiv. While he was there, he was given, perhaps by the saint herself, an icon of the Theotokos painted after the type of Our Lady of the Gate of Dawn and inscribed in Slavonic with the refrain of the akathist hymn: *Rejoice, O Unwedded Bride.*

At the advice of St. Dosithea, young Prókhor pursued the monastic life in the wilderness of Sarov, where he was tonsured with the name Seraphim. Saint Seraphim of Sarov became perhaps the greatest of all the Russian mystic saints, burning brightly like his namesake with the fire of God's love.

Throughout his life, this icon of the Theotokos, which St. Seraphim called the "joy of all joys," remained constantly with him, often his only possession. In his later years, when the saint (at the insistence of the Mother of God herself) broke his long solitude to begin the work of a spiritual father, he kept a lampada (a small oil lamp) burning before her icon. He would use oil from this lamp to heal the sick and to anoint those who came to him for confession. At the end of his life, St. Seraphim reposed kneeling before this icon.

Through the copy of Our Lady of the Gate of Dawn icon that St. Seraphim of Sarov possessed—love for this icon and through it—devotion to the Theotokos has spread across the Orthodox world, including to America.

Parish churches as far away as Dallas, Texas, have this icon on their walls, a constant reminder of her obedience and prayerful submission to the will of God. For Lithuanians, this icon—with its mysterious origins and its ubiquity in Lithuanian churches—is iconic of the growth of Christianity in their country.

She who bore Christ into the world in a particular time and place now bears Christ to a particular people in another particular time and place, and we, her people, say: *Rejoice!*

117

LITHUANIANS HAVE MANY HYMNS TO the Mother of God. Here is one of them, *Sveika, Aušros Žvaigždė, šviesi*, of the musical type called a *kantička*:

> Hail, O thou bright Star of Dawn,
> Thou art our radiant joy:
> O Virgin Mary, most holy Lady,
> most dear Mother of Jesus!
>
> We cry out in supplication,
> As we pass through the woes of earth:
> Guard us from evil, send blessings to us,
> Banish all suff'rings of Hades.
>
> Virgin, our consolation true,
> Oh, let not mankind perish!
> O Brightest Star, shine down on our journey,
> By mighty grace light all our way.
>
> Glory be forever to the Trinity:
> Father, Son and Holy Spirit!
> Let us all sing an unceasing praise to
> The most dear Mother of Jesus!
>
> Let us all sing an unceasing praise to
> The most dear Mother of Jesus![1]

Father Andrew: After we got back home to America, I couldn't stop humming and singing this song to myself. A *kantička* is a kind of religious folk song, and knowing how folk songs tend to evolve, I found myself adding a couple verses of my own:

> Behold, a great and heavenly sign:
> A Woman clad in brightest sun,
> Moon under her feet, crowned with stars twelvefold,
> Mother of One Who rules nations.

---

1   Transcribed and translated by Fr. Gintaras Sungaila, adapted for English meter by Fr. Andrew Stephen Damick.

Hail, O Dawn Gate of Christ our God:
The Sun of Righteousness will rise,
With holy angels, coming in power,
The most dear Offspring of Mary.

As I am writing this, I remember again the Gate of Dawn, and I cannot help but feel the desire to weep in the memory, the ache to be there again, to know that joy.

MUCH OF THIS PART OF our tale has been about the relationship between Orthodox Christians, Roman Catholics, and Greek Catholics in Lithuania. At times, these relationships were very warm and at other times quite cold and even violent—especially in the early years.

The question of how these communities relate and should relate to each other is quite old—stretching back to the eleventh century, the time of the Great Schism—and it is not unique to Lithuania. Yet there is something about the Lithuanian attempts to live out this reality that can be instructive to those of us who live in multicultural, multireligious contexts.

As is true nearly everywhere Orthodox Christians are found in the West, the boundaries between these communities in the Lithuanian context can sometimes be quite fluid. While we were in Lithuania, we heard, for instance, how one family included Orthodox Christians, Roman Catholics, and Old Believers all quite close together.

We also learned the story of Our Lady of the Gate of Dawn, an icon that resides above a Catholic altar with little to no evidence that it ever resided in an Orthodox Church, yet it has its own feast day on the Orthodox calendar. Music, greetings, language, ritual, and culture all cross these boundaries throughout Lithuanian history, often without much sense that a particular tradition belonged solely to one religious community.

What should we make of this permeability? Is the Orthodox history of Lithuania a history of massive canonical failure and capitulation to ecumenical compromise? That conclusion would be both anachronistic and also a myopic way to see it. So how should we understand it?

In Philippians 4:8, St. Paul said: "Finally, brothers, whatever is true, whatever is honorable, whatever is just, whatever is pure, whatever is lovely, whatever is commendable, if there is any excellence, if there is anything worthy of praise, think about these things." And St. James said in his epistle: "Every good gift and every perfect gift is from above, coming down from the Father of lights" (James 1:17).

So that means if we see something good, it belongs to God, and if it belongs to God, it belongs to the Orthodox Church, which is the body of Christ. An icon of the Theotokos is an icon of the Theotokos. A hymn that sings the truth is a hymn that sings the truth. And Christian love is Christian love.

That does not mean that we ought to cross boundaries that we are forbidden to cross—it would be wrong, for instance, for two clergy who are not in communion with each other to concelebrate divine services together. It would be wrong to accept heresy for the sake of togetherness.

But we also do not need to erect barriers that our Fathers did not erect. Like them and like the apostles, we also can see that whatever is true and good is indeed praiseworthy, wherever we find it.

PART IV

The Cuckoo and the Serpent

The Legends of Lithuania

CHAPTER 18

Legends, Lore, and the Life of a People

O UR LAST THREE PARTS HAVE focused mainly on the great natural
beauty of Lithuania, its important cities and churches, and its complicated religious history as a borderland between the Orthodox East and the
Latin West. But these descriptions and accounts have also been interwoven
with stories of another kind—legends, hagiography, and the stories of Lithuania's wonder-working icons.

And although there is a real difference between mythology, folklore, and
hagiography, they are all part of a collective "lore" that has an important place
in the life of a people—far more important than yesterday's news or even the
history of recent decades. In the ancient and medieval world, people groups
understood themselves as a body, held together not just by relationships to
their living contemporaries but also to the past and to their future. Another
essential dimension was their relationship to the land.

It might be hard for us to imagine this as modern people. After all, the small-
est unit we usually conceive for a people is the nation-state. What is more, the
"melting pot" of American society and the untethering effect of suburbia and
of economic realities such as the "housing ladder" mean that, for many of us,
our identity as part of a family, tribe, or clan is not tied to any particular place.

The very idea of *place* in the modern world has given way to *space*, in which
any place is as good as another, its relationship to your story more or less arbi-
trary. Thus, the house you grew up in was just a stepping stone, a place your
family lived while your father had a particular job, something you outgrew as

123

the family became too large or wealthy enough to buy a different house, which was in turn sold to you by another family who had outgrown or aged out of their house—and on and on. In this paradigm, modern suburban churches take the name of the street they're on or of the neighborhood they're in, and if the church ever moves to a new building, they change their name for the new street or neighborhood.

In the premodern world, the lore of a people formed the connective tissue between place and time, between their past and present. This lore was made up of myth and mythology, of legends and hagiography, of history and things which were not quite history, all of which together manifested the pattern or blueprint by which their future would be built. If places and events were connected to each other on the horizontal axis of chronological history, they were also connected along a vertical axis of stories, songs, and rituals to the "sacred time" of the Gospels and to the *illo tempore*, the "great time" of their people's founding.

Thus, from ancient times, Christians dedicated their churches to the great feasts of Our Lord, of His Most Pure Mother, and of His saints, making ordinary "spaces" into "places" under the protection and patronage of members of the Divine Council. When those churches celebrate their patronal feast days, local history is caught up into the history of redemption in a way that saves not only the souls of those who participate but also the history, in chronological time, of a people.

For examples of this, we may consider the feast days of Our Lady of the Gate of Dawn and Our Lady of Trakai, which we discussed in previous chapters. These feast days are a source of unity among Orthodox and Roman Catholic Christians in Lithuania, even though they are sundered by a thousand years of painful religious history and schism.

Hagiography, relics, and wonder-working icons function in this way at the highest level of reality—at the summit of the mountain, so to speak. Legends, folktales, and fairy tales function in a similar way down at the mountain's roots.

The Legend of the Iron Wolf transforms Gediminas Hill from simply one of a thousand hills into the birthplace of the Grand Duchy and especially of Vilnius. Without the tale of the giantess Neringa, the Curonian Spit is simply an interesting geological formation, instead of the site of a primordial battle

124

against chaos. The legendary connections between ancient Roman patricians fleeing the tyranny of Nero and the Gediminid Dynasty may not be strictly historical, but they have informed the self-understanding of a pious and freedom-loving people for generations.

Stories like this are the narrative equivalent of a pilgrimage, revealing the heart of a people. These stories often take on a highly symbolic form, distilling the complexities of historical realities into universal patterns.

In the chapters that follow, we will take a closer look at the stories and legends of the Lithuanian people that connect them to their past and inform their future.

CHAPTER 19

The Palemonid Dynasty

WHEN THE ENGLISH PRIEST AND poet Layamon began writing his great alliterative chronicle at the end of the twelfth century, he began where earlier chroniclers such as Wace and Geoffrey of Monmouth had begun—the fall of Troy.

According to these medieval chronicles, the island of Britain had been founded by Brutus of Troy, a descendant of the legendary Trojan hero Aeneas. According to ancient Roman legends later immortalized by the poet Virgil, Aeneas had been one of the great heroes of the city of Troy, spared from death by his mother, the goddess Venus (or Aphrodite), to lead a remnant of the Trojan people to Italy where his descendants would eventually found the city of Rome.

Thus, the English chroniclers tied the history of the island of Britain (named after Brutus, according to ancient etymologies) back to the most important mythic-historical cycle of the medieval world, the fall of Troy and the founding of Rome.

Modern historians, of course, dismiss these claims out of hand. Regardless of their empirical, historical value in the modern sense, they tell us something very important about the medieval world and how medieval people conceived of themselves as the successors of the classical world and of the vast inheritance of culture and literature that begins with Homer.

It is also important to understand that for them, this was part and parcel with their Christian inheritance. In the world of early Christendom and the

Middle Ages, when a people converted to Christianity, that also meant finding themselves in the story of Troy and Rome. Perhaps there is no clearer example of this than the fact that St. Constantine the Great, when he built his city of New Rome or Constantinople in near proximity to the site of ancient Troy, intended that it should be from the beginning a Christian city, the first city in the ancient world built without any pagan temples.

Over the course of early Christendom and the Middle Ages, various cities, provinces, and peoples wrote themselves into the ancient stories, connecting their legendary ancestors to the descendants of great Hellenic or Trojan heroes as well as to the sons of Noah and the Table of Nations found in Genesis 10. The Lithuanians were no exception.

IN THE FIRST TWO PARTS of this book, we focused primarily on the history of Lithuania leading up to Jogaila, who ruled over a unified Poland and Lithuania and made Roman Catholicism the official religion of his kingdom. As with other European peoples, such as the Kyivan Rus', the large-scale conversion of the Lithuanian people to Christianity was also the beginning of another very important addition to their society—literacy. And one of the first things a newly literate people does is begin to write their own chronicles.

By the fifteenth century, a chronicle that showed the way in which the Lithuanian people were connected to the larger, universal story of Europe and of the Christian world had become increasingly important.

Beginning in 1385, the Grand Duchy of Lithuania was connected to the Kingdom of Poland via the personal union, a single monarch holding both states. This relationship was eventually formalized at Lublin in 1569, when the Polish-Lithuanian Commonwealth took its most durable shape. The interim period of nearly two centuries proved to be critical for the formation of Lithuanian national identity.

During this time, Poland was Lithuania's gateway into Western Europe, and interactions with Latin Christian civilization were at first filtered through that lens. This led to claims on the Polish side that they had brought civilization to a barbaric land, that the Lithuanians were thus the main recipients of all of the benefits of the personal union with the Kingdom of Poland. At least partially in response to this, between 1420 and 1520, the first Lithuanian chronicles were composed.

Sometimes scholars lump all of these chronicles into one, but they should be understood as three works building upon one another. The first, the short *Chronicle of the Grand Dukes of Lithuania*, was composed in Smolensk and has a particularly Orthodox flavor to it. It survives only in later compilations, the earliest of which was put together in 1446 by Gerasim, the Orthodox Christian Bishop of Smolensk, along with the help of his clerk Timofei.

This chronicle was probably composed when Vytautas the Great had temporarily converted to the Orthodox Christian Faith as part of his bid to be crowned King of Lithuania. Although history eventually took another path, Gerasim was effusive in his praise of Vytautas, and he supported the claims of the Grand Duchy of Lithuania over against the Kingdom of Poland in the Lithuanian Civil War, which threatened to tear apart the personal union after Vytautas's death.

In the late 1400s, a second chronicle, *The Chronicle of the Grand Duchy of Lithuania and Samogitia*, was compiled, elaborating and expanding upon the earlier work. This second chronicle makes the most important addition to Lithuania's connection to the universal story of Europe, laying down the foundation for the story of Lithuania's Roman heritage—the Palemonid Dynasty.

ACCORDING TO THE SECOND CHRONICLE, Palemon was a first-century Roman noble, a relative of the Roman Emperor Nero, who had fled Italy along with five hundred other Roman nobles to escape the persecution. Settling in Baltic lands, they built a settlement on the hill later known as *Palemono kalnas*, where they ruled for many generations until the emergence of the Gediminid Dynasty.

It is important to note that the only other chronicle that had been written up until this time concerning the emergence of the Gediminid Dynasty was from the Teutonic Order, the long-standing Crusader enemies of the Grand Dukes of Lithuania. According to the Teutonic chronicle, Gediminas had begun his career as a stablehand. This new chronicle instead linked the Lithuanian rulers not only to a noble bloodline, but ultimately to Rome itself, and via Rome, to the story of the Trojan War, giving the Lithuanian rulers a pedigree as prestigious as any European dynasty and bolstering their claims against their Polish and Russian rivals.

Contrary to what many modern scholars have thought, this account was not fabricated out of thin air. It has its roots (somewhat ironically) in the fifteenth-century *Annals or Chronologies of the Illustrious Kingdom of Poland* of Jan Długosz. Długosz, whose twelve-volume work was really a synthesis of various medieval chronicles (including several Ruthenian chronicles that have not otherwise survived), was interested in tracing the origins of the peoples of Poland and Ruthenia.

He recounts that the Roman noble Vilia was the original founder of the country that later became known as the Grand Duchy of Lithuania. Vilia had left Rome in the time of Julius Caesar (not Nero) because he had been a follower of the Roman general and statesman Pompey. He left Italy with five hundred other Roman nobles, eventually settling in Lithuanian lands. The city he founded was called *Romnove* or *Roma Nova* ("New Rome") but was quickly renamed to *Vilnus* (later *Vilnius*) in honor of Vilia, in much the same way that Rome took the name of Romulus or Constantinople that of Constantine.

By this account, then, Vilnius was both the original site of Lithuanian civilization as well as a continuation of Rome. According to Długosz, the sound "L" was added to *Italia*, rendering the name of this new people first *Lithalia*, then *Litualia*, and finally, *Lithuania*. All of this was more or less in line with Italian historians of that time, who believed that followers of Pompey had settled along the Baltic, and it is among these same historians that we first find the name Palemon.

Rather than inventing a link between Roman and Lithuanian culture, then, the second and third Lithuanian chronicles expanded upon this legend and tried to bring it into line both with Lithuanian legends about their own history as well as their growing awareness of the classical world. For instance, the third chronicle, called the *Bychowiec Chronicle*, further updates the legend of the Palemonids, having them flee Italy after the invasion of Attila the Hun.

Although the legend of the Palemonids has not been accepted as historical fact since the beginning of the twentieth century, it proved durable enough to have a profound impact upon the collective Lithuanian consciousness. For instance, as Lithuanian scholar Artūras Vasiliauskas has noted, the number of the five hundred nobles, one of the most persistent elements found in every version of the legend, is a number associated in the ancient and medieval worlds with the resistance of citizens to despotism. It dates back to the Athenian boule, a council of five hundred citizens, who opposed the tyranny of Peisistratos in the sixth century BC. The second chronicle's change, which has these five hundred nobles leaving in the time of Nero, makes for an important difference—nobles fleeing the persecution of Nero were probably Christians.

These themes, the ancient Christian character of the Lithuanian people and a cultural predisposition to resist tyranny, became extremely important to the consciousness of the Lithuanian people in the late sixteenth century. These same themes would continue to echo loudly in the twentieth century, when the struggle to resist tyranny and defend the Christian faith became one and the same. But that's a story for another time.

CHAPTER 20

Eglė, Queen of Serpents[1]

L ONG AGO, IN ANOTHER TIME, there lived an old man and his wife. They had twelve sons and three daughters. Their youngest daughter was named Eglė, and she was the most beautiful girl in the whole countryside.

One day, Eglė and her two older sisters decided to go swimming. They laughed and bathed and splashed about in the river, and when they were done they climbed up onto the riverbank to dress and to comb their hair. But when Eglė was about to put on her clothes, she saw something wriggling in her blouse. To her disgust, she found that a sea serpent had slithered up one of her sleeves!

Her older sisters threw the blouse down and jumped on it, doing anything they could to dislodge the serpent. But the serpent would not leave. Finally, the serpent turned to young Eglė and spoke to her with the voice of a man: "Eglė, Eglė, promise to marry me and become my bride, and I will gladly come out of this blouse."

Eglė began to cry. How could she agree to marry a serpent? "Please, O serpent," she wept, "go back to where you came from, to the deep sea, and leave me in peace."

---

1   Paraphrased and adapted from Zheleznova, "Spruce, Queen of Grass Snakes," *Tales of the Amber Sea*, 164–171.

But the serpent would not listen, only calling to her again: "Eglė, Eglė, promise to marry me and become my bride, and I will gladly come out of this blouse."

Finding there was nothing else she could do, Eglė agreed, promising the serpent that she would become his bride. Her sisters, however, thought little of this, for how could a serpent ever take a human girl as his bride? When they went back and told their parents, they too thought little of this, for how could a little snake press his claim? By the next day, everyone had forgotten about the incident—everyone except Eglė.

On the third day after the engagement, the family found that all of the serpents in the land had gathered and overrun their farm, bringing a wagon with them. The whole family was terrified as the serpents slithered in heaving masses across every inch of the barn, the farm, and the house.

One of the serpents entered the house itself, addressing himself to the old man to discuss the terms of the marital union. At first, the old man hemmed and hawed, refusing to believe this was really happening and hoping it was all a dream. But when every serpent in the land is overrunning your farm, the reality of things soon sets in, and it does not matter how one feels.

So it was that the old man agreed to give his youngest and most beautiful daughter over to the serpents. But he had treachery in his heart: "I will give you my youngest daughter, my sweet and beautiful Eglė, only you must give me a little time so that she can be properly adorned as a bride, and so that the wedding gifts can be prepared."

The serpent agreed to this, but as soon as the old man could get away, he went to a wise woman who lived on the edge of the forest and asked her what he should do. "It's easy to fool the serpents," the wise woman said. "Load up the wedding gifts in the wagon, but instead of your daughter, dress up your goose in her clothes and give him the goose as a bride."

The old man went home and did as the wise woman had advised. He took his fat white goose and dressed it up in Eglė's clothes. When the serpents came with their wagon, he placed the goose and the wedding gifts in it, and climbed into the wagon with his "daughter" to begin the journey to his new son-in-law's home. But as they were beginning their journey, they heard a cuckoo bird singing in a tree nearby: "Cuckoo! Cuckoo! You've been fooled! Instead of a bride, he has given you a goose! Cuckoo! Cuckoo!"

The serpents returned to the farm, threw the goose, the old man, and the wedding gifts out of the wagon, and demanded the real bride. The old man begged for more time. "Please," he said, "I will give you my daughter, but you must give us another day to finish her bridal gown." The serpents agreed to this, but as soon as he could get away, the old man went to the wise woman who lived on the edge of the forest and asked her what he should do.

"It's easy enough to fool the serpents," the wise woman said. "Load up the wedding gifts in the wagon, but instead of your daughter, array a white sheep in the new dress, and give her as a bride."

The old man went home and did as the wise woman advised. He took a white, wooly sheep and dressed it up in Eglé's new wedding finery. When the serpents came with their wagon, he placed the sheep and the wedding gifts in it, and climbed into the wagon with his "daughter" to begin the journey back to his new son-in-law's home. But as they were beginning their journey, they heard the cuckoo bird singing in a nearby tree: "Cuckoo! Cuckoo! You've been fooled! Instead of a bride, he has given you a white sheep! Cuckoo! Cuckoo!"

The serpents returned to the farm, threw the white sheep, the old man, and the wedding gifts out of the wagon, and demanded the real bride. The old man begged for more time. "Please," he said, "I will give you my daughter, but you must give us another day to finish arraying her in her bridal finery." The serpents agreed to this, but as soon as he could get away, the old man went to the wise woman who lived on the edge of the forest and asked her what he should do.

"It's easy enough to fool the serpents," the wise woman said. "Load up the wedding gifts in the wagon, but instead of your daughter, array a white cow in the new dress and wedding finery, and give her as a bride."

The old man went home and did as the wise woman had advised. He took the family's white cow and dressed it up in Eglé's new wedding finery. When the serpents came with their wagon, he placed the cow and the wedding gifts in it, and climbed into the wagon with his "daughter" to begin the journey back to his new son-in-law's home. But as they were beginning their journey, they heard the cuckoo bird singing in a nearby tree: "Cuckoo!

Cuckoo! You've been fooled! Instead of a bride, he has given you a white cow! Cuckoo! Cuckoo!"

The serpents returned, and this time they were in a white-hot rage. They threw the white cow, the old man, and the wedding gifts out of the wagon, and demanded that they be given Eglė at once. Otherwise, they threatened that the next year there would be no rain, followed by a year of flood and then a year of famine.

Seeing there was nothing else they could do, they arrayed Eglė in all of her wedding finery. They put on her new dress and prepared her to meet her new husband. And Eglė wept within the house.

When all had been made ready, they put Eglė and the wedding gifts into the wagon, and the serpents took her away. As they drove, they heard the cuckoo singing from a nearby tree: "Cuckoo! Cuckoo! Drive, drive! The groom awaits his bride! Cuckoo!"

EVENTUALLY, EGLĖ AND HER WAGON full of writhing chaperones came to the edge of the sea. There, instead of the sea serpent, she met a handsome young prince. "I am the snake who crawled into the sleeve of your blouse," he said. "My name is Žilvinas, and I have come to take you to my palace beneath the sea."

Then he took her by the hand and brought her to a certain island, from which they descended to his realm beneath the sea. Žilvinas showed Eglė his palace, which was made of amber, and there the wedding was held. For three weeks they drank, danced, and feasted. There were many beautiful guests in the serpent's palace, and Eglė became happy and forgot her sorrows, her family, and her homeland.

Nine years passed, and Eglė bore her husband four children: three sons named *Ąžuolas* (meaning "Oak"), *Uosis* (meaning "Ash"), and *Beržas* (meaning "Birch"), and one daughter named *Drebulė* (meaning "Aspen"). Eglė had all but forgotten her family until one day, when she was playing with her oldest son Ąžuolas, he asked her: "My dear mother, where do your parents live? I would like to go and visit them."

In that moment, Eglė remembered her sorrows, her family, and her homeland. She remembered her father, her mother, her brothers, and her sisters, and she began to wonder how things were going for them. Were they in good health? Had they prospered in the nine years she had been gone from the world beneath the sun? Perhaps they had all died after so many years. She yearned to see her family and her homeland again. But her husband, the serpent Žilvinas, would not even listen to her entreaties.

She asked him again and again, and finally he showed her a spindle of silk and told her: "Very well. But first you must spin this tuft of silk. Afterward, I will let you go and visit your family and your homeland."

Eglė sat before the spindle. She spun all day. She spun all night. She spun and she spun, but the silk would not spin. "Spin, spin, spin," she said, "but it will never be spun." And she knew that she had been tricked. So she went to an old woman who lived beneath the sea, who was known to be a witch and a sorceress.

Eglė asked her: "Grandmother, dear heart, please teach me how to spin this tuft of silk. I spin and spin and spin, and yet it will never be spun."

And the old woman told her how to accomplish this task: "Cast the silk into a new-kindled fire. Otherwise, you will never be able to spin it."

Eglė returned home and cast the silk into the flames of an oven that had recently been kindled. The silk went up in flames, and when the flames died down, where there had once been a bundle of silk there was now a toad. But when Eglė picked up the toad, she found it was making silk from its body. Having spun and woven the silk, she returned to her husband and said: "Now, husband, please let me go and visit my parents and my homeland."

Then Žilvinas the serpent drew out a pair of hard metal boots from beneath one of the drinking benches of his palace, and said, "Very well. But first, wear these boots down. Afterward, I will let you go and visit your family and your homeland."

Eglė put the boots on her feet. She stomped around the palace and even dragged her feet along the stone floor, but the boots were thick and were not at all worn down. "Stomp, stomp, stomp," she said, "but they will never be worn down. Walk or do not walk, but these boots will last forever." So she went back to the old woman who lived beneath the sea, who was known to be a witch and a sorceress.

Eglė asked her: "Grandmother, dear heart, please teach me how to wear down these boots of iron. I stomp and I stomp, and yet they will never be worn down."

And the old woman told her how to accomplish this task: "Go to a blacksmith and wear them down in his furnace," she said. "Otherwise you will never be able to wear them out."

Eglė did as she was told. She took them to a blacksmith and wore them down in his furnace. After three days of stomping, the boots were worn down. Then she returned to her husband and said: "Now, husband, please let me go and visit my parents and my homeland."

The serpent said to her, "Very well, but you must bake at least a rabbit pie for the journey, otherwise what will you have to give to your brothers and their children?" But the serpent had ordered that all of the cooking utensils in the palace be hidden so that Eglė could not cook. Eglė thus found that she would have to bring in water without a bucket and make the dough without a bowl.

Once again she returned to the old woman who lived beneath the sea: "Grandmother, dear heart, please tell me, how will I bring in water without a bucket, and how will I mix the dough without a bowl?"

And the old woman told her how to accomplish this task: "Spread out the sifted leavening, immerse the sieve in water, and with it mix the dough."

Eglė did as she was told. All day long she mixed and baked until the pies were ready. Having completed all of his stipulations, she bid farewell to her husband and took her children to visit her homeland.

The serpent went along part of the way with them, getting them across the sea. Then, he said to her: "Now, my wife, you should be no longer than nine days in visiting your family and your homeland, and at the end of those nine days you must return here, to the edge of the sea. When you return, you must come alone, just yourself and the children. When you approach the sea, call for me like this:

Žilvinas, dear Žilvinėlis,
If alive, may the sea foam milk,
If dead, may the sea foam blood.

If you see foaming milk coming toward you across the waves, then know that I am alive. But if you see blood, then you will know that I have reached my end. While you are at your parents' home, neither you nor the children should let this secret be known—don't tell anyone how to call for me!"

Having said all of these things, the serpent bid farewell to his family and wished them a swift and safe return. For her own part, Eglė felt great joy in returning to her homeland. All of her relatives, in-laws, and neighbors gathered around to ask question after question. Everyone wanted to know what it was like living with the serpent and what her life was like beneath the sea. She described every aspect of her life, and everyone offered her wonderful hospitality: good food and good talk. Eglė hardly even noticed the nine days passing.

During all this time, Eglė's parents, brothers, and sisters had been scheming about how to keep Eglė from returning to her husband. They decided to question the children to find out how, when their mother returned to the beach, she was supposed to call for her husband. Once they knew this, the family could go down to the seashore, call for the serpent, and kill him.

First, they called upon Ąžuolas, trying to flatter him by telling him how clever and handsome he was. They questioned him all day, but he said that he did not know. Having failed, they threatened the child not to tell his mother of their actions. The second day they tried the same thing with Uosis, and then with Beržas, but they would not divulge the secret.

Finally, they took Eglė's youngest child and only daughter, Drebulė, outside. At first she did as her brothers had done, claiming not to know. But they threatened to beat her with a rod and, being young and frightened, she told all.

Then all twelve brothers took scythes and went down to the edge of the sea. Standing upon the shore, they called out:

Žilvinas, dear Žilvinėlis,
If alive, may the sea foam milk,
If dead, may the sea foam blood.

Then the sea began to foam white with milk, and the serpent came to the shore. But as he was swimming up, the brothers stood around him and hacked him to pieces with their scythes. Then they went home, but they did not tell Eglė what they had done.

After the nine days of Eglė's stay were ended, she bade farewell to her father and mother and brothers and sisters, and to all of her family and friends, and went down to the seashore. She called for her husband as he had taught her:

Žilvinas, dear Žilvinėlis,
If alive, may the sea foam milk,
If dead, may the sea foam blood.

The sea shook and the thunder rolled, and a great wave of foaming blood washed toward Eglė. Eglė heard the voice of her beloved husband crying out to her amid the storm: "Your twelve brothers with their scythes cut me down, for the secret of calling out to me was given to them by our own Drebulė, our most beloved daughter!"

Then Eglė turned to her children, storming with wrath. To Drebulė she said:

May you become a quaking aspen,
May you shiver day and night,
May the rain cleanse your mouth,
May the wind comb your hair!

But to her sons, she said:

Stand, my strong sons, as strong as trees.
I, your mother, will become a spruce.

Then all became as Eglė had said. She became the spruce. Her sons became the oak, the ash, and the birch, the strongest of our trees. Her daughter became the quaking aspen, which trembles even in the slightest breeze, for she shook before her uncles and gave away her true father.

CHAPTER 21

The Curonian Spit and Its Spirits

RICHARD: KURŠIŲ NERIJA, OR THE Curonian Spit, is a thin, curving spit of sand and forest. Some sixty-eight miles long, it shelters Lithuania's Baltic coast. As with many places in Lithuania, it is steeped in history and legend. According to local folklore, it was raised by a giantess to protect her people from the raging storms sent by a sea serpent.

Since those days, its dunes have seen Vikings and Teutonic Knights; they have moved to swallow villages, stood in silence as European luminaries from Napoleon to Thomas Mann marched, and lived and found beauty in their dancing trees and fine, sandy beaches. For me, it was one of the most beautiful and eerie places we visited during our pilgrimage.

Currently, the territory of the Curonian Spit is divided between the modern state of Lithuania and Russia's Kaliningrad Oblast. To get to the spit, we took a ferry from the city of Klaipėda, then drove across the spit to the town of Nida, the largest settlement on the spit and a popular resort destination for Lithuanians and Germans.

As we drove, we passed log homes and fishing shacks built in a style that reminded me of traditional German homes colonial settlers built in Pennsylvania. These, along with the presence of a Lutheran church and graveyard in Nida, are a testament to the ongoing German presence on the spit going back hundreds of years.

In the Middle Ages, the Curonian Spit was the site of Kaup, a major trading settlement occupied by pagan Old Prussian tribes, the first stop on the

Baltic trade route sometimes called the Amber Road. It is difficult to overstate the ubiquity of amber on the Curonian Spit and elsewhere in Lithuania—in well-trafficked areas, booths and shops advertise amber wares every few dozen yards!

Because of its wealth and importance, Kaup was a frequent target of Viking raids. Sometimes these raids were successful. Other times—not so much. As we stood on the deck of the ferry taking us from the mainland to the Curonian Spit, Fr. Gintaras told us tales of how the Vikings would come over from Sweden. When they landed on the Spit, they met the Curonians. While in many other places in northern Europe and Great Britain they were able to establish footholds or conduct regular raids, faced with the ferocity of what roughly amounted to tribes of Baltic Vikings, they decided to leave Lithuania alone.

One of the impressions of the Curonian Spit that is the most difficult to convey is the utter silence of the place. Perhaps you've taken a walk in the winter right after a fresh snowfall. Do you know the hush that falls over the landscape as the snow muffles everything except the soft crunch of your footfalls as you walk?

The Curonian Spit is really a series of massive sand dunes, some of which have moved in the past, thanks to deforestation and other factors, and swallowed up whole villages. The pine forests that cover most of the Spit today thrive in the sandy soil, protecting it from erosion, and the sand swallows up the sounds of the forest.

As you walk through the forest of the Curonian Spit, you will encounter strange pine trees whose trunks grow in graceful S-shapes, hearts, spirals, twisting corkscrews, or run like writhing serpents along the ground. These are the "dancing trees" of the dunes, and astonishingly, in an age of scientific discovery and explanations, nobody knows exactly why they do this.

There are theories. Some scientists believe, for instance, that it has to do with the life cycle of a certain kind of caterpillar. Somewhat more intuitively, local legend simply holds that the forest is walking or dancing, following the dunes in a stately procession. Janina Degutytė, a twentieth-century Lithuanian poet, saw these trees as symbolizing Lithuanian culture, driven and storm tossed, but still proud:

On and on they march

Over Neringa quicksands,

Bent and sped on by the westerner,

Tall, speechless and boughless pine trees,

With crowns tossed and shaken

Burdened with the storm's wailing and the seagulls' sobbing.

Like ancient rust-eaten statues—

A multitude sombre and silent—

They march on, Neringa pines,

Over the quicksand landward,

My sisters

Tall.[1]

The largest of the dunes on the Curonian Spit is called the Parnidis Dune (*Parnidžio kopa*), called so (it is believed) because it has passed over the town of Nida many times over the course of the last few centuries. This dune, which rises up nearly two hundred feet above sea level, overlooks the border that divides the Spit between its Lithuanian and Russian halves.

The climb up to Parnidis took us on a long path through the forest, until we finally reached a long wooden stairway that had been built into the base of the dune. Here, it's important to keep on the path. A misplaced foot on Parnidis can move several tons of sand, something that could have devastating long-term consequences.

I still have very distinct memories of that climb. We had taken off our shoes, and after a quick dip in the waters of the lagoon we began to hike up through the forest toward the dune. The cool sand felt good on our feet, which were tired and blistered after several long days of walking. A cool, bracing wind was blowing in from the sea, and we had to hurry to try to get to the top of the dune before the sun set.

At some point during the climb, someone started beating a drum a long way off in the trees, and the sand strangely muffled and distorted the sound. The place felt wild and ancient. One person in our group said, "I feel like I'm

---

1   Degutytė, "Neringa Pines."

in Narnia." And as I said to someone else: If I had met a faerie at that moment, or a white stag had run across my path, I would not have been at all surprised.

At the top of Parnidis there is a massive granite sundial that was built there in 1995. The feat of engineering that must have been necessary to build such a large granite structure at the top of an ambulatory dune without disturbing it is, even now, difficult to imagine.

The sundial is some forty-five feet high and accurate to the half hour, with notches that also indicate the month of the year as well as the solstices and equinoxes. It was the largest of the many sundials we would see during our pilgrimage. The granite stones of the sundial are engraved with Norse runes, which seem to be an attempt—perhaps like the Hill of Witches, about which I will say more in a moment—to make a nod toward the area's pre-Christian past.

There is also a phrase engraved on the sundial in Latin: *LUCEM DEMONSTRAT UMBRA*—"The Shadow reveals the Light."

The Tale of the Giantess Neringa[2]

LONG AGO, IN ANOTHER TIME, there was a young girl named Neringa. Neringa was found by the kindly fisherfolk who lived on the coast between the forest and the sea, near the mouth of the River Nemunas, in a land that is now known as Lithuania.

Neringa was a surprising child in many respects. Not only was she very clever and very beautiful, but she also quickly outgrew every other child in the village. Before long, she had outgrown all of the women in the village. Before much longer, she had outgrown all of the men in the village!

At this point, there could be no doubt: She was a giantess. However, she was kind, and she used her strength to help and protect the fisherfolk. Some even said that she was the daughter of the god of the sea.

When it came time for Neringa to marry, it was clear that no ordinary groom would do. Any man who would marry such a strong and beautiful

---

2   There are multiple conflicting versions of this story. This one is Richard's telling adapted from oral versions we were told while in Lithuania, supplemented with other material found in research.

woman must be quite strong himself. So a contest was held, and word of it went out to all of the surrounding towns and villages: Whoever could cast a stone the farthest could marry the beautiful Neringa.

A suitor—some say he was himself a giant—threw a stone all the way from Klaipėda to the village where Neringa lived. He won the contest, and the two were betrothed.

But Neringa had also attracted the attention of Naglis, a dragon or sea serpent, and in his rage he sent great and violent storms to batter the fisherfolk of the coast.

In her love for them, Neringa raised up a great spit of earth and sand to shelter the people who had taken her in and cared for her as a child, and this land became known as the Curonian Spit.

But some say that Neringa and her lover fought and killed the sea serpent, and built the great dunes of the Curonian Spit over his body, forever freeing her people from the terror of the dragon.

The Hill of Witches

ON THE CURONIAN SPIT, THERE is a site near the village of Juodkrantė known as the Hill of Witches (*Raganų kalnas*). It is one of the most distinctive sites on the dunes and consists of nearly one hundred traditional wooden sculptures—many of them carved by Samogitian folk artists. These sculptures line various trails and hiking paths in the area, and they depict scenes from Lithuanian mythology, folklore, and legend. And the most important legends these sculptures depict are those of the giantess Neringa.

The Hill of Witches has its origin in an ancient summer solstice festival known as St. John's Night (*Joninės*). On St. John's Night, the eve of the Christian feast known as the Nativity of St. John the Baptist, it was customary to build great bonfires, around which the villagers would dance and feast. At these feasts, the rich would feed the poor, and wild herbs would be gathered to be woven into crosses and taken to the church to be blessed.

Although some scholars simply see this (and other Christian festivals tied to the agricultural or solar cycle) as a holdover from paganism, for the ancient Christians who celebrated them, they were an affirmation that the gospel was real and not unconnected with the ebb and flow of a life lived close to the earth. Saint John's Night is still celebrated, both by Christians as well as by the Romuva, Baltic neopagans who have attempted to reconstruct the lost pre-Christian solstice festival.

In the nineteenth century, the area was romanticized as part of a growing Lithuanian nationalism, and the sites of the old St. John's Night bonfires were made the gathering places of "witches"—a term that, when translated into English from Lithuanian, might mean a witch but might also describe what we would call dwarves, fairies, and other mythological creatures. The sculptures there only date to the second half of the twentieth century, however, when they were added during the Soviet occupation.

One might wonder why the Soviets, being generally anti-religious, would permit the sculptures to be erected, since their content was related to ancient pagan religion. It is because they saw these stories as anti-Christian, and since Christianity was a living "problem" for the Soviets while Baltic paganism was long dead, the folk art served their interests.

That conclusion reveals something of the banal stupidity of Soviet leaders, however. As we ascended the hill, passing by numerous sculptures of Neringa and her story but also of various other figures—even the thunder-god Perkūnas—we finally arrived at the top of the hill, the highest point amid these dozens of sculptures. There at the top is the most striking image of them all—a great dragon flying through the air, and it is in the process of being defeated by a knight that to almost any Christian is quite obviously St. George, an ancient Christian image of Christianity triumphing over paganism.

Even if one interprets the sculptures as authentically pagan, they are not the oldest "religious" installments on the spit by a long shot.

There are several Christian churches on the Curonian Spit. Not far from the Hill of Witches, for instance, there is a Lutheran church and cemetery dating back to the 1850s. Walking up the hill toward the old graveyard, you will encounter more traditional Lithuanian carvings, now depicting Christ on the Cross.

As I walked alone through the old Lutheran cemetery, I came across a grave marked by a distinctive three-barred cross, the resting place of my own

Orthodox Christian brothers and sisters. I stopped and said a prayer for them, and for all of those who had been buried in that place.

Not far from there, there is another church, a Roman Catholic parish run by the Franciscan order. Once again, you can see traditional Samogitian carvings outside this church, this time depicting Christ, Francis of Assisi, and other Christian figures.

Lithuanian Paganism and Neopaganism

IN THE FIRST PART OF this book, we gave a general outline about the ancient Indo-European origins of Lithuanian paganism as well as notes about a few of the Baltic gods the Lithuanians worshipped. We also learned about the first written-down piece of Lithuanian mythology, the Myth of Sovijus, which is said to introduce the practice of cremation and sacrifices to the various Baltic gods.

To get a sense of the framework within which we can understand Lithuanian paganism, we have to point out a few facts about the known sources. Lithuanians and their early tribal forebears were pagans until the late fourteenth century, when Christianization began under Roman Catholicism. The Myth of Sovijus was recorded in a Slavic chronicle in 1261, and the earliest known written sources of the Lithuanian language itself date only from about 1500.

What this means is that we have no writing from Lithuanian pagans themselves detailing their gods, their myths, their worship practices, and so on. All that we have prior to Christianization are a handful of testimonies from people who are not Lithuanians or even Balts—mainly Slavic Orthodox Christians or Catholic Crusaders.

In addition to the Sovijus story, the Teutonic Crusaders mention in a peace treaty with Prussian tribes that the Lithuanians worshipped a harvest god named Kurkas, whose priests were noted for performing certain burial rituals. There is also a reference in the twelfth-century Book of Roger, an atlas written for King Roger II by a Muslim cartographer living in Sicily, that the Baltic tribes worshipped fire, possibly a reference to worship of Perkūnas, the god of thunder and lightning. A number of other fragmentary references exist from

THE WOLF AND THE CROSS

the pre-Christian period of Lithuanian history, but none are from works dedi-cated to describing Lithuanian pagan religion—its myths and its rituals.

There is also some archaeological evidence that reveals a handful of details about Lithuanian pagan religion, including that its adherents practiced human sacrifice. That is hardly unique to Lithuanian paganism, however. Archae-ology reveals that pagans practiced human sacrifice not only in the Baltic lands, nor only throughout northern Europe generally, but nearly everywhere paganism existed in the world. Human sacrifice lasted among the Balts for a long time, too. There are indications, for instance, that St. Adalbert of Prague, a tenth-century missionary to the Baltic Prussians, was killed with an axe in a ritual manner by a pagan priest.

The other sources for Lithuanian paganism are folktales whose earliest attestations are from centuries after Christianization. They cannot therefore be relied upon as accurate witnesses to pagan myth or ritual, though a number of interpreters have attempted to reconstruct such things by extracting pieces from the context of these later stories. It remains guesswork, however, based on very little information.

So what was Lithuanian paganism like? We honestly don't know much at all. That said, if it was anything like the paganisms we know more about from the same region or even elsewhere in the Indo-European world, it was a religion that included constant interaction with the gods through ritual sacrifice—including humans in some cases—and in which tribal leaders often functioned as the center of religious practice, perhaps thought to be divine themselves.

BEGINNING IN THE NINETEENTH CENTURY, a few attempts have been made to reconstruct Baltic paganism. The most notable of these is Romuva, which takes its name from an East Prussian Baltic sacred grove. Romuva sees a Prussian-Lithuanian philosopher and theosophist called Vydunas—born Wilhelm Starost in 1868—as its founding father, though Vydunas him-self never said that he was trying to revive a pagan religion. A leader of the Lithuanian national revival in Lithuania Minor (then part of the Kingdom of Prussia), he praised ancient Balts as having a high spirituality, with the divine represented by fire. He died in 1953.

Other attempts to recreate Baltic pagan practice were made in the early twentieth century in both Lithuania and Latvia, relying significantly on adaptations from the much better attested and still extant Hindu religion, whose Indo-European roots in ancient Sanskrit texts were taken to represent a common heritage. The influence from Hinduism continues even to the present day, using Indian mythology and ritual to fill in the numerous gaps that a reconstructed Baltic neopaganism suffers.

During the Soviet occupation beginning with World War II, what practitioners of Romuva there were suffered persecution by the Soviet authorities, both because of its religious nature and also because of Romuva's emphasis on Lithuanian nationalism.

With Lithuanian independence in 1990, Romuva came out into the open again and has since been trying to be recognized as one of the traditional religions of Lithuania, a legal classification that would give it certain privileges and funding alongside the existing nine recognized religious groups. Recognition has not been given, however, as the Lithuanian government does not recognize Romuva as an authentic Lithuanian traditional religion but as a modern neopagan reconstruction. According to the 2021 census, fewer than four thousand people in Lithuania identify with Romuva.

CHAPTER 22

Jūratė and Kastytis[1]

L ONG AGO IN ANOTHER TIME, a young man named Kastytis lived beside the shore of the Baltic Sea. Kastytis was a fisherman, and deeply afflicted with the sea longing. It is important to this tale that you know that Kastytis was a handsome young man, some say a giant or the son of a giant, and that beneath his proud and noble forehead, his eyes blazed like coals.

He would sail out over the deep for days on end, seeking its mysteries and treasures, and drawing up its fish into his nets. You might say that Kastytis was too successful, for all of the sea creatures began to complain. "Soon, the sea will be empty of fish," they said, "if someone does not make Kastytis go home to his mother!"

All the sea creatures complained, and the complaints came down to Jūratė, the Queen of the Sea, who lived in her great palace of bright golden amber beneath the waves. So Jūratė sent her mermaids to warn Kastytis that if he did not stop at once and go home to his mother, there would be trouble.

But Kastytis only laughed, and the mermaids blushed and scattered, afraid of the young man's eagerness and of the light in his eyes. The beauty of the mermaids and the mysteries of the deep only made him more eager, and he gathered up all of the fishes and sea creatures into his nets, and he did not go home to his mother but continued on in this way for many nights.

---

1   This story is another written by Richard based on oral recountings we were told in Lithuania, as well as other versions found in research.

At last, the situation in the kingdom under the sea became untenable. Jūratė herself now felt that she had to intervene. And so it was that one night, when the moon was full and shining upon the dark, still water of the sea, the stillness was broken as the Queen of the Sea herself arose out of the churning brine and foam. Her skin was as white as alabaster, and she was clad from the waist down in green that sparkled like emeralds. Pearls and iridescent shells adorned her comely neck and shapely arms.

The moon shone upon her and the stars crowned her hair, and she greeted the young Kastytis with all of the terrible splendor of the queen she was: "Hail, sweet Kastytis! Isn't it immodest of you, night after night, to drag your nets through my domain? For I am Jūratė, the Queen of the Sea!"

Jūratė had thought to overwhelm and shame the young fisherman with her beauty and her glory—but when Kastytis saw her, he took his oar and swiftly began to row his small ship toward her.

Seeing his eagerness, his noble forehead, his flashing eyes, his powerful limbs—in that instant, so the songs tell us, Jūratė forgot herself, her innocence and her divinity, and fell in love with this young giant, so that he caught her (or she caught him), and they met in a lover's embrace.

Then Jūratė took Kastytis down to her home beneath the waves, to her palace of golden amber with its many rooms and treasures and secrets, and Kastytis forgot his home and his mother and the dry land, forsaking it all for that world of wonders and for the love of Jūratė.

And for her part, Jūratė found that his coal-bright eyes had here become a lovely blue, bluer than the sea or the sky, and she kissed them, and forgot her realm. So the waves rose and threatened the land, and all of the creatures of the land and sea cried out in fear lest the natural order should be overthrown.

Perkūnas the Thunderer heard their cries and looked down on Jūratė and saw that she had abandoned the rule of her realm for the love of the handsome young giant.

He hurled one of his thunderbolts, and there was a flash of blinding light and a crack of deafening sound as the golden amber palace of Jūratė, with its many rooms, its treasures, and its secrets, shattered into a thousand thousand gleaming pieces of amber.

The songs say that in the storm that followed, Kastytis was washed up on the shore and lay there dead under the moonlight, his beautiful face still caressed by the waves.

But Jūratė was chained to the ruins of her palace. Some say that when a storm rages across the Baltic it is Jūratė struggling against her chains and weeping for her lover. After these storms, pieces of gleaming amber can be found washed ashore, the broken fragments of the golden palace of the Queen of the Sea.

CHAPTER 23

The Swan Queen[1]

LONG AGO IN ANOTHER TIME there lived an old man and an old woman. Every morning they went out to the nearby forest to gather kindling for their fire, and the moment they left the house a white swan would come flying there. She would fold and put aside her wings and, turning into a beautiful maid, she would light the stove, cook the dinner, clean and wash everything, and then fly away again.

The old people had not a care in the world, for they returned home each day to find everything done for them. But they were filled with wonder as to who their kind helper was.

One day the old man remained home alone. He hid behind a tub and waited to see what would happen. After a time who should come flying into the hut but a swan! She folded her wings, laid them aside and, turning into a maid, went to the well for water, and the old man at once took the wings and burnt them.

The maid returned with two pails of water; she looked and she saw that her wings were gone! She burst out crying and wept long and bitterly, for this meant that she was parted from her mother and father and her own dear love as well. But there was nothing she could do, so she stayed with the old people, living with them as their daughter.

---

1   Adapted from Zheleznova, *Tales of the Amber Sea*, 140–143.

Now, the king himself was once out hunting near the forest not far from where they lived. He saw the maid and liked her well, and he said to the old people: "I must have the maid for my own. Give her to me and you can have as many pieces of gold as you like."

The old people were filled with sorrow at this, but it is not good to refuse a king in such matters. So the old people gave him the maid. The king brought her to his palace and married her, and in due time a son was born to them.

One day the queen came out into the garden with her baby son. Looking up, what did she see but a flock of swans flying near. At their head flew her old father himself, singing as he flew:

> In that garden bright my daughter I see;
> Though she has no wings, yet swan is she.
> Her fingers are covered with golden rings,
> To her little son a song she sings,
> From a little gold book she reads him a tale,
> A kerchief of silk behind her trails.
> A pair of white wings to her I'll throw,
> And she'll leave her son and with us she'll go!

The queen's heart grew heavy; the tears poured from her eyes and she sang out in reply:

> Do not throw me the wings, for you come too late—
> I won't leave my son to an orphan's fate.

Just then the king came up to her. "Why are your eyes red with weeping?" he asked, for he could see that something was wrong.

"Our little son cried, and it made me cry, too," the queen replied.

On the next day her mother flew over her and, on the days that followed, her brother and her sisters, and they all sang the same song, but the queen refused to heed any of them.

The last to come flying over her was her own dear love, and he sang as he flew:

> In that garden bright my beloved I see;
> Though she has no wings, yet swan is she.

> Her fingers are covered with golden rings,
> To her little son a song she sings,
> From a little gold book she reads him a tale,
> A kerchief of silk behind her trails.
> A pair of white wings to her I'll throw,
> And she'll leave her son and with us she'll go!

The queen could contain herself no longer and sang out in reply:

> A pair of wings throw down to me,
> And with you I'll fly beyond the sea!

The swan who was her own dear love threw a pair of wings down to her, and she left her son and flew away with him. But her love met his death soon after, and her heart filled with sorrow again.

As for the king, her husband, he waited and waited for her, but as she did not come back, he married Laumė the Witch.

The new stepmother took a dislike to her stepson and treated him very badly. But every night, the Swan Queen would come flying to the palace at night, fold her wings, wash and cradle her son, and then fly away again, singing:

> The King and his wife
> Repose in their bed;
> The palace guards, too,
> Sleep the sleep of the dead.
> But every night and without fail
> My only son, he sobs and wails!

Then, before flying away she would lull her son to sleep and he would not wake till she came back again, till at last the king was filled with wonder as to why his son slept so long.

One night he saw the swan come flying into the palace. She changed into human shape, lulled her son to sleep, and then turned back again into a swan and flew away.

The king thought and thought how to keep her with him, but he could not think of anything. He thought of setting his hunters upon her, but he loved the queen still and was not willing that any harm should come to her.

So things proceeded in this way: Laumė the Witch mistreated her little stepson, the Swan Queen came each night to dry his tears and put him to sleep, and the king watched and loved her from afar.

As I said, things went on in this fashion for many nights, until one day an old man came to the palace. Seeing he was wise, the king asked him what he should do to catch the swan.

The old man told him: "Watch and see which of the windows the swan flies out of and put some tar on the sill. Her wings will be glued to it, and if you seize her with your left hand and tear them off with your right hand, she will return to her human shape."

The king did as the old man said. He put some tar on the windowsill, and when the swan's wings were glued to it, he seized her with his left hand and tore off her wings with his right hand, and lo!—the swan turned back into his own dear queen again.

The king had Laumė the Witch put to death and, three days later, he held a great feast. People came from near and far, and mead and ale were there in great quantities. The Swan Queen lived in joy with her own dear son and never left her husband's people again.

PART V

The Cross and the Empire

Lithuania in the Russian Empire (1795–1915)

CHAPTER 24

Partition

I N THE LATTER HALF OF the seventeenth century, the Commonwealth of Two Nations began to suffer setbacks, both externally and internally. While the theory of the Commonwealth was based on a unity in diversity, including religious tolerance, the reality for ethnic and religious minorities was an increasing domination by the Polish Catholic nobility.

While Swedes invaded from the north in a series of incursions known to history as "The Deluge," in the easternmost lands of the Commonwealth, in what is now Ukraine, the Khmelnytsky Uprising began in 1648 with a group of Orthodox Christian Zaporozhian Cossacks along with Crimean Tatars and Ukrainian peasants rising up against Polish rule. The uprising was named for its leader Bohdan Khmelnytsky, a Ruthenian nobleman and military commander.

Some say the insurgency began when a Polish nobleman attacked Khmelnytsky's farm and even carried away his bride. This second wife of his, Olena Czaplińska, was known as "Helen of the Steppe." Like the Greeks of old sailing to Troy, the aggrieved Khmelnytsky gathered an army of Cossacks and went to get her back. Resentment against the Poles helped to spread violence and ignited the fires of rebellion.

Historians doubt this story, but whatever Khmelnytsky's motives, this insurgency shook off the Commonwealth's control of the region, but the new regime did not show tolerance for minorities, and the Cossacks massacred both civilians and Roman and Uniate Catholic clergy as well as Jews. The local

Ruthenian Voivode, the representative of the Commonwealth, responded with equal savagery against even civilians aligned with the uprising.

The success of the uprising led to an autonomous Zaporozhian Cossack state, called the Cossack Hetmanate, which pledged its allegiance initially as a vassal of the Ottoman Empire during the Uprising and was centered in Kyiv, governing what is now central Ukraine. Eventually realizing that the Ottomans could not be counted on for support against the Commonwealth, Khmelnytsky turned to Moscow, and the Hetmanate was by 1654 aligned with the tsar. Over time, however, its autonomy eroded.

By the early eighteenth century, the Hetmanate, in lands that had been part of the Grand Duchy of Lithuania since their conquest by Algirdas in the late fourteenth century, had been fully incorporated into the Russian Empire as the Kyiv Governorate. As a result, the Greek Catholic churches that had flourished in the region during the Commonwealth period declined steeply and Orthodox Christianity was firmly reestablished.

While the Commonwealth was losing the heart of its Ruthenian lands to the east, The Deluge flooded the Commonwealth with an invasion of Swedes from the north, supported by the Hungarian Calvinist Duke George II Rákóczi, Prince of Transylvania, and Frederick William, Elector of Brandenburg.

The result was that in 1657 the Commonwealth had to renounce its over-lordship of Prussia, the heirs of the Northern Crusaders the Lithuanians and Poles had defeated in 1410. In addition to lands that are now part of western Poland, Prussia controlled the region traditionally known as Lithuania Minor (now mostly included in Kaliningrad Oblast) as well as the Curonian Spit up to Klaipėda. By the early eighteenth century, the Prussian Duchy became the Kingdom of Prussia, a major European power that eventually would unite Germans in the late nineteenth century.

After these losses to the Russians and Swedes, the Commonwealth had lost nearly one third of its population, and its reign as one of the great powers of Europe was over.

The Commonwealth's last great victory came in 1683 at the Battle of Vienna. There, Polish King John III Sobieski, allied with the Holy Roman Emperor Leopold I, turned back the Ottoman advance into Europe. In the sixteen years that followed, this alliance, together with the Russians, Venetians, and

Hungarians, pushed the Turks south of the Danube River. They were never to enter Europe again.

It was the end of a 250-year struggle between Christian Europe and the Muslim Turks, and it was a moment that defines the map of Europe even today. For its efforts at Vienna, the Commonwealth was called *Antemurale Christianitatis*—"the Bulwark of Christendom."

WITH THE DEATH OF THE heroic John Sobieski in 1696, the Golden Liberty of the Polish-Lithuanian Commonwealth—that system by which thousands of nobles participated in the szlachta, the legislature—could no longer hold the country together. Factionalism took hold, and neighboring powers continuously meddled, attempting to get their own candidates elected to be the next sovereign as King of Poland and Grand Duke of Lithuania. Bribes flowed freely to corrupt nobles from sources such as France, Austria, and Russia, who all had interests in who ruled the Commonwealth.

Merely functioning as a parliament was difficult. Any one of the thousands of nobles could either stop a meeting of the legislature or exercise a veto, a privilege referred to by the Latin phrase *liberum veto*. All the noble had to do was shout out in Latin *Sisto activitatem!*—"I stop the activity!"—or say "I do not allow!" in Polish, and the whole session was officially annulled.

This parliamentary device, in place from the mid-seventeenth century until the end of the eighteenth, was designed to promote unanimity and to check the power of the monarchy, but in practice it prevented about a third of the parliamentary sessions from passing any legislation at all. The expression *Polish parliament* began to appear in northern Germanic languages, referring to paralyzed legislatures governed by chaos and disorder.

Despite this governmental gridlock and chaos, as well as periods of civil war, the eighteenth century was a time of flourishing throughout the Commonwealth in Baroque art and architecture, perhaps as a result of its rulers' need to be popular to remain in power or even to have any influence at all with the szlachta.

With the weakness of the state and the interests of the surrounding and expanding empires, the Commonwealth's neighbors began to no longer be content with just influencing the Commonwealth of Two Nations. The last

King of Poland and Grand Duke of Lithuania was Stanisław August Ponia-towski, elected in 1764 through the support of Catherine the Great, a German noblewoman who two years before had become Empress of Russia and had been, coincidentally enough, his lover.

IN 1730, THE THREE NEIGHBORS of the Commonwealth—Protestant Prussia, Catholic Austria, and Orthodox Russia—signed a secret agreement to not allow the laws of the Commonwealth to change, in order to keep the balance of power between them. Thus, even though Stanisław tried in the 1760s to initiate reforms, the entrenched interests of these great powers as represented in the szlachta prevented any real change.

In 1767, through the influence of Catherine, a new law was forced on the Commonwealth to codify this status quo, but with several pro-Russian provisions, including that the next king and grand duke would be a member of the Russian royal family. In response, an uprising occurred that attempted to force the Russians out of the country, but failed. Almost simultaneously another Cassock insurgency arose in eastern Ukraine, and there was also an incursion of Ottoman Turks that was put down by a combination of Commonwealth and Russian troops.

Prussia, Austria, and Russia finally decided they were done with half measures and meddling and in 1772, in Vienna, against the will of the helpless Commonwealth government they signed an agreement shaving off parts of the Commonwealth for themselves—the First Partition. Prussia took the northwest part of Poland, uniting its Baltic coast territories. Austria took Lvov and western Ukraine, and Russia took Polotsk, Vitebsk, and what is now eastern Belarus.

In 1790, the Commonwealth was forced into an alliance with its old enemy Prussia, and in 1793, the Second Partition gave western Belarus and southwest Lithuania to Prussia, while Russia took Minsk, Slutsk, and more of Belarus.

A final uprising began in 1794 under Tadeusz Kościuszko—an engineer and statesman who had fought in the American Revolutionary War. His armies had some success for about six months, but finally the superior Russian forces defeated them. In 1795, Prussia took southwest Poland and Warsaw, Austria claimed Krakow and more of southeast Poland, and Russia claimed all of Belarus and the remainder of Lithuania. The three powers, in signing this agreement, especially wanted to make sure that the memory of "Poland"—by which they meant the Polish-Lithuanian Commonwealth—would be erased:

> In view of the necessity to abolish everything which could revive the memory of the existence of the Kingdom of Poland, now that the annulment of this body politic has been effected . . . the high contracting parties are agreed and undertake never to include in their titles . . . the name or designation of the Kingdom of Poland, which shall remain suppressed as from the present and forever.[1]

King Stanisław was taken to St. Petersburg where he lived out the rest of his days. His paramour the Empress Catherine died the next year in November 1796, and a little over a year after, he himself died in February 1798.

WITH THE FINAL PARTITIONING OF the Commonwealth—the Third Partition—the Grand Duchy of Lithuania came to an end. It was once one of the largest states in Europe and, during its union with Poland, indeed the largest—a multicultural, multilinguistic, multireligious country that was governed with an early form of European democracy—and it now had fallen before the ambitions of rising imperial powers.

With Lithuania's lands on the coast under Prussian control and the majority of its traditional lands including Vilnius itself part of the Russian Empire, the core of this Baltic Empire was now relegated to the status of a region. Would its identity be erased or reemerge? What about its Orthodox history? Would it become Orthodox while under Russian imperial control?

All these questions would be decided over the next 120 years.

---

1   Quoted in Davies, *God's Playground*, 408.

CHAPTER 25

The Russian Orthodox Diocese of Lithuania

I N THE YEAR THAT STANISŁAW, the last King of Poland and Grand Duke of Lithuania, died, on December 25 in the village of Pavlivka, about 135 miles south-southwest of Kyiv, was born a Ruthenian who would alter the history of the Orthodox Church in Lithuania—a man named Joseph Semashko.

Before we get to his story, however, we should consider the state of Orthodox Christianity in Lithuania—and from here on out when we say "Lithuania," the territory we usually mean is roughly that of the small modern nation-state—what was once called "Lithuania proper." Since the Third Partition, the expanded Ruthenian lands of the Grand Duchy and of the Commonwealth with Poland have all remained in the hands of other nations.

By the time of the Third Partition in 1795, the institutional presence of Orthodox Christianity in Lithuania was almost nonexistent. There remained only one parish and one monastery, both in Vilnius. The parish was dedicated to St. Euphrosyne of Polotsk, a twelfth-century Ruthenian saint who is now the patron saint of Belarus. The current building is a small, round church situated southeast of the old city of Vilnius, and it dates from 1837.

The monastery that remained Orthodox was the Monastery of the Holy Spirit. It had been stavropegial, directly under the Ecumenical Patriarchate, but in 1721 became stavropegial under the Russian Orthodox synod, having received financial support from Moscow for some decades. After the Third Partition, the monastery was subordinated to the Russian Orthodox Metropolitan of Minsk.

By 1795, after two hundred years of the Unia all other Orthodox churches in Lithuania had been turned over to the Greek Catholics. Despite this lack of functioning Orthodox parishes in the country, were there still Orthodox Christians? It is difficult to say, but there must have been some at least around Vilnius, perhaps largely among the Ruthenian population, though likely a tiny minority. Eastern Christian worship continued to have a significant presence in Vilnius, however, through the presence of the Holy Trinity Greek Catholic Monastery as well as the Orthodox churches that had been in Uniate hands for some time.

This remained the state of things largely until 1839, when Joseph Semashko was granted the throne of the Russian Orthodox Bishop of Vilnius. It was not the first time he had been there, however, though it was his first time there as an Orthodox Christian.

Joseph had been born to a Uniate family, though because of the lack of any Catholic churches in his area, he largely attended Orthodox churches in his youth. When he was twelve his father, also named Joseph, became a Uniate priest. The younger Joseph eventually attended the Catholic seminary in Vilnius, graduating in 1820 and being ordained a Uniate deacon and celibate priest over the following year at the age of twenty-one.

By this time, Uniates within the Russian Empire worshiped in over 1500 parishes and seventy-five monasteries across four dioceses—mostly in Volhynia in western Ukraine and in Belarus, yet with a number of communities in Lithuania, especially around Vilnius. Scattered across Lithuania were also a number of small Russian Orthodox Old Believer communities who had fled into the Commonwealth in the seventeenth century before the partitions of the eighteenth.[1]

In 1827, Joseph Semashko, now a Uniate priest, wrote a memorandum in which he urged the incorporation of the Greek Catholic churches of the empire into the Russian Orthodox Church. He included in his suggestions their submission to the Procurator of the Holy Governing Synod—the lay government official to whom the Church reported as a department of the

---

1   For an overview of the history of the Old Believers, see Meyendorff, *Russia, Ritual, and Reform.*

Russian state, a situation imposed upon the Russian Church by Tsar Peter I in 1721 when he replaced the Patriarchate with the Synod.

At about the age of thirty, Joseph was consecrated as Greek Catholic auxiliary Bishop of Mstislaw in Belarus in 1829, then named Bishop of Lithuania in 1832. And while there were few Uniate parishes in Lithuania proper at the time, the Vilnius governorate included considerable parts of what is now Belarus, so he governed some 1600 parishes.

During his episcopacy in the Ruthenian Uniate Church, he worked to make liturgical life conform to Russian practice. When he took office, the Uniate tradition consisted of native Ruthenian Orthodox elements mixed with Latinizations.

Ruthenian iconostases, which in the earlier, Orthodox period likely were smaller than the towering Russian edifices familiar today, had gradually disappeared under Latin influence, flowing from the sixteenth-century Council of Trent, which emphasized removing visual obstructions near the altar. Nineteenth-century Uniates continued to use Greek-style vestments, an inheritance from their Orthodox heritage, but with certain Latinizations added.

Further, the Synod of Zamość, which met in southeastern Poland in 1720, had decreed certain Latinizations for the Uniates such as introducing the *filioque* clause into the Creed, forbidding the use of the liturgical sponge and hot water in the liturgy, and forbidding Communion to infants and small children. It also forbade veneration of St. Gregory Palamas, a saint who symbolized resistance to Roman Catholic theology. The Synod emphasized retaining certain distinctives, however, such as the use of leavened bread.

Instead of seeking to sift out the Latinizations and restore Ruthenian Orthodox practices through a process of study and engagement, Joseph Semashko's reforms essentially treated everything that differed from Muscovite practice as a Latinization and simply replaced the Uniate customs—whatever their origin—with Russian Orthodox customs. This made sense, since one of his goals was to integrate the people of these western lands into the whole way of life of the Russian Empire.

Thus, Joseph decreed the building of iconostases and required the use of service books from Moscow. He replaced the vestments that Ruthenians had been using with the Muscovite style and the music with compositions from St. Petersburg.

In this way, with his reforms Joseph both removed certain Latinizations that had accrued and also introduced the Muscovite tradition, which was different from the native Ruthenian Orthodox traditions that had been retained in the Unia. He also decreed that sermons should be preached in either Russian or Belarusian and that sacramental records should be kept in Russian, although in many cases the language of the people was Polish.

In 1830, the November Uprising began, lasting for almost a year as it attempted to shake off Russian control. It started in Warsaw but spread throughout the former lands of the Polish-Lithuanian Commonwealth, including in Lithuania itself. While the rebels had some local successes, ultimately the powerful imperial army crushed the insurgency.

In the wake of this rebellion, the semi-autonomy that formerly Polish lands had enjoyed was severely curtailed. This semi-autonomous region was so-called "Congress Poland," named for the Congress of Vienna at which its status had been outlined in 1815, a major European diplomatic meeting held in the wake of the fall of Napoleon. This territory included most of modern Poland but also southwest Lithuania, the Suvalkija region.

In the aftermath of this rebellion, the often-Polish cultural character of the Greek Catholic Church was even more suspect in the Russian Empire. Many of its clergy spoke Polish—including Joseph Semashko, though Ruthenian was his first language—and identified as culturally Polish, though the word *Polish* here was really a shorthand for the conglomerate identity of the Polish-Lithuanian Commonwealth.

Between 1831 and 1836, Russian imperial authorities closed forty-four Uniate monasteries and nearly all the schools run by the Uniate Basilian order as they were seen to be sympathetic to the rebellion. Many Uniate clergy were accused of having participated in it.

In 1835, Joseph was invited to join a secret committee that included the Procurator of the Russian Synod, the Uniate Metropolitan of Kyiv and head of their church, and St. Philaret, Orthodox Metropolitan of Moscow. The purpose of this group was to work on the unification of the Uniates with the Russian Orthodox Church.

In 1837, the imperial government placed the Uniate Church under the control of the Procurator, effectively incorporating it into the apparatus of the state like the Russian Orthodox Church. The following year, Metropolitan Josaphat of Kyiv and his vicar (another Josaphat), the two primary Uniate opponents of reunification, died of natural causes, clearing the way for the end of the Unia in Russian imperial territory.

Finally, on February 12, 1839, a council was held at the Cathedral of Holy Wisdom in Polotsk, now in northern Belarus, on the Sunday of the Triumph of Orthodoxy, the first Sunday in Lent. The council's purpose was to unite the Greek Catholic churches in the former lands of the Grand Duchy of Lithuania with the Russian Orthodox Church. In attendance were three Uniate bishops—Joseph Semashko as Bishop of Lithuania, Bishop Vasiliy Luzhinskiy of Orsha, and Vicar Bishop Antoniy Zubko of Brest, along with many other clergy and laity.

The council solemnly called for the abolition of the Union of Brest that had taken place in 1596. It also formally petitioned Tsar Nicholas I to reduce the number of dioceses of their church to two—in Lithuania and Belarus—and to join them to the Russian Orthodox Church.

While for Joseph this council was the culmination of years of work, it apparently took many of the Uniate clergy by surprise. Some 111 of these clergy began circulating petitions immediately to call for the prevention of reunification with the Orthodox.

The clergy of the Belarusian diocese did not receive the council well—out of nearly seven hundred clergy, not even two hundred signed on to reunification. A number fled, while others tried to join the Roman Catholic Church (a move the imperial government made illegal ten years before). Other sources say that most of Joseph's clergy were in favor of reunification, with only 2 percent opposing.

When recounting the synod in Polotsk, Joseph Semashko talked about his motivations:

This is my position! Feeling from childhood an attachment to the Greco-Russian confession, experiencing doubts about this subject in the distant past, and finally, completely convinced of the purity of this confession, I decided to abandon my former rite, which was both removed from the ancient spirit of Christianity and inappropriate for the good of my fatherland—Russia.[2]

The council's deliberations, accompanied by over 1300 letters of support, were accepted by the Russian imperial government and the Holy Synod of the Russian Orthodox Church. Saint Philaret, the Orthodox Metropolitan of Moscow, concelebrated with Joseph Semashko and the other bishops in Vilnius in March of 1839.

There were no baptisms or chrismations of these Greek Catholics to make them Orthodox, nor were there lines of people making a profession of faith. Rather, with the stroke of a pen, roughly 1600 parishes and about 1.5 to 2 million people were joined to the Orthodox Church that year. An Orthodox diocese of Lithuania was reestablished, and Joseph Semashko was named the first Orthodox Bishop of Lithuania in centuries.

The official account from the Russian Church of the events of the reunification is as follows:

An immense number of people came to witness this solemn festival of the Church . . . and when, after the conclusion of the liturgy and the vespers, the Decree of the Most Holy Synod for their reunion was read, concluding with those touching words of the monarch—'I thank God and accept it'—they who were present were so affected that their eyes were bedewed with tears of joy.[3]

Commemorative coins were issued that included the motto: "Severed by Violence (1596), Reunited by Love (1839)."

The bigger picture was of course rather more complicated. While the Unia had been enforced through government coercion and persecution under the Polish-Lithuanian Commonwealth, beginning in 1596, its abolition under the Russian imperial government in 1839 was also accompanied by state coercion.

---

2   Semashko, "A work on the Orthodoxy of the Eastern Church," 309.
3   Quoted in Mouravieff, *History of the Church of Russia*, 439.

Even at the time of the council in Polotsk itself, the 29th Russian Cossack regiment was present to make sure things went the government's way.

It seems that nearly a third of the clergy refused to become Orthodox—again, depending on which sources you read—and many were exiled to Siberia in response. Possibly as many as one hundred thousand Uniates refused to join the reunification, and there were clashes with the Russian army.

Various stories about the harshness of Joseph Semashko in his zeal against the Uniates were circulated in Poland and even became the subject of poetry. He became notorious in Catholic circles. While the stories were later debunked by a Jesuit scholar, they nonetheless left an impact, and bitterness lingered for a long time.

You may remember that Bishop Joseph's father was a Uniate priest, Fr. Joseph Semashko. Even into the 1840s, with his son now his Orthodox bishop, he continued to offer liturgy in the Greek Catholic style. His son subsequently transferred him from his parish in Ukraine to a parish near his see in Vilnius, where he finally began using the Russian liturgical books that were official in the new diocese.

It's worth noting that not all of Semashko's actions as an Orthodox clergyman toward Catholics were negative. Among other things, he petitioned the tsar that the icon of Our Lady of the Gate of Dawn remain in Catholic hands, despite its veneration by the Orthodox, because Catholics had revered it and cared for it for so many centuries themselves.

After the reunification, only a few Uniates then remained in the Russian Empire, concentrated in northeast Poland. On the basis of the Synod of Polotsk they were joined by the government to the Russian Orthodox Church in the 1870s, while many refused and became Roman Catholic. Thus, within a few decades, the last remnants of the Union of Brest were now within the borders of the Austro-Hungarian Empire.

The Russian Orthodox Diocese of Lithuania was now established, and it remains the primary presence of the Orthodox Church in Lithuania to this day. Joseph Semashko was elevated to the rank of metropolitan in 1852 and governed the diocese until his death in 1868. He was buried beneath the relics of the Three Martyrs of Vilnius.

CHAPTER 26

Our Lady of Pažaislis

O N THE CALENDAR OF THE Russian Orthodox Church are feast days for many icons, especially for icons of the Theotokos, the Mother of God. Perhaps best known among them is the icon of Our Lady of Vladimir, which has three feast days, and earlier in this book we mentioned Our Lady of the Gate of Dawn, whose feast day is December 26. On July 2 is the feast of the *Pozhaiskaya* icon of the Theotokos.

From the name, we might think it is a Russian icon, but that is simply its Russian name, like how Our Lady of the Gate of Dawn is called Ostrobramskaya in Russian. There are certain legendary origin stories for Ostrobramskaya that could point to an Orthodox origin in Crimea, but the Pozhaiskaya icon's origins are not Orthodox at all. So how did this icon come to be celebrated in the Orthodox Church?

This is one of the many complicated stories about the Orthodox Church in Lithuania during the Russian imperial period. But the story itself begins about 130 years before Lithuania was annexed into the empire—in 1664, when Lithuania was still part of the Commonwealth of Two Nations.

IN THAT YEAR, KRISTUPAS ZIGMANTAS Pacas—known more commonly by the Polish version of his name, Krzysztof Zygmunt Pac—founded a monastery in the forests near Kaunas, which is today the second-largest city in Lithuania, located south of the center of the country. The name is a form of Christopher. Christopher's brother Michael Casimir Pac would become the

Grand Hetman of Lithuania, the senior military commander of the Grand Duchy. The monastery was given the name "Mountain of Peace" in Latin—*Mons Pacis*, a pun on the family name *Pac*.

The monastery was given as a hermitage to the Camaldolese Order, a small monastic order founded in the eleventh century, and its main church, a Lithuanian Baroque masterpiece, was dedicated to the Visitation of the Mother of God to St. Elizabeth. The monastery is now known as Pažaislis Monastery, named for the neighborhood in which it resides. The name itself comes from a Polish name for a small tributary of the Nemunas River, which is next to the neighborhood.

In 1812, when Napoleon came into Lithuania and temporarily occupied it during his invasion of the Russian Empire, his army entered the monastery and began plundering its treasures. While they engaged in this plunder, it is said that they accidentally dropped one of the monastery bells, which rolled into the Nemunas River. Since then, whenever the monastery celebrates its feast day on July 2 and rings its bells, some say you can also hear a drowned bell reverberating under the water in response.

DURING THE EARLY YEARS OF the construction of the monastery, which lasted from the 1660s until 1712, Pope Alexander VII gifted to it an icon of the Mother of God.

This icon, painted in the seventeenth century, is said to be from either a Flemish or Italian painter, and it depicts the Virgin Mary holding Christ in a distinctly Western style, though restrained and with none of the Renaissance sensuality that one often finds in Western religious paintings of the period. She and her Son are surrounded by an oval of pink, white, and red roses. Around the icon is a gilded oval frame.

Over time, the Catholics of Lithuania came to revere the icon, and it was associated with many miracles, so the Catholic Church set a feast day for it on July 2, a day of pilgrimage to the monastery.

During the uprising of 1830–31 against the Russian Empire, a meeting of rebel commanders took place in 1831 on the monastery grounds. Thus, after the Empire had put down the uprising later that year, the imperial government closed it on the grounds that it had collaborated with the rebellion. It was handed over to the Russian Orthodox Church, and in 1842, it was made into an Orthodox monastery, rededicated to the Dormition of the Mother of God.

DURING ITS TIME AS AN Orthodox monastery, many notable Russian Orthodox Christians visited, including visits in 1837 and 1847 by Tsar Nicholas I. Further, Alexey Fedorovich Lvov, the composer of the national anthem of Tsarist Russia, "God Save the Tsar," was buried there.

During this period, a number of the church's frescoes were painted over, and much of its statuary was destroyed. But what happened with the very Western-looking icon, the Virgin Mary and Christ ringed in roses? Did the Russian monks destroy it as well, a Catholic religious picture unfit for an Orthodox monastery?

That is, in fact, not what happened. They did not destroy it, perhaps because the icon was so revered for its miracles, perhaps because its style was not really that distant from the nineteenth-century Russian iconographic style, or perhaps because the Russian monks saw something in the icon itself—we may never know. What we do know is that they venerated this image themselves.

We also know that they welcomed pilgrims on July 2 to venerate the icon and pray before it, and that this Catholic feast day was simply adopted onto the Russian Orthodox calendar, with the icon carried in joyful procession around the monastery. In addition, they also encouraged pilgrims to come on the new feast day of the monastery—August 15, the Dormition of the Theotokos—and so this day became a secondary feast of the icon and also a day of pilgrimage.

Just as the monastery had become Orthodox, the icon had also become Orthodox—not because it was changed in some fundamental way but because it was treated as an Orthodox icon. Thus, Our Lady of Pažaislis came to be known as Pozhaiskaya (Пожайская) in Russian.

IN 1893, AN OUTBREAK OF cholera threatened Kaunas, and numerous people fled into the forests near the city. However, many believers, both Catholic and Orthodox, went to the monastery to pray before the icon and ask the Virgin for deliverance. By her prayers, the disease receded and with it came relief of suffering.

In gratitude, a copy of the icon was made and the memory of deliverance from cholera was included on it in an inscription. In 1898, restoration work was done on the icon to return it as much as possible to its original condition. With the feast firmly established on the Russian calendar, more copies of the icon were made, and variations—almost always with the oval of roses—can be found throughout the Russian Church.

In 1915, with the collapse of the Russian Empire during World War I Lithuania was again becoming independent, and the Orthodox monks of Pažaislis Monastery fled to Russia, taking many of its treasures with them—including Our Lady of Pažaislis. The German army occupied Lithuania, including the monastery, from 1917 to 1918, turning it into an army hospital and ransacking whatever they could.

With Lithuanian independence established in 1918, the monastery was given back to the Catholic Church, and in the 1920s a group of Lithuanian-American nuns from Chicago took up residence. In 1928, Our Lady of Pažaislis was returned to the monastery from Russia.

The monastery operated peacefully until World War II, when in 1940 the occupation forces of the Soviet Union confiscated it, and its buildings served variously as an archive and a home for the elderly. In 1947 Our Lady of Pažaislis was moved to the Catholic cathedral in Kaunas, and then in 1949, the monastery church was closed by the Soviet authorities. It then later served as a tourist attraction and art gallery. In the 1970s the icon was stolen from the cathedral in Kaunas.

When Lithuania again regained its independence in 1990, the monastery was returned to the Catholic Church, and a group of nuns renewed monastic life. Finally, Our Lady of Pažaislis was found and returned to the monastery in the year 2000. It now serves as the altarpiece in the main church, visible immediately behind the main altar. The oval frame is itself framed with an additional rectangular frame on which are placed many votive offerings, given in thanks for answered prayers.

SO NOW THAT THE MONASTERY and the icon have been out of Orthodox hands for roughly a century, has the Russian Orthodox Church removed the feast from its calendar, perhaps considering it an embarrassment to have ever included it in the first place?

Again, no. July 2—on the Old Calendar—remains the Orthodox feast of the Pozhaiskaya icon for the Russian Orthodox Church, even while the Catholic Church celebrates thirteen days earlier with July 2 on the New Calendar.

There is no sense that this feast is a mistake or embarrassment, and Orthodox Christians continue to make pilgrimage to this again-Catholic monastery. There, they make their petitions and there, prayers are answered, while they kneel before the image of the Mother of God and her divine Son, ringed in roses.

CHAPTER 27

Russification and National Awakening

O N MARCH 4, 1894, THOUSANDS of Lithuanian-Americans, along with numerous other sympathetic people, marched in protest through the blustery early springtime streets of Wilkes-Barre, Pennsylvania—possibly as many as ten thousand in all. About six weeks before, in the frigid streets of Chicago in late January, six thousand Lithuanian-Americans gathered in a similar rally. These were the two largest, but there were gatherings of thousands of Lithuanians all over America in early 1894.

It was a turning point in Lithuanian history, and its effects were being felt—and assisted—right here in America. A little over twenty years later, everything in Lithuania would change.

But what had happened that brought so many thousands of Lithuanian-Americans into the streets? Why were the Lithuanian-language newspapers of America buzzing with anger and calls to organize, calls to action, rousing members of church and ethnic societies?

To understand these protests and what happened in their aftermath, we have to understand the latter half of the nineteenth century in Lithuania and how Lithuanians related to the Russian Empire within which they were still a provincial governorate.

THE NOVEMBER UPRISING OF 1830–1831 was not the last such uprising. While across the Atlantic America was engulfed in civil war, in January of

174

1863 another insurgency began, called the January Uprising. It lasted until June 1864, and clashes between rebels and the Russian Empire happened in what is now Poland, Lithuania, Latvia, Ukraine, and Belarus—the former lands of the Polish-Lithuanian Commonwealth, which by that time had been under Russian imperial rule for some seventy years. It was an attempt to shake off Russian rule and reestablish the Commonwealth, but once again rebellion was put down by the Empire.

From the imperial point of view, what inspired these people to turn against their Russian masters is that they did not feel they were part of a single people, a single great Russia. And of course they were right.

The language on most of the streets was still Polish, though Lithuanian still lingered on in the Lithuanian countryside, particularly in Samogitia in the west. The religion of Lithuanians and Poles was still Catholicism, and of course their culture—its music, art, clothing, etc.—was not Russian. Generally, the Russians referred to them collectively as "Poles," a concept that conflated multiple identities, usually clustered around Catholic religion.

Historian Theodore Weeks writes:

For official Russia and indeed for a very great part of Russian society in the mid-late 19th century, Poles and Catholicism were regarded as a kind of dual conspiracy against—to use the contemporary phrase—"all things Russian" (*vse russkoe*). The place of Catholicism in the 19th-century Russian psyche surely deserves a study of its own; suffice it to say that Catholicism was almost universally regarded with suspicion, fear, and even loathing by Russian administrators as well as Russian conservatives and nationalists. In official documents as well as in the press, the link between the Polish nation and the Catholic religion appears again and again. While official policy and laws did differentiate between the concepts "Pole" and "Catholic," in practical matters the two labels were usually treated as equivalent. The presence of many hundreds of thousands of Catholic Lithuanians, Belarusians, Latvians, and Germans in the empire did little to change this perception, in particular in the western provinces (roughly comprising present-day Lithuania, Belarus, and western Ukraine). Indeed, Russian nationalists tended to explain the Catholicism of these peoples in great part as a result of Polish missions (which, to be sure, has some historical basis).[1]

That many Catholic clergy and seminarians joined the January Uprising only proved to Russian authorities that to be Catholic was to be against the empire.

Though historians will rightly point out that there was not a carefully planned and executed program throughout the empire to make non-Russians into Russians, there nevertheless were various policies designed to privilege Russian culture—including language, education, and religion—that made it advantageous to assimilate and difficult to maintain non-Russian identity. These policies are referred to as Russification.

Though the details are too numerous to go into here, it's worth noting that there was often a gap between official policy and the ideology that backed it on the one hand and the practical reality of attempting to implement policy on the other. Again, Theodore Weeks writes:

> While at certain moments Russian officials expressed a desire to see the region Russified, when it came to attempting the cultural transformation of an entire population, they nearly always balked for both practical and ideological reasons. To be sure, this presents a contradiction: how could this "eternally Russian land" (*iskono-russkaia zemli*—a very typical phrase in the writings of nationally minded officials) be "re-Russified" without Russifying the present inhabitants—Lithuanians, Poles, Jews, and Belarusans? The contradiction was a very real one and reflects the gap between mythology ("eternally Russian land") and reality—cities dominated by Jews and Poles and a countryside populated mainly by Lithuanians and Belarusans. Hence when speaking in broad, general terms mythology dominated, but when forced to deal with specifics (for example, funding schools, enforcing restrictions), reality came to the fore.[2]

That said, in the wake of this second rebellion in the 1860s, the Russian Empire began to intensify policies of Russification.

---

1   Weeks, "Religion and Russification," 91.
2   Weeks, "Russification and the Lithuanians," 97.

Some such policies had been put into place in the 1830s, such as renaming Polish voivodeships to Russian governorates, introducing Russian currency, and liquidating the Polish parliament and armed forces, as well as confiscating the property of anyone who had participated in the insurgency. And no doubt the incorporation of the Uniate Catholics into the Russian Orthodox Church was seen as low-hanging fruit, since culturally and liturgically, Uniates were more similar to Orthodox Christians than to Roman Catholics. Now, however, these policies were increased and escalated.

Numerous towns were renamed with Russian names. Polish was removed from its primary place in the educational system and relegated to a second, optional language used only for teaching religious classes. History textbooks were replaced with books supporting the imperial narrative, and there was even an attempt to replace the Latin alphabet for Polish with the Cyrillic alphabet used for Russian and some other Slavic languages.

Orthodox churches began to be built throughout the lands of the former Commonwealth, even in places where there were few or no Orthodox Christians. They were often connected with garrisoned military units and attended mainly by soldiers, and thus were a direct symbol of imperial power.

Many Lithuanians were also conscripted to fight and die in the wars of the Russian Empire, which was a constant demoralizing drain on families as their young men were taken from them and gave their lives for an empire they did not believe in and in which they were second-class citizens.

One song, "Užuolėlio šakos linko" ("The Oak Branches Were Bending"), was composed during this period to lament the loss of these young men:

The oak branches were bending, / When they took us young men to war.

They took us, lined us up, / Equipped us with guns.

Guns out of solid steel, / Will kill all the enemies.

They put us in the wagons, / Where they are taking us no one knows.

While we sat in the wagons, / We watched through the window.

We saw the meadows and the valleys, / Never seen in our own land.

The oak branches were bending, / When they took us young men to war.[3]

---

3   Traditional, translated by Fr. Gintaras Sungaila.

Beginning in May 1864, Tsar Alexander II decreed that in the former lands of the Commonwealth the Polish language would be eliminated from public life, Catholics would be barred from government employment, the Catholic Church would be controlled and restricted, and favorable conditions would be created for the spread of the Orthodox Church. Lithuanian parish schools would be replaced with Russian grammar schools, ethnic Russians would be encouraged to resettle in Lithuania, the Latin alphabet would be replaced by the Cyrillic alphabet, and there would be a ban on the publication of any Lithuanian books using the Latin alphabet.

The Lithuanian Press Ban

IT WAS THIS LAST PROVISION that history remembers as the Lithuanian press ban. It was a direct restriction on a core facet of Lithuanian culture—reading and writing books in their language with the traditional alphabet that most people knew. Literacy was also growing in this period, reaching between 70 to 80 percent by the end of the nineteenth century in Lithuania proper. Meanwhile, to the west of Lithuania proper in the lands of East Prussia, also known as Lithuania Minor, where many Lithuanians lived, literacy had reached the same rates decades before—although in those areas there was increasing encroachment by German language and culture.

That said, although Lithuanian literacy was rising, those who enacted the press ban could see that the eastern parts of Lithuania had been largely Slavicized, with Polish and Belarusian more commonly heard on the streets. Lithuanian itself was, it seemed, becoming extinct, as it was confined mainly to peasants living in the western regions. So perhaps the ban would simply hasten the demise of an identity that almost no one in power seemed to care about preserving.

During the years of the ban, about fifty-five books were published in Lithuanian using the Cyrillic alphabet, with about half published in the ban's first decade. They were often given away for free, including, for instance, Catholic prayer books. Lithuanians largely did not accept them, however. The Cyrillic alphabet was not part of their culture, and of course it represented a capitulation to the imperial Russian culture.

Seeing that this publishing project wasn't working, imperial authorities in Russia then focused mainly on eliminating illegal publications. But where were these illegal books being printed in the traditional alphabet coming from? Were there hidden printing presses in Lithuania? It's possible that there might have been a few, but in fact the majority of such contraband was being printed in Lithuania Minor, those lands under Prussian control just to the west of Lithuania proper. Furthermore, a few were being printed by Lithuanian immigrants in America.

So how did they get into the hands of Lithuanians living in the Russian Empire? Dozens of small societies were formed, with organizing begun and sponsored by Motiejus Valančius, the Catholic Bishop of Samogitia. These societies had a single purpose—to travel secretly to Lithuania Minor, pick up sacks full of books, then smuggle them across the border and get them into the hands of Lithuanians so they could use them to pray, to learn, and to educate their children.

During the decades of the ban, some 829 smugglers, 859 distributors, and 1,359 people possessing banned books were arrested by the imperial government for the crime of seeking to preserve their religious and cultural identity through literature.

Did the ban work? It did not. And now the smugglers are seen as cultural heroes.

It turns out that when you tell people they can't have books that they can read and instead have to learn another alphabet or even another language, it may not have the effect intended.

ULTIMATELY, THE PRESS BAN INSPIRED the resurgence of Lithuanian national identity—not just a linguistic or cultural identity, nor even a religious one, but a sense that one could be a Lithuanian. That identity was not bound up with the former Polish-Lithuanian Commonwealth, nor was it confined to being one group in the old multicultural Grand Duchy that had fallen centuries before. Nor, increasingly, was it confined to peasants living in the countryside.

Rather, a number of men began to rise up and call for Lithuanians to embrace self-determination. They would not be subject to Polish nobles nor to

Russian bureaucrats. Instead, they would seek to have their own nation with their own religion, their own language, and their own culture.

Foremost among those who led what is now called the Lithuanian National Revival were Jonas Basanavičius and Vincas Kudirka, intellectuals who had risen up from within the peasantry. Kudirka himself was a doctor who practiced medicine in the small towns of Šakiai and Naumiestis, which was in those days often called Vladyslavovas.

Besides being a doctor, Kudirka was a writer and became the publisher of *Varpas* (*The Bell*), an underground newspaper dedicated to increasing Lithuanian national consciousness. He also wrote poetry and eventually in the 1880s wrote the poem "Lietuva, Tėvyne mūsų," that is, "Lithuania, Our Fatherland," accompanied by music he wrote himself. This is how it reads in English translation:

Lithuania, our homeland, / Land of worshiped heroes! / Let your sons draw their strength / From our past experience.

Let your children always follow / Only roads of virtue, / May your own, mankind's well-being / Be the goals they work for.

May the sun above our land / Banish darkening clouds around, / Light and truth all along / Guide our steps forever.

May the love of Lithuania / Brightly burn in our hearts, / For the sake of this land / Let unity blossom.[4]

It later became the national anthem of Lithuania, titled "Tautiška giesmė" ("The National Hymn"). Kudirka published the words and music in *Varpas* in 1896, and it was first performed publicly in 1899. In that same year, Vincas Kudirka died of tuberculosis at the age of forty. He was buried in Naumiestis, and part of the anthem is inscribed on his grave, which is shaped like a tree stump.

---

4   Kudirka, "National Anthem of Lithuania."

The Kražiai Massacre

Father Andrew: Kudirka did not live to see an independent Lithuania. But he did live long enough to hear about an event that brought thousands of Lithuanian-Americans to protest in the streets of American cities—an event in the small town of Kražiai, on November 22, 1893. And when I heard the story myself, I knew I had to go there. So I asked Fr. Gintaras to take me there, and it turns out that, although he knew the history well, it was his first time visiting himself.

In 1891, Tsar Alexander III ordered the church closed. It was a Benedictine women's monastic church, though it served the townspeople as well. The nuns tried to remain, and multiple petitions to the regional governor were filed, but eventually the nuns were forcibly moved to Kaunas in 1892 and 1893, and word came to Kražiai that their church would be demolished.

To try to save their church, the people gathered inside it, and they took turns inside, praying and keeping watch. They hoped that if the church was occupied by people praying, it would not be destroyed.

In November 1893 the police arrived, but they were repelled by the townspeople. The governor ordered in a regiment of three hundred Don Cossacks, who attacked the people, recklessly riding their horses even inside the church. In the days that followed, many people were arrested and flogged for their resistance, and a number of people were killed. The Cossacks were allowed to pillage the town itself under the pretense of looking for escaped rebels, and more people were beaten and a number of women were raped.

KRAŽIAI IS WELL OUT INTO the countryside in the eastern part of Samogitia. In 1893, it had over three thousand residents, which is quite small, but now it has fewer than six hundred. As such, there are not many buildings, and the tall, broad, white Catholic church dominates the view. A small chapel stands next to it in the grass.

When we went inside the church, we found one very old wooden pew off to the side and roped off. Next to it was a sign indicating that this was a pew from the 1890s, and the Don Cossacks had tied their horses to it while they ransacked the church. They had smashed statues and shot religious paintings with guns. The place of prayer had been filled with mayhem. The church was not demolished, however, though its interior needed to be restored.

LITHUANIAN-AMERICAN NEWSPAPERS, HAVING GOTTEN WIND of what had happened, exploded with rage and indignation. They circulated a political cartoon in which you see two churches. On the left is the Catholic church in Kražiai, shining with light and with Christ in the sky above it. On the right you see an Orthodox church, and people are being hanged on gallows next to it.

In the center is the Russian Tsar holding an Orthodox cross, saying "Long live Orthodoxy!" He is surrounded by Orthodox clergy and Russian nobles and soldiers. Hovering over the Orthodox church and the tsar is a flaming devil, grinning and licking his fingers gleefully.

As an Orthodox Christian, it is a shocking image for me, the association of Orthodox Christianity with the devil. Yet for the people whose church was desecrated by Cossacks and many of whom were massacred, raped, beaten, prosecuted, and executed, it would be hard for them to see the Orthodox Church in another way. For them, it was a symbol and instrument of persecution.

The Kražiai Massacre galvanized the Lithuanian national revival. Lithuanians living abroad demanded that the governments of their adopted homelands pressure the Russian Empire to end the persecutions against Catholics.

International outcry began, but the pope at the time, Leo XIII, issued an encyclical titled *Caritatis*, which urged obedience to the tsarist government. Vincas Kudirka's *Varpas* angrily thundered that the pope had betrayed the blood spilled in Kražiai.[5]

It was not the first such event in Russian-occupied Lithuania, but its timing in the midst of the revival of Lithuanian identity as well as the support given by Lithuanians abroad made it a turning point in the history of the country. Lithuania would soon be reborn.

---

5   Žaltauskaitė, "Catholicism and Nationalism," 120.

CHAPTER 28

The Domeikai of Kudirkos Naumiestis

Father Andrew: Beginning in 1867, crop failures throughout Lithuania led to starvation and outbreaks of cholera. As Lithuania was beginning to reawaken its sense of national identity, many of its poorest people began to wonder if they would even be able to survive.

Into the midst of this time of woe and want came American and British visitors, who spoke to the peasants in regions such as Suvalkija in the west and Kaunas closer to the center of the country. They told of opportunities in Great Britain and America, centered largely on huge coal mining operations that had opened up in places like Glasgow in Scotland or Scranton in northeastern Pennsylvania.

And so it was that from the 1860s until World War I, about 635,000 people, some 20 percent of the population of Lithuania, left their homeland, looking not for wealth or prestige but simply for survival. This was the time of great immigration to the West. Many young men came with young families or by themselves, hoping to marry after they arrived, hoping to stay alive.

With these hopes in mind, they descended into the depths of the mines of Scotland and Pennsylvania. Many men became sick and died young due to the toxic conditions of coal mining, and many walked into the dark underground and never came out again. Mining accidents were common—explosions, cave-ins, and inhalation of deadly gases.

Yet many survived. Wherever Lithuanian immigrants went, they formed families, they built churches, and however they could, they stayed in touch with their brothers and sisters, their parents and cousins who remained behind. They continued to make their Lithuanian cuisine but began to adapt it to life in America, often including new ingredients.

An example of this adaptation is in a certain alcoholic drink. Lithuanians make a liqueur called *Krupnikas*, a spiced honey drink, but the Lithuanian-Pennsylvanian coal miners started adding orange peel and lemon—fruits that they probably saw for the first time in America. With a couple pounds of honey, they would boil it all up in a pot along with the cheapest liquor they could find—usually some kind of whiskey—and serve it for holidays. Thus was born a drink called *Boilo*.

ONE YOUNG MAN NAMED ANTANAS, a peasant laborer, made the journey in the 1890s, arriving first in Scotland to join his brother Juozapas and sister Ona, who had settled there and married other Lithuanians. Antanas did not stay there long but eventually boarded a boat in Glasgow and arrived in New York City on November 13, 1905.

He was twenty-two years old and had $15 in his pocket, and he told the dockmaster that he was going to join his cousin in Throop, Pennsylvania, to become a coal miner in Scranton. They misspelled his first name on the passenger manifest, but he probably didn't notice—because he couldn't read.

His full name was Antanas Petras Domeika, and he was my great-grandfather.

He wasn't the only one who left, either. In 1892, his hometown had nine thousand people in it. By 1897, it was just 4,600. Half the town left. Many went to northeastern Pennsylvania.

I don't know how long he spent in Pennsylvania. The next record I have of his life is from January 1913 when he got married in Worcester, Massachusetts, to Olga Weiland, who was just a few months older than him. They were both thirty—well, not quite. He got married the day before his birthday. And they misspelled his last name on the marriage record, but again, he couldn't read.

Olga was also from Lithuania, but her family name—Weiland—was something of a mystery to me. Where was she from? Why did she have that Germanic last name?

My family passed down almost none of this information to me. I knew only that they were from Lithuania. It took me years of research even to discover what I have just written.

Over time, I found that Antanas—who went by Anthony here in the US—had siblings. At first there was just his brother John—or Jonas—who apparently also was in the Scranton area at some point. But what happened to him?

And Olga had a brother Theodore, who came to America in 1913. But what happened to him?

For a long time, this was all I knew. I didn't know about my great-grandfather's Scotland connection, just that he had arrived in the US in 1905.

But with years of research, asking many questions and with a lot of patience—not to mention the help of strangers on the internet in genealogy forums—gradually the picture emerged.

ANTANAS WAS ONE OF NINE children, possibly the youngest. And he had a sister named Antanina who was born in the same year—could they have been twins? Their names certainly suggest it.

Besides his brothers Juozapas and Jonas, there were also Augustinas and Pranciškus. Besides Ona and Antanina, there were also sisters Agota and Petronėlė. How many emigrated? How many stayed behind? I still do not really know.

Jonas himself settled in Worcester. I don't know why he and my great-grandfather went there or even if they went together, but the conditions of the Pennsylvania mines would probably have been enough. Jonas was also married, and he had four children—maybe five.

I actually discovered that there was a whole other Domeika side of the family in Worcester because a stranger happened to take photos of their graves and post them on a website. And where were they buried? They're in the cemetery right across the street from my great-grandparents. And I have learned that I have living third cousins here in America.

It also turned out that my great-granduncle Theodore was in the same cemetery as his sister Olga.

Within the space of perhaps a year or two, a flood of information started opening up in front of me. The key question for me, though, was this: Where in Lithuania were the Domeika family from?

Finally, in my research I discovered my great-grandfather's draft card, filled out when he was fifty-nine years old. His signature is almost illegible, and you can't tell if he's trying to write Domeika or Damick, which is how the name is spelled at the top. It seems he never did learn how to read, and it looks like he got help filling out the card because there are three distinct handwritings on it.

In the box that reads "Place of Birth," there is a name written—Maunistis. So I looked that up. It certainly sounded Lithuanian. But it turns out that there is no such town in Lithuania, not even in the world, at least not as far as the internet seems to know. Where could that be?

It was then that I started thinking with my philological brain. A passion of mine for a lot of years has been how words form and are connected to each other and the stories that are told in their various languages. A phenomenon of word history is what is called metathesis, which is when syllables or sounds in a word switch places, like when people say "aks" for *ask* or mispronounce *Barclay* as "broccoli."

What if whoever filled out the card misheard my great-grandfather? It would not have been the first time, looking at the wreck of how the family name of Domeika got spelled over the years by various government agents—Domoko, Domaka, Dormic, Demick, and so on. I don't know when he finally changed it to Damick, but it eventually stuck.

So, could Maunistis be a case of metathesis? I made a guess and switched the M and the N, then searched the internet. Was Naumistis a thing?

Then, there it was—not Naumistis but *Naumiestis*, a Lithuanian word meaning "New Town." There were two places with this name in Lithuania—one in Samogitia and one in Suvalkija on the border with Kaliningrad Oblast—what was Prussia in the nineteenth century. Which could it be? Family lore that I half remembered hearing years before said that Antanas had worked at the estate of a Prussian noble. And an encyclopedia entry I came across said that Glasgow's Lithuanian population was mostly Suvalkijan peasants. But I wasn't sure.

Then, I started getting responses to queries I had made in genealogy groups, and I suddenly had a small pile of documents to sift through: birth and death records, marriage records—and my great-great-grandparents' names! They were Matas Domeika and Apolonija Adomaitytė, and they had indeed lived in what is now called Kudirkos Naumiestis, the old Vladyslavovas where Vincas Kudirka himself had lived.

In 1934, they had renamed the town after Kudirka, who had penned the national anthem and done so much to revive Lithuanian identity. Was it possible that the Domeikai had known Kudirka? Did they meet the book smugglers as they crossed over the border?

While I don't know for certain, it seems possible that the answer to both questions was "yes." In the late 1890s, almost five thousand people lived in the town, but some 45 percent were Jews, while only 22 percent—about one thousand people—were Lithuanian. So the actual Lithuanian community was rather small and likely all knew each other. There were also some four hundred Russians and almost three hundred Ukrainians, so it's likely that the Domeikai knew some Orthodox Christians, as well.

What about my great-grandfather's possible twin Antanina? It seems she never married, and she died at just age fifty. And at forty-one years of age, she had a son who died at just two months old. She named him Antanas.

IT WAS THESE DISCOVERIES THAT, more than anything else, led me to conceive of making the journey to Lithuania. The idea was not simply to visit the country of my ancestors but the actual place where they had lived and died, the place where my great-grandfather said farewell forever to his family.

So it was that when we made the pilgrimage to Lithuania, I had to go there. I had to go to Kudirkos Naumiestis. I was not able to make contact with any living relatives—though I am sure they are there, and I am still working on this—but I knew that I could certainly find some who had departed this life. So we drove to this little town of now less than two thousand people, walked around a little, and found the cemetery. And we started looking.

Lithuanian cemeteries are remarkable places. Each plot is outlined, sometimes in stones, sometimes in small fences, sometimes in concrete. The plot itself is planted—often plentifully—with flowers, and everything is kept in good order. It is not cemetery staff who do this work but rather the relatives of those at rest there, who traditionally visit their departed family at least twice a year—once on the anniversary of the death and then also for Vėlinės, the first two days of November on which the dead are honored and commemorated. In those days, the cemeteries are filled with candles, at least one flickering on every grave, a kind of city of souls.

We walked and walked, scanning the graves for probably close to an hour, haphazardly dividing up the cemetery between four people. And then Richard spotted it—*Domeikių šeima*. Father Vladimir, who had driven us to Naumiestis, confirmed that the inscription we saw on a gravestone indeed meant "Domeika family."

So then, there we were. My daughter and I stood over the bones of our ancestors. And we did what we had to do.

Father Vladimir lent me his priestly stole; I put it on, and together all of us began to sing and pray. We prayed for every member of my Lithuanian family whose names I had discovered over the years.

We prayed the prayer of Orthodox Christians for our departed: *Amžinas atminimas*—"memory eternal."

After we were done, I knelt next to the grave and wept. At the time, I couldn't explain exactly why. But I have come to realize that I wept for people I had never met. I wept for the brokenness of family separated by thousands of miles and by generations who never knew each other. I wept for a past that had been invisible to me but came rushing in all at once. I wept for the love of God given to me that I was able to be there. I wept because something had been healed.

ON SUBSEQUENT TRIPS BACK TO Lithuania, I went to Kudirkos Naumiestis twice more, and both those times we were able to enter the surprisingly large Catholic church that serves the whole town. There, with my sons and also with my father, we stood in the place where over 150 years before my great-great-grandparents had been married. And we touched the baptismal font where in 1883, my great-grandfather had been baptized.

Late in 2023, a woman in a Lithuanian Lutheran genealogy group contacted me. She told me where my great-grandmother Olga was from—the village of

Valdomai, near the city of Šiauliai. She sent me a family tree. I saw new names. She told me that Olga's family were Latvians who had come south into Lithuania and settled there.

Another piece of the puzzle came into place. So now I have another place to go and pray, another place to touch the earth and weep for what was lost.

CHAPTER 29

St. John of Kronstadt and Fr. Pontius Rupyshev

MUCH OF THE STORY OF Orthodoxy in Lithuania during the Russian imperial period is difficult to hear, bound up as it was with the priorities of an imperial government. However, the place where our attention really should rest is on the holy people, those who with grace from God were working out their salvation and bringing that salvation to others.

One of the stories from this period is about an Orthodox Christian man named Pontius Rupyshev. You might not have heard of him, but when he was sixteen years old and living in Vilnius, someone you might have heard of came to town—a priest named Ivan Ilyich Sergiyev, who was visiting Lithuania from the Russian port city of Kronstadt, on an island off St. Petersburg. He is known to history and to Orthodox Christians as St. John of Kronstadt.

BEFORE I TELL YOU THAT story, however, a little background on Pontius: He was born to a Russian family on August 5, 1877, in the city of Ašmena, an ethnically Lithuanian city in what is now Belarus but was then part of the Vilnius governorate of the Russian Empire. When he was born, he was so sickly that everyone thought he would die, so his parents did not think of a name to give him. The priest attending the family at the birth—who was the baby's grandfather—looked at the church calendar and picked an otherwise obscure name from one of the saints of the day: Pontius.

Pontius did not die, however, and while he was still young, his father, who worked for the government, was promoted and transferred to Vilnius. Pontius struggled with his health all his life, and the death of his mother and remarriage of his father made him something of an unwanted child in his own home. Yet he struggled onward.

So in 1893 when St. John of Kronstadt came to Vilnius, Pontius was just sixteen years old and eager to meet this famous priest. But so was everyone. Newspapers of the time reported that for days prior to his arrival, hundreds of people gathered at the train station to get a glimpse of him.

Everywhere he went in Vilnius, the saint was trailed by thousands of people and accompanied by influential figures from both the church and government. It is said that some of the local priests were competing to see if they could somehow get St. John to stop in to their churches for just a little while.

There are remainders of St. John's visit to Vilnius present there to this day—he was made an honorary member of the Cathedral of the Dormition, and he signed a photograph there of himself, which hangs in the presbyterion where the clergy get vested. He also collected funds and gave them to the St. Nicholas Church in Vilnius so that they might construct a chapel dedicated to the Archangel Michael, which still stands to the left of the church.

In the midst of all this hubbub, the teenaged Pontius actually met this renowned priest. When the saint saw the young man, he stopped, took off his hat, and gave him a respectful bow. The young man would never forget it.

Pontius later went on to study in places such as Moscow University and St. Petersburg University, where he met the saint once again. He was unable to finish his studies in either place, however, due to his health, and desired to become a monk, an ambition his father disapproved of.

In order to support himself, he served as a reader at various parishes and lived at different monasteries. Seeing his dedication and piety, his superiors recommended him to study for the priesthood, and during a visit to St. Petersburg, Pontius asked for and received the blessing of St. John of Kronstadt to walk the priestly path.

In 1901, he was married at twenty-four and then ordained to the priesthood. Over the next few years he served in various parishes and taught in schools in both Lithuania and Belarus, making occasional visits and, for a time, living in St. Petersburg in Russia. During his times in St. Petersburg, he served the

Divine Liturgy alongside St. John of Kronstadt, whom he considered his spiritual father, and spent time alone with him. During one of their visits, the saint gave him his own cassock. And then St. John died in January 1909 at the age of seventy-eight.

In 1911, Fr. Pontius was assigned to be a naval chaplain and was serving in this capacity when the Bolshevik Revolution in 1917 swept away the Romanov monarchy and brought atheistic ideologues into power following two years of civil war. In 1919, being warned by workers at a hospital that the Bolsheviks planned to arrest him, Fr. Pontius fled for his life from St. Petersburg, saying farewell to his wife and children. He would never see them again.

He arrived in Daugavpils—a city in the southeast corner of Latvia close to both Lithuania and Belarus, and at the time part of the newly created Soviet Socialist Republic of Latvia—and he served there for a time. In 1920, Polish troops temporarily occupied the city, and with that local shift of power Fr. Pontius took the opportunity to flee even farther away from the Bolsheviks.

So it was that Fr. Pontius arrived back in his childhood home of Vilnius.

DURING WORLD WAR I, GERMAN forces occupied Lithuania from 1915 until November 1918, the end of the war. With the Bolsheviks in control in the Russian capital of St. Petersburg and the Russian Empire in tatters, Lithuanians saw the opportunity, after more than 120 years of occupation, to reassert their independence in February of 1918, even while still occupied by the German army.

But independence was not to be had merely by declaring it. Lithuania had to fight three wars over the next two years to reclaim it—with the Bolsheviks themselves, trying to hold onto what had been Russian imperial territory; with the Bermontians, a pro-German military group in Lithuania and Latvia; and then with Poland, which was trying to reconstitute the old Commonwealth. In the end, Lithuania was a newly independent state that contained most of its oldest ethnically Lithuanian territory, except for Vilnius and a stretch of land to the southwest of it, which remained in Polish hands. The capital of the new Lithuanian state was Kaunas.

So when Fr. Pontius arrived in Vilnius in 1920, he was in Polish-controlled territory. The state of the Orthodox Church in Lithuania was in disarray—both scattered and also divided. A number of the Orthodox churches had been abandoned during the two years of war for independence.

Many Orthodox Russians, including clergy, had fled Lithuania, heading east into Russian territory, and ethnic Lithuanians were a small minority of the remaining Orthodox flock—just 8 percent. What Russians remained were often afraid of retaliation from Lithuanians and Poles who now were ascendant and resented imperial rule. During the wars, Orthodox churches were destroyed on the one hand by Lithuanians and Poles because they were associated with Russia and on the other hand by the Bolsheviks because they were churches.

Because Vilnius was controlled by Poland, the Russian bishop in Kaunas could not travel to those parishes, so he asked Fr. Pontius to visit them and see how the people were doing. In this way, Fr. Pontius soon became well known to the local Orthodox Christians.

Because there were so few priests in the area, Fr. Pontius was given the blessing to serve and preach at any church. He thus became a traveling missionary priest, preaching, catechizing, baptizing, and caring for this broken flock, not in the Vilnius region only but throughout Lithuania, crossing the border between the new Republic of Lithuania and the territory controlled by Poland.

ONE OF THE COMMUNITIES FR. Pontius encountered during this missionary work consisted of a widow of the Koretsky family and her three daughters who lived on a private family estate. They had built their own church dedicated to the icon of the Mother of God, called "Joy of All Who Sorrow." The four Koretsky women lived together as an intentional community with many church services and assigned duties, in some ways reminiscent of a monastery—and they begged the bishop to send a priest to them. Father Pontius finally was the one who accepted this assignment.

Over time, others joined the community and were regarded as new sisters and brothers. They held all their possessions in common, and subsistence farming was their main occupation. This estate was at a place called, in Russian, Mikhnovo, but in Lithuanian, Mikniškės. Father Pontius became so beloved that often the church would be flooded with worshippers, with many having to stand outside. At first other priests were envious and suspicious of him, but eventually they began to invite him to their parishes because of the effect he had on the faithful.

In 1924, just a few years after Fr. Pontius's return to Vilnius, the Orthodox Christians of Poland became part of the newly proclaimed Polish Autocephalous Orthodox Church to which the parishes in Polish-controlled Lithuania were subordinated. This was against the will of the Russian Orthodox Church, which itself was wracked with schism because of the Renovationist "Living Church" that took command in Moscow with the backing of the Soviet Union.

Rather than abandon his flock to move into an area where the parishes belonged to Moscow, Fr. Pontius chose to belong to the newly formed Polish Church. Because the autocephaly was controversial, he was asked about it and had only this to say:

> As for autocephaly, it is a matter of no importance for our salvation, not concerning faith and piety. Of course, the question of the position of our hierarchy will sooner or later be resolved at the All-Russian Local Council.... It is enough for us to know that such a position does not violate for us the state of faith and piety, which we need to hold to with all our might for salvation. Therefore ordination from our hierarchy also brings down the grace of the priesthood upon the one being ordained.... Any separation of the faithful from the Orthodox Church in Poland, in which they reside, tears its Body and brings sorrows, and therefore is displeasing to God, since He has Love above all things and by it we must be united in one common life in Christ.[1]

He also once wrote in his diary:

> Church autocephaly, as the adaptation of ecclesiastical boundaries to political boundaries, like the elective beginning in the Church, is an indulgence to the weakness of man, harmonizing the life of the Holy Church with the conditions and circumstances caused by these weaknesses.[2]

---

1   Rupyshev, "Spiritual Diary," 197–198.
2   Rupyshev, 195.

With this practical and humble sensibility, the Mikhnovo community flourished and grew under his care. We can see that his ministry resembled that of his spiritual father St. John of Kronstadt, whose preaching and pastoral care led many to convert in their hearts and become very active in the church.

Clearly, St. John remained on Fr. Pontius's mind long after he had died in 1909. In 1923, for instance, Fr. Pontius wrote about him in his diary:

> Fr. John of Kronstadt overcomes passions and tramples the enemy. I am liberating myself from passions and overcoming the enemy. He rules over his nature, I am still rising above it. This and the other difference comes from the difference of spiritual nature and mental makeup. The end is one—abiding in God, he in the fiery zeal of the spirit, I in the deepest peace of it. This is the heart, the life. They determine the direction of the will—love....
>
> Fr. John has the boldness of faith as a gift of God for the attainment of the fullness of Truth through it. I have simplicity of faith as a gift of God to guard against errors and mistakes or to get out of them safely when the Providence of God allows me to fall into them for the sake of my humility. Fr. John therefore has decisiveness in action, while I have discretion and caution until I have grasped the whole situation of the action. Fr. John needs to uphold purity of heart, I need to attain it.[3]

Like St. John, he also encouraged frequent Communion for his flock. The norm in that time and place was to commune just one to four times a year, but Fr. Pontius himself communed daily and many in the Mikhnovo community communed three times a week.

In this manner he was the spiritual father of this community for eighteen years. Finally his weak health caught up with him in the early days of 1939. On the tenth of January, he sat down on his bed, and the sisters read the prayers of the departure of the soul from the body. He then lifted up his eyes to heaven and seemed to be viewing the unseen realm itself. He then fell asleep peacefully in the Lord.

---

3   Rupyshev, "Personal Notes," 183–190.

His funeral services took five days to conduct, and crowds of people came to bid him farewell. The sisters remembered afterward that even in his final days in this world he said to them, "Don't worry if I depart! I will be able to help you even more!"

His body is buried in a chapel next to the church where he served, and witnesses say it remains incorrupt to this day. That chapel is named for St. John of Kronstadt.

The unusual manner of life that Fr. Pontius organized for the community providentially helped them to survive what was to come in just a few years. With the coming of the Soviets during World War II and their general persecution of Christianity, the community's life essentially as a kind of collective farm—highly productive, in fact—made them the pride of the Communists, who ironically saw them as model citizens.

In 2021, the Mikhnovo community celebrated one hundred years of common life in work and prayer.

CHAPTER 30

The Hill of Crosses

L ITHUANIAN ETHNOGRAPHER BALYS BURAČAS TRAVELED throughout Lithuania taking photographs and collecting stories, songs, dances, and games through writing and recording and making wood carvings. Born in 1897, he lived through a vast swathe of tumultuous history, until he died in 1972. He is renowned for having recorded and preserved an inestimable treasury of the old culture of his homeland.

One of the thousands of stories that he wrote down goes like this:[1]

THERE ONCE WAS A MAN who had a beloved young daughter, the delight of his life. To his sorrow and the sorrow of her mother, the girl became seriously ill. The father began to search for every remedy that he could, bringing each of them to her so that she might get well.

Yet nothing worked, and every day her condition grew worse. She suffered more and more, and it became clear that the day of her death drew near.

One night, the father was sitting by the bedside of his daughter, filled with anxiety and love for her. At the moment of midnight, he found that he could no longer stay awake, being filled with a great urge to sleep, and he lay down with his head next to his daughter's and he began to dream.

---

1   This version of the story is adapted from accounts we collected in Lithuania as well as through subsequent research.

In his dream, a woman in shining clothing appeared to him and said, "If you wish your daughter to be made well, fashion a wooden cross and bring it to the old hillfort near Meškuičiai, the small village northeast of Šiauliai. Climb the hill and place the cross at its top, and your daughter will be healed."

The woman then disappeared and the father woke up, unsure of whether he had been awake or asleep, so vivid was the dream.

Whatever the case, one thought remained: He must make a great cross, beautiful to behold, and carry it to the mound of the old hillfort at Meškuičiai. He set to work immediately, constructing not merely two beams of wood fastened to each other but beautifying it with carving and all his care and love for the Savior by whose Cross the world is healed.

Finally, the cross was complete. Taking up the heavy cross upon his shoulders, the father began carrying it to the hill. As he walked, he prayed for his daughter, and his soul ached for her recovery. He began to grow weary, but love compelled him to carry the cross until he reached the hill.

Finally, after thirteen hours of walking, he arrived. The hill rose up before him, just a green mound in the middle of level fields. Was this once a place where his pagan ancestors had erected fortifications and defended themselves against the Livonian Crusaders coming from the north? If so, nothing remained now on the old hill's head but two small peaks at the top of a gradual slope.

He carried the cross up the slope, set it down, then dug a hole for its base. Planting the cross in the hill, he kissed it fervently with tears, praying to God that his daughter would again be made well.

He turned back toward home, exhausted but with his load lightened. As he reached the halfway point, suddenly he saw an image running toward him. He stopped and looked, and as the figure gradually came into view, he recognized who it was—his daughter! And she was on her feet—running!

He couldn't believe it. Was this another vision? Was she dead and this was her spirit? But then she was embracing him, tears in her eyes. It was her. And she was whole.

As she spoke with him, she revealed that when her father had set out on his journey she had begun to feel gradually better. And when he reached the hill and placed his cross on its apex, she stood up out of bed.

So it was that they met halfway, having begun their journey at the same time.

News of this miracle spread throughout Lithuania, and so was founded the great pilgrimage site of the land, with Christians from all over the country—and now, all over the world—making the journey with their crosses. Some are small, only a prayer rope or rosary. Many are a little larger. Some tower as high as thirty feet over the hill. And each one comes and places their cross in the hill, says their prayers, praying to the Savior who died and rose for us.

Father Andrew: While Buračas said he saw about 250 crosses, the Hill of Crosses—*Kryžių kalnas*—is now home to hundreds of thousands of crosses. Most are wood, but they are made out of nearly any material you can think of. Some are very professionally made with amazing carved designs, while many are simpler and even crudely constructed. As the weather and occasional fires wear them down or destroy them, they are replaced almost as quickly by more pilgrims coming to say their prayers.

Historians believe that the Hill first became a place of pilgrimage during one of the nineteenth-century uprisings against the Russian Empire, though no one really knows. We do know for certain, however, that in the twentieth century, the Soviets hated this place. They would bring in bulldozers and fire to destroy it, wiping it clear of the memorials of the prayers of pilgrims. Authorities would block access to the hill and would even arrest and imprison those found carrying crosses nearby.

Nevertheless, sometimes in the middle of the night the pilgrims would return, risking their freedom. The crosses seemed to grow up out of the hill, with the seeds of faith planted deep, invincible against even the demonic hostility of atheistic Communism.

With this history and these legends in mind, we pilgrims went to the Hill of Crosses ourselves. My daughter and I had brought olive wood crosses all the way from America, which were sourced in the Holy Land, a tribute to my daughter's Palestinian heritage from her mother.

We wrote names on our crosses, listing family and friends. Our fellow pilgrim Richard was able to get a cross on the outskirts of the site. And we made the final walk down the long path to the Hill.

It is in the middle of an open field and so it is fully visible, rising up in front of the pilgrim with crosses sprouting all over it as though they are trees and bushes, extending outward far beyond the Hill itself in two long arms stretching out into the grass, reaching out and forward to embrace the one who comes in prayer.

There are paths, but between the paths is a crowded jumble of crosses, some planted so closely together it is impossible to pass. Of course, most of the crosses were brought by Catholic pilgrims, but it is clear that Orthodox Christians and Protestants come here, too. And written on the crosses are names—mostly in Lithuanian but in dozens of languages from all over the world. A few evergreen trees are scattered between the crosses, enhancing the general feeling of being in a kind of forest.

Amidst the crosses are traditional Lithuanian wood carvings of the Lord, His Mother, and the saints, as well as icons. They are reminiscent of the style of the sculptures out on the Curonian Spit, but here there are no mythological characters—this place is exclusively sacred to Christ and His saints. These are *koplytstulpiai*, standing wooden columns with Christian devotional carvings. Most common is *Rūpintojėlis*, the "Pensive Christ" in His suffering before the Crucifixion, but His mother, St. George, and other saints are seen, as well.

Many larger crosses have rosaries, prayer ropes, and smaller crosses with strings attached draped all over them, and they move with the wind. One has the impression that these many smaller crosses are almost the clothing of the larger ones.

We approached the main path, and a woman was showing her son around a corner. "Here is the cross that your father and I placed here when you were born," she said.

Before climbing the hill, we walked around the perimeter, which is ringed with towering wooden shrines featuring scenes from the Catholic Stations of the Cross devotion. As we were taking it all in, looking at all the names with all the prayers, Fr. Gintaras turned to me and said, "There are different intentions written on these crosses. Some people come to ask for health, for guardianship. Some people are saying thanks to the Lord for something He did for them, and some people pray for the departed. It's as if you hear what God hears."

He went on: "There are a lot of different petitions to God. Some are sorrowful, some are happy, and when you make a pilgrimage here, you can put that on your cross—whatever is on your mind, whatever is in your heart. Then you place your cross as an external sign of your prayer."

We walked up the Hill, and I remembered my great-grandmother Olga, who came from the village of Valdomai, just twenty minutes away. Could she have come here? Did she come with her family to place her cross? What names would she have had in mind? Did my great-grandfather Antanas ever come from hours away to do the same thing? Could he have imagined when he came here that his future wife lived so nearby but that he would not meet her until he was in America?

We reached the summit. We placed our crosses. We prayed our prayers. And we joined many generations of our ancestors in praying to the Christ who was crucified for us and rose from the dead for us, who hears us in every generation and in every place, and gives healing to the world.

And in the days that followed, with the prayers we had offered, we learned of a miracle of the healing of a child whose tongue was silent for years, but now . . . he spoke.

A Difficult Story to Tell

THIS STORY OF THE ORTHODOX Church in Lithuania during the Russian imperial period has been one of the hardest to tell. Like so much of history, it is complicated, and while it would be convenient to look at such difficult times and say, "Look, the Church was unwavering and stayed true and perfect in the midst of troubles," as we have seen, that is not always the case.

In this story, the Church had to contend with an empire, and the desires and methods of empires do not always—in fact, do not usually—harmonize with those of the Christian tradition. And so there was distortion.

The beginning of the story of the Unia involved government persecution *of* Orthodox Christians. Here, the end of the story of the Unia in Lithuania involved government persecution *by* Orthodox Christians. Being a religious minority is rarely easy in the history of the world.

It would be easy to look at this use of state power and to condemn whatever came out of it as tainted, especially if what came out was not advantageous to our own side. But we Christians have to remember that what humans mean for evil, God can turn to good. And so, even if the restoration and continuation of Orthodox Christianity in Lithuania had a troubled path, it is nevertheless a good thing that it again became present in this land.

Even more, this was the context in which we met St. John of Kronstadt and Fr. Pontius Rupyshev, the context in which the Domeika family made the immigration to America, the context in which rose up the Hill of Crosses, that great beacon of hope in the midst of suffering. The path is not always clear, but if we keep the vision of the Cross before our eyes, we will see the One to whom it belongs.

PART VI

The Stork and the Bear

Lithuania in the Twentieth Century (1915–1991)

CHAPTER 31

From America to Lithuania: St. Tikhon

THE TWENTIETH CENTURY IN EASTERN Europe was a time of colossal change. For Westerners who remember the 1980s, that vast region behind the Iron Curtain was, up until that time, something of a mystery—an opaque, impenetrable landscape ruled by totalitarian governments preaching the glories and benefits of Communism. Here and there, amid the brutalist, gray, utilitarian architecture of the Soviet system rose the golden and copper onion domes of the Orthodox churches as well as the baroque spires and cupolas of Catholicism in the nearer countries such as Poland and Lithuania.

When the Iron Curtain fell in the 1990s, Protestant missionaries from America flooded the East, eager not only to spread their version of the gospel but also to see this hidden world that had suffered decades of mechanical atheist trauma. What many of them did not know—or in some cases did not care to know—was that the world they were now exploring already had heard the name of Christ, though in many places speaking it had fallen to a whisper. Faithful Christians hid their icons and their rosaries away from the eyes of Communist party informers, and they made the sign of the cross only where trusted family and friends might see them.

Many, of course, had fallen away from the Christian faith as the new gospel of Marxism converted the hearts of whole generations. Communism had indeed given rise to a New Man, the Soviet Man (or Person), and he existed in Lithuania, too.

A FEW YEARS BEFORE THE rise of the Soviet Union, however, a young archbishop arrived in Vilnius. It was a cold January day in 1914, and he was just forty-eight years old, though in another week he would turn forty-nine. Vilnius was his third episcopal assignment in the Russian Orthodox Church, which governed the diocese that had been formed in 1839 when the Lithuanian and Belarusian Uniates were joined to the Orthodox.

Prior to his arrival in Vilnius, the bishop had served for six years in the Russian city of Yaroslavl, about 170 miles (270 kilometers) northeast of Moscow. His first assignment, however, from 1898 to 1907, was tending a flock that was mostly former Uniates, though much more recently converted and across an ocean from the European world.

The archbishop was named Tikhon Bellavin, remembered among the saints as the Enlightener of North America.

American Orthodox Christians know St. Tikhon well, of course, but his years in Lithuania are far less well known, eclipsed as they are for us by his service on our continent and also his martyric struggle as the first Patriarch of Moscow in the modern era. But before he became Patriarch of Moscow, he was Archbishop of Vilnius.

When St. Tikhon took up his see in Vilnius in 1914, about 10 percent of the population of Lithuania was Russian while the majority were Catholics with many Jews present as well, at 8 percent of the population. In the city of Vilnius itself, however, 40 percent were Jewish, with Polish people at 30 percent and Russians at 20 percent. The remaining 10 percent were Lithuanians, Belarusians, and others.

A key piece of context is the 1905 Act of Religious Tolerance, a law of the Russian Empire that loosened up restrictions on non-Orthodox religions. In Lithuania, this led to the large Polish Catholic population pushing back on the Russian Orthodox minority with slogans such as "Poland for the Poles."

Saint Tikhon's diocese included two provinces of the Russian Empire—Kovno (Kaunas) and Vilna (Vilnius), with most of the latter including territory inside modern Belarus. In the Kovno province, the population were mainly Lithuanians, while in the Vilna province, most were Belarusians.

He set immediately to work, not only fulfilling the customary administrative duties of a bishop but also with the pastoral attentiveness that his sixteen years of experience had taught him. He paid special attention to the young in his parishes and, where he saw a skillful iconographer or a diligent choirmaster, he encouraged them. He was found among simple villagers and with the powerful, visiting not only the monasteries and churches of the cities but also distant rural parishes who had never seen an episcopal visit.

He was not there only for the Russian minority, however. As he had learned in America, Tikhon knew that the integral missionary work of the Church was impossible without focus on the local language. Shortly after his arrival, he convened his clergy together and, in addition to the usual logistical matters, he introduced the idea that the Lithuanian language should be taught at the Orthodox theological school in Vilnius, because many of the Russian clergy did not know it.

Saint Tikhon also made a point to participate in the public cultural life of Vilnius, attending not only Russian cultural gatherings but also concerts of sacred music in the municipal buildings of the capital. He came to be respected throughout Lithuania, and not only by his own Orthodox flock but also by Catholics and Jews.

His cathedral in Vilnius, directly next to his residence, was named for St. Nicholas, but it was not the currently known Orthodox Church of St. Nicholas in the city but rather a converted Jesuit church dedicated to the Catholic patron of Lithuania, Casimir. A plaque on the residence next to the church marks his presence even to this day.

In July 1914, just six months after the archbishop's arrival, the Great War—World War I—erupted in Europe. This war would form the backdrop for the rest of St. Tikhon's ministry in Lithuania.

With many soldiers passing through Lithuania to fight on the western front, the saint organized both donations and hospitals to care for the wounded. This work included setting up a two-hundred-bed hospital in St. Mary Magdalene Convent, an Orthodox women's monastery that depended on cooperation between the Orthodox, Catholics, and Jews in Vilnius to help the suffering. Saint Tikhon himself took responsibility for two of the beds, and many doctors worked for free. He ministered to many of the sick and wounded, both at the Orthodox hospital and at other places.

As the battle lines shifted eastward, St. Tikhon took the relics of the Three Martyrs of Vilnius—Anthony, Eustathius, and John—and on the feast of the Exaltation of the Cross in September 1914, he carried them in a solemn procession around the Monastery of the Holy Spirit. About this same time, Tsar Nicholas II visited Vilnius and venerated the relics alongside the holy Archbishop, who said to the tsar, "From the relics of the holy Vilnius martyrs we draw lessons of courage and patience that are so necessary now."[1] A month later the relics were venerated by Grand Duchess Elizabeth, later known as St. Elizabeth the New Martyr, killed by the Bolsheviks in 1918, as well as Archimandrite John Pommers (St. John of Riga), who would go on to become the archbishop of the Church in Latvia and would also be martyred, in 1934.

Meanwhile, at the Orthodox hospital at St. Mary Magdalene convent, St. Tikhon and his clergy were ministering to the sick and dying, hearing confessions, praying memorials, distributing crosses, Bibles, and other spiritual books, as well as feeding patients and tending the wounds of the injured. Divine services were held in the hospital as often as possible, and when the fast of Great Lent in 1915 was broken, the saint himself served the festal meal in the hospital.

WORD BEGAN ARRIVING IN LITHUANIA of what the Kaiser's army was doing in Poland—ransacking and desecrating Orthodox churches and their contents. Would the same happen in Lithuania?

That spring, shortly after Pascha, the German army invaded Lithuania, and by August the city of Kaunas fell. In September, the German army arrived in Vilnius with the Russian imperial forces fleeing eastward before them.

The archbishop could see the battle raging around his cathedral and finally obeyed the order from the Russian military to evacuate, leaving the day before the Germans entered the city. To prevent their destruction, he took with him the wonder-working Zhirovits icon of the Theotokos as well as the relics of the Three Martyrs of Vilnius, bringing them to Donskoy Monastery in Moscow.

His administration-in-exile was set up for a while in Moscow, but he eventually moved to Belarus (which was part of his diocese) to be nearer to his Lithuanian flock—many of whom had fled with him as refugees—then on to

---

1   Arefieva, "From here, from Lithuania, he entered glory."

Ryazan, trying to find shelter somewhere. He spent much of his time in St. Petersburg, doing work with the Holy Synod. As he was sojourning, he prevailed upon the central church administration to pay for the needs of his clergy on the front lines, writing, "Both the pastors and the flock drag out their existence in crying need, in the abyss of grief, misfortunes and illnesses, in conditions of fabulously high prices for basic necessities."[2]

Though he was never able to return his headquarters to Vilnius, St. Tikhon nevertheless continued his ministry to other places within his diocese, particularly in Belarus, and he still made visitations to Lithuania proper. At one point during the war, he consecrated a refugee shelter in Vilnius and donated to the care of orphans. While shells were exploding not twenty miles away, he encouraged the graduates of a school in western Belarus, telling them, "The sorrowful time of war is only a temporary test, a chastisement for sins, which strengthens our faith and hope in God's providence for us."[3]

He would often visit soldiers on the front lines and celebrate the Divine Liturgy for them in the open air among the evergreen trees of the vast forests of the region. Throughout 1916, the saint thus lived as a refugee himself, traveling among his flock as he could and ministering to them in the midst of many dangers.

FINALLY, IN FEBRUARY OF 1917, amid the chaos of the war, the Russian monarchy was overthrown. The government of the church was also thrown into disarray as the Ober-Procurator, the government official appointed to oversee the Holy Synod, began to force many bishops from their sees, including the Metropolitan of Moscow. Tikhon found himself in St. Petersburg, renamed Petrograd at that time, right in the midst of it all.

Five months later he was elected as the new Metropolitan of Moscow. That fall, the infamous October Revolution occurred in Russia. On November 5, in a moment that must have seemed throughout Europe like the world itself was on fire, Tikhon, the Archbishop of Vilnius and Lithuania, was named the first Patriarch of Moscow and All Russia since the year 1700.

---

2   Arefieva.
3   Arefieva.

That is the story of how an American Orthodox saint brought what he had learned in America to Lithuania. Then, through the purification of suffering in his Lithuanian diocese, he was raised to even greater heights of holiness, becoming one of the great Orthodox saints of the twentieth century. He suffered greatly under the Bolshevik government and, after an illness, surrendered his life for Christ on March 25, 1925, at the age of sixty.

CHAPTER 32

Independence (1918–1940)

A T THE DAWN OF THE twentieth century, Lithuania had been part of the Russian Empire for over one hundred years. Despite that century of incorporation into the tsar's imperium, a growing sense of Lithuanian national identity had been expanding for some decades, as we detailed in previous chapters.

The Great Seimas of Vilnius

SO IT WAS THAT TOWARD the end of 1905, on December 4, about two thousand Lithuanians arrived in Vilnius from all over Lithuania and beyond, including from areas that now are part of Poland, Ukraine, Belarus, Russia, Estonia, and Latvia. Some even came from Lithuania Minor, those western lands that at the time were part of the German Empire. Most came from the ancient Lithuanian heartlands of Aukštaitija and Suvalkija, but also Žemaitija (Samogitia) in the west as well as other regions such as Dzūkija in the south.

They had been summoned to the Great Seimas of Vilnius, and they came together in a grand white palace in the heart of the Old City, a building now home to the Lithuanian National Philharmonic Society. Just up the same street, a little higher on the hill, looking down on them was the great icon of Our Lady of the Gate of Dawn.

In January of that year, the events of Bloody Sunday in St. Petersburg had sparked a revolution, and Tsar Nicholas II was cornered into making a variety of concessions that weakened his government's control. Among those listed in a decree called the October Manifesto were a guarantee of freedom of religion, including the study of religion in local languages, as well as the right to form regional political parties. The Manifesto also said that elections would be held for the Russian Duma (parliament), and it was on this basis that the Great Seimas organizers made their plans—Lithuanians, they said, needed to prepare to participate in those elections.

The thousands who gathered in Vilnius on that cold December day had been selected by their local communities, about half through election and the rest via various methods. They were drawn from multiple social classes and occupations, though the majority, 60 to 70 percent, were ordinary peasants, with some 30 to 40 percent coming from the intelligentsia. Only a handful of artisans or landlords were selected for the assembly.

The Great Seimas was thus the result of the first popular election in the history of Lithuania. It was a parliament of sorts that, perhaps for the first time in European history, would include women. They were not many, but seven of them showed up, having been chosen by their towns and villages.

When the delegates arrived, they read telegrams from Lithuanians in America. They spoke of their excitement for this moment in Lithuanian history and about how they were holding various meetings and rallies in the United States in support of their relatives and friends in the homeland.

The Seimas elected Jonas Basanavičius, the famed leader of the national revival, to preside over its proceedings, and they debated over two days. Though there were various factions and viewpoints, on everyone's mind was how Lithuania might reemerge and come once again into its own. The Seimas was a clamor of loud, raucous debate, reminiscent of the unruly szlachta of the old Commonwealth days, but in the end far more focused and determined.

Finally, the Seimas issued a four-point document. The resolution begins with a bold proclamation that the imperium of Russia was the enemy of Lithuania:

> Taking into consideration the fact that the current tsarist government is our deadly enemy, that now all lands of the Russian state have risen against this

government, and that better life can be won only in the struggle against the old order, the Lithuanians, taking part in the assembly, announce the need to educate themselves, to unite and together with the insurgent nations of Russia join battle.[1]

Second, the Seimas demanded autonomy for Lithuania, ruled by a Seimas (parliament) elected through universal suffrage, and they also demanded the conversion of the empire into a federation. Third, they outlined the means toward achieving this autonomy, emphasizing only nonviolent means such as cessation of paying taxes, abandoning Russian schools, refusing conscription, implementing a workers' strike, and generally ignoring the imperial government. The last paragraph insisted that children should be taught in their native languages by teachers chosen by the local people.

After this document was agreed to, Basanavičius put forward a motion that the Catholic Church authorities, based in Poland, be condemned for suppressing the Lithuanian language in churches in Lithuania, which was approved without much discussion.

In the middle of the night, between December 5 and 6, thirty-six thousand copies of the resolution were printed and began to be distributed. What would happen? How would their fellow Lithuanians—not to mention the Russian government—respond?

So what did come in the immediate aftermath of this Seimas? Not much, it seems—at least politically. A number of the delegates went home and began electing their own local leaders and organizing their own schools, and they stopped paying taxes to the Russian authorities. But, after an initially confused response, the imperial powers brought things back to what they had been.

More importantly, however, Lithuanians had learned they could organize, form political parties and associations. They had come together—thousands of them—from all over their homeland, and they had looked into each other's eyes and seen that they were a people.

1   Miknys, "Decisions of the Lithuanian Assembly," 152.

Independence

NEARLY TEN YEARS LATER THE Russian Empire entered World War I, mobilizing its army in defense of Serbia, and Germany declared war on the empire on August 1, 1914. A little over a year after that, on September 19, 1915, the German army entered Vilnius. Seeing the Russian army retreating from his city, the man who had presided over the Great Seimas in 1905, Jonas Basanavičius, saw an opportunity.

Although originally from a small village in the Suvalkija region, Basanavičius had become deeply entrenched in Vilnius life. He founded the Lithuanian Scientific Society there in 1907, and in the years leading up to and during the war he had been working to defend its properties and interests as well as aiding Lithuanian refugees and those wounded by war.

As the war wound on, the military occupation authorities approached men like Basanavičius and his associate Antanas Smetona to participate in a rubber-stamp advisory council of Lithuanians, but they refused. Eventually, the refugee aid organization that included Basanavičius negotiated with the Germans to allow a conference of delegates from throughout Lithuania. They agreed, but no elections would be held. Instead, a committee would be permitted to choose delegates directly.

Two hundred fourteen delegates came together on September 18 to 20, 1917, with no Germans in the room looking over their shoulders, meeting at what is now the Old Theatre of Vilnius. They discussed a number of topics, but most notably, they elected twenty people to what was called the Council of Lithuania, an executive authority for the Lithuanian people. The Council included lawyers, Catholic priests, agronomists, financiers, a doctor, a publisher, and an engineer, ranging in age from twenty-five to sixty-six. Antanas Smetona was elected as the chairman of the Council.

Earlier that year, Tsar Nicholas II had abdicated, and within weeks of the election of the Council of Lithuania, the October Revolution erupted in St. Petersburg and the Bolsheviks, led by Vladimir Lenin, swept away the old order of the Russian Empire. The Empire began to collapse. The Bolsheviks signed a truce with the Germans on December 4.

With this news ringing in their ears, and with the presence of the occupation forces of the German Empire still in control of Vilnius, the twenty men of the Council of Lithuania met in the Lithuanian capital and on December 11 signed a declaration of federation with Germany with a certain autonomy for a new Lithuanian state. Germany would nonetheless control Lithuania's foreign policy.

This arrangement was unpopular with Lithuanians both in Lithuania and abroad, and the Germans for their part broke their promise to recognize the new state. The Council was treated as purely advisory, and these developments threatened to tear the Council apart.

Demoralized and divided, yet with a sense of perhaps muted determination, the Council again convened on February 16, 1918, this time under the chairmanship of Jonas Basanavičius. They prepared a one-page document, written in both Lithuanian and German, just four sentences long. In it, the Council wrote:

> The Council of Lithuania, as the sole representative of the Lithuanian nation, based on the recognized right to national self-determination, and on the Vilnius Conference's resolution of September 18–23, 1917, proclaims the restoration of the independent state of Lithuania, founded on democratic principles, with Vilnius as its capital, and declares the termination of all state ties which formerly bound this State to other nations.[2]

With all twenty signatures affixed to the document, Lithuania's independence was declared. As the twenty men looked at each other, considering the weight of what they had said together, they wondered whether the world would listen, whether they would truly be free.

News of the declaration reached the German Reichstag, and it was largely ignored. The Germans acted as though the December 11 document determined Lithuania's future.

Although the presence of German troops prevented them from forming any of the usual machinery of government, in June the Council again met. This time, the name of their ancient ancestor Mindaugas was on their lips— the first and only King of Lithuania, crowned in 1253. But why? Lithuania

---

2   "Act of Independence of 16 February 1918."

THE WOLF AND THE CROSS

ought to be a monarchy again, they said, though a modern monarchy with a constitution.

To this end, though they were divided on the question, they voted to invite Wilhelm Karl, Duke of Urach, a German Roman Catholic prince and descendant of Lithuanian Grand Duke Casimir IV, to be the second King of Lithuania. In July, he accepted and took the name Mindaugas II. The Council hoped his German background would secure German cooperation and protect against the return of Russia.

Duke Wilhelm began to learn the Lithuanian language at his home in southern Germany and made plans to visit his new realm. But then the war turned against Germany as it also suffered its own revolution in November 1918. The Council met again on November 2 and adopted a provisional constitution, rescinding its invitation to the German noble. He never was crowned, and so Lithuania never did have a second king.

To the west, the German Empire was collapsing. To the east, Russia burned with the flames of the Bolsheviks. So it was that, for the first time in well over a century, Lithuania was free.

That freedom would be dearly bought, however. A series of wars were fought on Lithuanian soil over the next two years, between the new Lithuanian state and the newly formed Soviet Union, between Poland and the Soviets, between Lithuania and a group of pro-German militants known as the Bermontians, and between Poland and Lithuania. Collectively, these conflicts are known as the Lithuanian Wars of Independence. In Lithuanian, they are called *Laisvės kovos*—the Freedom Struggles.

The Orthodox Church in Interwar Lithuania

BY THE END OF 1920, the new state controlled most of modern Lithuania, but the Suvalkija region in the southwest, as well as Vilnius itself and the lands east and north of it, were in the hands of Poland. The capital and government of the newly independent Lithuania thus rested in its second city, Kaunas.

The Orthodox Church in Lithuania now found itself outside the empire that had supported it and established the diocese in 1839. Many of its parishes, especially in the Vilnius region and to the north and east, were inside a newly independent Poland.

In 1924, with the persecution of the Orthodox Church inside now-Soviet Russia, the Orthodox Church in Poland, including the parishes in the Vilnius region under Poland's control, asserted its independence and became the Autocephalous Orthodox Church of Poland. Thus, the Lithuanian diocese of the Polish Church based in Vilnius during this period was headed by Archbishop Theodosius Feodosiev, while the diocese of the Russian Church based in Kaunas was governed by Metropolitan Eleutherius Bogoyavlensky. As we said in a previous chapter, it was between these two sets of parishes that the revered Fr. Pontius Rupyshev made his ministry, crossing the border between the newly established independent states of Lithuania and Poland.

Now that the Orthodox churches of Lithuania were outside the Russian Empire, would they turn their attention to Lithuanian culture and society?

In this period leading up to World War II, the diocese established programs for clergy to teach them the Lithuanian language. The state itself established incentives, offering social security and even parish funding for clergy who learned Lithuanian and kept their records in Lithuanian. Evidence shows that it did not make much impact, however, as documents from that period continued to be written in Russian, and worship (as in Russia) was conducted in Church Slavonic. Old habits were maintained, and the Orthodox community in Lithuania remained mainly ethnically Russian.

That said, there was at least one Lithuanian priest serving in the diocese at the time, a prominent priest named Fr. Jonas Korčinskis (or Ivan Korchynsky), himself the son of a priest with Belarusian roots. He was born in Ukraine in 1864, about 150 miles south of Kyiv, was ordained in 1888, and served in what is modern Ukraine, Belarus, Russia, and Lithuania, including in the ancient village of Merkinė. He was briefly imprisoned in Poland as a "Russian agitator" before he moved to Lithuania in 1920.

Father Jonas was involved in both Belarusian and Lithuanian politics and served as a Lithuanian army chaplain. Among many other texts, he wrote a history of the Orthodox Church in the Grand Duchy of Lithuania, a book about Vytautas the Great, and another about Grand Dukes Algirdas and Kęstutis, as well as hagiographical texts for St. Gabriel of Bialystok (which is in

Poland) and St. Athanasius of Brest. He received multiple awards and recognitions from both the Church and state authorities for his work. He died in 1935 and was buried at the Orthodox cemetery in Kaunas. The cemetery was later destroyed by the Soviets.

In the interwar period, around 8 percent of the Orthodox population were ethnically Lithuanian. There also seem to have been majority-Lithuanian parishes. One priest even asked the Lithuanian Ministry of Internal Affairs for permission to serve in the Lithuanian language, and the ministry replied that this wasn't the Russian Empire anymore, so they didn't regard it as any of their business what language was used for worship.

CHAPTER 33

Our Lady of Surdegis

S URDEGIS IS A SMALL VILLAGE of about 150 people in the Aukštaitija region of Lithuania, situated roughly twenty miles northwest of the great forest of Anykščiai and twenty-five miles east of the city of Panevėžys. The first mention of this village in any document comes from 1510, during the time of the Grand Duchy, when a wealthy Orthodox Christian Ruthenian noble named Bogdan Shish-Stavitsky had an Orthodox church built there.

Not far from this church was a spring of water, welling up from the ground and bringing life to the place. In 1530, on the feast of the Dormition of the Mother of God, an icon of the Virgin herself suddenly appeared above the spring. In the icon, the Lord Jesus as a child is seated in the crook of her left arm. Her right hand reaches toward Him, and He is grasping one of her fingers. Their faces are distinctly wide-eyed, in an expression of wonder and innocence.

At the sight of this miraculous appearance, the local landowner Alexei Feodorovich built another church, made of wood and dedicated to the Holy Trinity, to be a home for the icon of Our Lady of Surdegis.

The Christian faithful of Lithuania began to make pilgrimage to this place, and so in 1550 (some sources say 1627) a monastery dedicated to the Holy Spirit was founded there, to house the icon and dedicate the place to continual prayer and to provide hospitality for the pilgrims. The brother-hood there was dependent upon the Holy Spirit Monastery in Vilnius. The reputation of the icon grew, and the stories of its miracles spread throughout Lithuania and beyond.

Because of its fame, it is said that once local Roman Catholics attempted to steal the icon to enshrine it in the Catholic monastery at Troškūnai, a few miles away. As the story goes, when the icon entered the monastery, its faces disappeared, and the jaws of the thieves became crooked and painful. Seeing this, the Catholic abbot ordered that the icon be returned to the Orthodox monastery in a great procession, during which one of the Catholic locals lost his sanity and shouted out blasphemies.

As the icon was being carried back to the monastery at Surdegis, a blind beggar approached the procession. He knelt down on the ground in prayer, and as the icon was held aloft it passed over him and he received his sight.

As the tales of the miracles spread, not only Orthodox Christians, including Old Believers, but also Roman Catholics and even pilgrims from the western coast of Lithuania—probably thus including Lutherans—came to Surdegis to pray and ask God that He would grant them their petitions. A group of Russian merchants from Riga in Latvia even made a yearly pilgrimage on the feast of the Dormition in August, the anniversary of the appearance of the icon.

There at the monastery they would celebrate an all-night vigil for the feast, with a blessing of water from the holy spring, an akathist to the Virgin Mary, and commemorations of all their departed in Christ. During their pilgrimage, they served in the church and throughout the monastery grounds, made and sold candles to support the monastery, and cleaned the holy objects of the church.

On the day of the Dormition, it became the custom to carry the icon in a great procession, with frequent stops to allow the faithful to pass under it, just as the blind beggar had done, so that they might also receive a blessing. The Surdegis Dormition pilgrims also had the custom of visiting the graves of all the brotherhood of the monastery, singing hymns and asking God to grant them rest with the saints.

Many benefactors gave to the monastery from throughout Eastern Europe, including Tsar Peter I, who visited the monastery in 1721. Among Russian Orthodox Christians, the icon came to be known as *Surdegskaya*.

In 1812, a new stone church was built with the support of pilgrims from Riga, and it included a narrow staircase on the left of the church leading under the altar. There at the bottom, to this day, still flows the holy spring above which the icon appeared in 1530. When the church was completed, the miraculous icon was enshrined in its iconostasis with a crown placed over the head of the Theotokos.

In 1916–17, with the advent of the First World War and the collapse of the Russian Empire, the brotherhood fled the monastery and brought the icon with them into Russia, where it was installed in an iconostasis in a church in Yaroslavl. In 1921, the icon was returned to Lithuania and placed in a church in Panevėžys. After World War II, the icon was moved to Annunciation Orthodox Cathedral in Kaunas, where it resides to this day.

The ruins of the Surdegis monastery, now abandoned for over a century, still stand, and the 1812 stone church became a Catholic church in 1940. A small, square Orthodox chapel built in 1869 stands nearby, where pilgrims still come and pray.

In an entry from the monastery chronicle, attempting to record some of the miracles that have happened through the holy icon of Our Lady of Surdegis, one of the monks wrote: "If we were to begin to describe all the blessings bestowed upon the human race of different confessions and different sexes and make a general search from ancient times about the miracles that occurred from the Surdegis Mother of God, then a large library of books would be compiled."[1]

So it is with many Orthodox pilgrimage sites in Lithuania, that the blessings of God, His Mother, and all His saints flow indiscriminately to all who approach in faith and hope.

---

1   "Icon of the Mother of God Surdegskaya."

CHAPTER 34

From Domeika to Damick

F ATHER ANDREW: IN JULY OF 1994, my grandmother Elizabeth sat
  down with my grandfather Albert, the son of Antanas and Olga Domeika,
and asked him to tell her about his parents. As she listened to his stories, she
sat at her typewriter and began to clack away at the keys, taking dictation
and setting down the only known record of the American life of my great-
grandparents. He died nine years later in 2003, and she followed him in 2021.

In recent years, as my father was sorting through my grandmother's belong-
ings he discovered the typewritten manuscript and sent me a copy. My grandfather wrote this:

> My father, Tony, came to the United States by way of East Prussia where he was
> working on a German baron's estate as an all around man. He had a brother, John,
> who had already emigrated to the United States and was supposedly living in the
> vicinity of Philadelphia. My future father soon came also. Not knowing much
> about the paperwork he was required to accomplish, his brother gave him help.
>
> He told his brother Tony he had a job for him in the coal mines of Scranton,
> Pennsylvania. My future father accepted the job. As to how he got to Scranton
> and how he began to live, all we know is, he just got there and began to live.

Just how long he worked in the coal mines is anyone's guess.

Earlier, you read about the many Lithuanians living in northeastern Pennsylvania, so many that thousands filled the streets of Wilkes-Barre in the wake

of the Kražiai Massacre in 1893. Most of them were there because of the mines. It was a dangerous business, but Lithuanians had flocked there, especially many from Kudirkos Naumiestis, the town of my Domeika ancestors.

Cave-ins, explosions, poison gas, lung diseases, and rampant cancer took the lives of many miners, leaving their wives widows and their children fatherless. Yet as the Pennsylvania mining companies dug deeper, their hunger for laborers only grew. So they began to send recruiters to Eastern Europe, looking for miners to send down into the tunnels in and around Scranton.

I don't know why my great-grandfather left Scranton, but I am glad he did. There were many coal miner widows and orphans in northeastern Pennsylvania, and when my great-grandfather worked there, he wasn't even married yet. If he had stayed, I might not have ever existed.

The next information I ever heard, he was working in Worcester, Massachusetts, in a furniture store. His brother John lived nearby. I am not certain, or even close to knowing, what kind of work Uncle John was doing.

From what I have heard, my future father worked diligently at his job in the furniture store. He was young, and strong as a bull, so they say. He had to walk only a short distance to his brother's house or place of residence. He had an observant eye as to who was walking on the sidewalks and people sitting by parlor windows looking out at the street. One day by chance he had his eyes looking at the parlor windows of the first floor of the houses he passed by. A nice young lady, busy at a sewing machine, raised her head and smiled at him as their eyes met. Now I need not go any further to tell you who she was. Need I say she came from Lithuania also? In Lithuania she had lived close to the Latvian border and used to go to work daily in the city of Riga.

We later learned that she not only lived near the Latvian border but that it was specifically the village of Valdomai, in a community of other ethnic Latvians that had come to Lithuania some generations before:

Her family lived on a farm in Lithuania. Her father died from cancer. One of her brothers, Teddy, also came to the U.S. He did not wish to become part of the Tsar's army. Though no war was taking place, all the main countries were

223

preparing for the event. The Kaiser, 'Uncle' Bill,[1] was becoming more aggressive year by year.

My mother's next move was to walk my future father down the aisle at the German Lutheran Church. She did. He didn't mind.

So on January 12, 1913, Antanas Domeika and Olga Weiland were married in Worcester, Massachusetts, by the Rev. Gerhard Rademacher. Antanas was Catholic and Olga was Lutheran, but they were both Lithuanian.

My mother handled all the finances of the family. My father would get—get this—a share of his pay, to buy a few cans of snuff, one pair of working gloves each week, and now and then enough to go to the movies with one son in tow. He was a wire temperer, which is to say, he ran coils of wire through a heated furnace, so as to heat the wire to a certain temperature, to give it the necessary tensile strength as needed by the customer.

My mother saw to it that all of us were well fed, our health was watched over, and our clothes were neat. Most of the children's clothes she made with her sewing machine. No electric sewing machines were to be found in the early 1900s. She loved to crochet and knit. All of her fancy dining room tableclothes were crocheted, as well as bedspreads and bureau covers. All the sweaters we wore were knitted by her, and she used the best of materials.

When she needed various supplies she used to walk to Water Street, the Jewish section of the city, and go to the stores which sold what she wanted. She never paid the price they asked. Sometimes she and the store owner would bargain for 15 minutes before he gave in, so he could wait on another customer. Very rarely did she pay the asking price. If she did, the sales person thought she wasn't feeling well. Any store in the Jewish section which sold yard goods, crochet materials and yarns, had to brace themselves in their determination to be firm, to not be outdone by Mother's verbal onslaught. As long as we lived near the Jewish section it became a ritual to go shopping at least once every two weeks. I often wondered what those Jewish salespersons did when we moved to the north end of the city. As far as I know, they did not go out of business.

---

1   Kaiser Wilhelm.

This image of my great-grandmother Olga as tough, diligent, and shrewd came as something of a revelation to me. Of course I had never met her, because she died in 1954 when my father was just two years old. I remember my grandmother describing her as a hard woman. It was no wonder, though. She had come to the United States at just seventeen years old, and it would be another fourteen years before she married my great-grandfather. So she had been thrust into American immigrant life as a single young woman without a husband or other family to support her. She was thirty when she finally got married.

My father didn't know how to read English. My mother did, but very slowly. She improved her reading as the years went by. My Uncle Ted was the smart man. We knew it and he knew it, but he would never become arrogant. The remainder of the Domaika clan, with the exception of Uncle Bill, never cared to know English.

It's still not quite clear to me how educated my immigrant family was. In the couple of documents where my great-grandfather signed his name, it is a mostly indeterminate scrawl. You can make out the initial A, but then it's anyone's guess what the rest of it says. Perhaps they were like many other immigrant families in those days, living among others of their culture and language and only stepping outside those circles when needed. Of course, Olga clearly had no problem taking the initiative:

My mother now lived nearer to the church she attended—the German Evangelical Lutheran Church. It was a small church; a new one was being built. Some of the church members lived nearby. She went to church faithfully each Sunday, weather permitting, and made certain we went there on our own. Sunday School was held after the church services were over. Some Sundays my mother would secure a ride home from some members who owned an automobile. We boys had to hoof it—you know, one foot in front of the other. By the time we got home, and we had to make sure, dinner was ready to be eaten.

My father attended his own "Sunday School" and "Church Services." He had his Saturday night bath, fresh undergarments, and clean shaved himself.

225

He put on his best suit, which included a vest, removed the shiny foil wrapper from the best cigar he had—usually 5¢ was allowed by my mother—and lit it.

He would lock the doors to the tenement, make his way out to the west side of the yard, and start his "Home Baptist services." He would walk the perimeter of the yard slowly puffing on his cigar. . . . Well, by the time my mother arrived home from church my father had smoked one-half of his cigar. He plunked himself into the rocking chair on the front porch and slowly rocked himself to sleep until his wife gave him a rousing homecoming welcome. He was ready to throw her off the porch. He had completed the Home Baptist service. He dropped 50¢ into his pocket and said this was the collection platter. My mother grumbled a string of Lithuanian words at him. We boys couldn't make out what she said. We never learned the language.

Why didn't my great-grandparents teach my grandfather and his two siblings, Robert and Bertha, the Lithuanian language? Why didn't they pass on Lithuanian identity and culture to them, especially considering how slow the clan was to master English? I don't know for certain, but perhaps they were like many immigrants of the early twentieth century in America—they had left the old world behind, and America was where their life was. There was no point in holding onto the old ties.

Perhaps this is why the family name began to change from Domeika (sometimes spelled Domaika) to the simpler, shorter, more American-sounding Damick. (My grandfather himself used both, including one for each of the two times he joined the military.) Perhaps this attitude is also why none of them ever went back, as far as I know, except for one visit in 1936:

My mother [once] went on a vacation to visit her mother in Lithuania. It was [August] 1936 when my mother returned from Lithuania. I was the sole greeter as she stepped off the train at the Worcester railroad station. My father said he was too tired to go and fetch her. My brother and sister weren't available. My mother had brought home many items. One I remember vividly was a sheep's skin. We did not know the size of the skin until it was spread out on the double bed in the guest room. My mother used it as a foot warmer during the winter months.

226

I just remembered why she went to see her people in Lithuania. I had been in the Army at Ft. Slocum, New York, only five days, when my company clerk notified me that my uncle had been killed by a milk-truck while walking along the side of the road [in 1933]. He was heading back to the farm he had recently begun working at.

His estate received more than $2000 from the milk company. My mother took care of all my uncle's affairs.

Instead of keeping the money for herself she went to visit her mother, and gave her his wealth. My grandparents were pleased, because the economic depression was in Lithuania as well as the United States. When my mother left her parents to return home, it would be the last time she would see them. She wrote letters occasionally until Hitler and 'Cousin Joe' initiated a real estate deal,[2] regardless of what the owners of the land thought.

I later looked up how much that $2000 would have been worth in 1930s Lithuania. For the average worker in Lithuania in the interwar period, $2000 was close to two years' worth of income. My tough, shrewd, thrifty great-grandmother, who had worked so hard to survive as an immigrant in America both before and after her wedding in 1913, would have had every right to take the money from her brother's estate and set it aside for herself. But instead she got on a boat and gave it to her parents in Lithuania.

She died in 1954, while my great-grandfather died in 1958, both buried in Hope Cemetery in Worcester, Massachusetts, where Olga's brother Theodore had been buried in 1933.

The Latvian Cousins

AROUND WORLD WAR II, THE remainder of my great-grandmother's ethnically Latvian kinfolk returned north to Latvia, leaving behind only those who had been buried in Lithuania.

As I mentioned earlier, in 2024 during one of my subsequent visits to Lithuania I went north into Latvia, along with my father and one of my sons. Early

---

2   He is referring here to the Molotov-Ribbentrop Pact, signed in 1939 by the governments of Adolf Hitler and Joseph Stalin ('Cousin Joe').

in 2024 I had received an email from an unknown woman named Mudīte titled "Family from Latvia." The email was in Latvian, so I ran it through a translator, and there I read that she had been working with a genealogist to find her "lost American cousins," descendants of her grandfather's sister Olga. She shared her family tree, and the details matched what I had only relatively recently learned about my great-grandmother.

We traded several emails, and then I told her I would be returning to Lithuania and would be near Latvia. Would it be possible to come for a short visit? She was overjoyed and started putting me in touch with her daughters and other family, making preparations for our arrival.

So it was that after visiting the Hill of Crosses near Šiauliai, we drove north across the border to the small town of Dobele and met our Latvian cousins, reunited after eighty-eight years. The last meeting between our two branches was during that 1936 visit when Olga brought the money to her parents.

Of course, even though we had compared family trees over email and all the parts of our stories matched up, there was still a nagging question in my mind as to whether we really were long-lost cousins, whether we truly were related. But then at one point, as Mudīte (who turned out to be my father's second cousin) pulled out a box from her closet and began emptying its contents onto her kitchen table, there was a scrap of paper. On it was written an address that she said was given to her grandfather Jānis when Olga visited in 1936. My father saw it and said, "That was my grandparents' address in Worcester!" That was the moment we knew for certain that we were among family.

It is hard to describe what it is like to meet a group of cousins you did not even know existed until a few months before, but I will give you one impression: How many times in your life have you met someone without having any expectations at all? That is how we felt.

We had no idea who they were or what their lives were like, what their histories were, what they thought about us Americans, or any of it. And yet when we saw each other and I stammered out *Labvakar—ir labi jūs visus satikt* ("Good evening—it's good to meet you all") in Latvian (having practiced it for hours before), there was simply one experience—acceptance. We simply accepted each other, because we were family.

CHAPTER 35

Chiune Sugihara

O UR NEXT STORY IS ABOUT a Japanese man. It may seem strange, but one of the brightest lights to shine in Lithuania before the darkness of World War II was a Japanese man named Chiune Sugihara.

Sugihara was born January 1, 1900 to a middle-class family in south central Japan, one of six children. His father wanted him to be a doctor, but he deliberately failed the required entrance exams by simply writing his name on them and leaving the rest blank. He instead majored in the English language while in university, and then at the age of twenty served in Korea in the imperial Japanese army, resigning his commission after two years.

Having mastered English, he also learned Russian and in 1922 entered the Japanese Foreign Ministry. The Foreign Ministry sent him to the Japanese Language Institute in Harbin, the capital of Manchuria in China, where he also learned German, became an expert in Russian matters, and was assigned to the Japanese Foreign Office of Manchuria. In Harbin, he met many "White Russians"—Russian monarchist refugees who had fled Russia in the wake of the Bolshevik military victory.

During Sugihara's time in China, at the age of twenty-four, he met and married a Russian woman named Klaudia Semionovna Apollonova. At this time, he was baptized into the Orthodox Church with the name Sergei Pavlovich. The old priest who baptized him said that Sergei sounded something like Sugihara, and since the priest himself was named Pavel, he gave Sugihara his own name for a patronymic.

Like most Japanese people at the time, Sugihara was raised a Buddhist—in fact, he had even been born in a Buddhist temple—so why would he convert? Klaudia apparently did not press him to become Orthodox, yet Sugihara was so impressed by her religion that he insisted on it.

By 1934, Sugihara became the deputy foreign minister serving in Manchuria, but he resigned his post in protest of how his countrymen treated the Chinese people. Around this time, Klaudia and Chiune Sugihara divorced, and he returned to Japan. In Tokyo, in February 1935 he remarried, this time to a Japanese woman named Yukiko.

Back in Japan, divorced from his Russian wife and now married to a Japanese woman, it would have been easy for Sugihara to return to the Buddhism of his youth. That is not what happened, however, and Yukiko herself was baptized, receiving the Christian name Maria.

With his multilingual capability, Sugihara was soon reassigned to the Japanese office in Finland, and then in March 1939 he was transferred to Kaunas, then the capital of Lithuania, and promoted to vice-consul. He worked alone without any staff, and his duties focused mainly on reporting on Soviet and Nazi German troop movements. He was also tasked with trying to discover whether the Nazis were planning an attack on the Soviet Union. While in Kaunas, Sugihara used an alternative version of his name, Sempo, since it was easier for Lithuanians to pronounce than Chiune.

SIX MONTHS AFTER SUGIHARA'S ARRIVAL in Lithuania, on September 1, 1939, Hitler invaded Poland, lighting the fires of the Second World War. Around the same time, the Slovak Republic (a Nazi client state lasting from 1939 to 1945) and the Soviet Union also invaded Poland, with this joint attack aimed at dividing Polish territory between them, much as had been done in the late eighteenth century with the partitions of the Polish-Lithuanian Commonwealth.

In October, the Soviet Union signed a treaty with the government of Lithuania, returning the old capital of Vilnius to Lithuanian control in exchange for allowing Soviet military bases on Lithuanian land, supposedly to protect them against Nazi incursions. Vilnius at that time was populated mainly by people of Polish and Jewish backgrounds.

With Nazi ideology driving not only territorial advances but also the persecution of Jews, Jewish refugees from Poland began to pour into Lithuania, which was then home to about 160,000 Jews, some 7 percent of the population. In Vilnius itself, Jews were about 30 percent of the population. The community was so large that Vilnius was called "the Jerusalem of the North," and the edition of the Talmud most Jews use today was compiled in Vilnius.

During the Russian imperial period, the government did not permit most Jews to live in Russia proper, so they had to live in the so-called "Pale of Settlement," which was roughly the lands of the old Commonwealth. This established and bolstered the largest community of Jews in Europe. As such, when the Jews fled Nazi-occupied Poland into Lithuania, they joined a long-established, stable community of Lithuanian Jews, known as Litvaks. Jewish refugees from Poland swelled their ranks to about 210,000 by 1941.

In June 1940, the Soviet Union broke the October 1939 treaty and invaded Lithuania. Unbeknownst to the Lithuanian people, on August 23–24, 1939, less than two weeks before Hitler invaded Poland, Nazi Germany and the Soviet Union had signed a secret agreement known as the Molotov-Ribbentrop Pact. This nonaggression pact divided Eastern Europe between the two military powers. Lithuania had been signed over to the Soviets.

Despite this nonaggression pact, tensions between the Nazis and Soviets remained high and would even escalate to the Nazis invading the Soviet Union in 1941, including an incursion into Lithuania and an occupation that lasted until 1945. With the Nazi threat from the west and historical memory of Russian persecution from the east, displaced Polish Jews and Litvaks living in Lithuania knew they were in a precarious position. Thousands began to look for a way out, and foreign consulates were inundated with requests for transit visas that would give permission for Jewish refugees to flee to or through the consulates' respective home countries.

IN JULY 1940, THE SOVIET occupiers of Lithuania ordered all foreign consulates to leave the country. Sugihara requested and received a twenty-day extension for his presence in Kaunas, and he contacted his superiors in Tokyo about the transit visa requests he was receiving.

Their response was that visas could be issued only to those who had visas for destinations beyond Japan, and they also had to have gone through an immigration process and be in possession of sufficient funds for travel. Suffice it to say that most of the refugees contacting Sugihara did not meet all or often any of these criteria. With the dust clouds of Nazi tanks rising to the west, Sugihara knew that the Holocaust was coming to Lithuania. And so he made a choice.

From July 18 to September 4, 1940, Sergei Pavlovich, known more commonly as Chiune or Sempo Sugihara, dedicated himself to a single task. He began to handwrite transit visas, giving them to anyone who asked, whether they could fulfill the Japanese Foreign Ministry's requirements or not. It is said that he often worked eighteen to twenty hours a day, writing visa after visa, often writing in a single day the number of visas that would normally have been a month's worth of work.

Finally, the Soviets came and closed his consulate in Kaunas. As Sugihara boarded the train to exit the country, he still had his stack of transit visas with him, and he continued to write them, one after another. His wife later wrote that he said, "Please forgive me," as he boarded the train, bowing low to the Jews gathered at the train station. "I cannot write anymore. I wish you the best." One replied, "Sugihara. We'll never forget you. I'll surely see you again!"[1]

The Jewish refugees pressed against the train, calling out to him in desperation. He kept writing visas and finally threw blank visas out the window, with only his signature and official stamp, where they were picked up as precious treasures by the desperate trying to flee the Holocaust.

THE NAZIS ARRIVED IN LITHUANIA in June 1941 and stayed through January 1945. During this time, they rounded up and shot some 95 percent of Lithuania's Jewish population—nearly two hundred thousand people—with most being killed in the first six months. They were all dumped into mass graves. In

---

1   Sugihara, *Visas for Life*.

many cases, local Lithuanians collaborated with the Nazis or turned a blind eye to them, leaving a shameful stain on Lithuania that is mourned to this day.

All over Lithuania, in both large cities and small villages, as well as out in the countryside, one can find mass Holocaust graves and memorial markers. In the space of just a few months, the centuries-old Jewish community of Lithuania was virtually erased. Today, it is estimated that there are about 2,400 Jews remaining in Lithuania.

WE DO NOT KNOW HOW many people's lives were saved by one Orthodox Christian Japanese man living in Kaunas for eighteen months from 1939 to 1940. Estimates range from 2,200 to six thousand. Some say as high as ten thousand. Certainly, some who received a Sugihara visa did not make it out in time, but it is now believed that there are between forty thousand and one hundred thousand living descendants of all those who escaped, with Sugihara's visas and through other means.

During the remainder of World War II, Sugihara was reassigned to Königsberg in East Prussia (now Kaliningrad), then later to Prague and then Romania. When the Soviet military entered Romania in 1944, Sugihara and his family were imprisoned in a camp for prisoners of war for eighteen months.

They were released in 1946 and returned to Japan. The Foreign Ministry asked him to resign in 1947, and although an official reason is not recorded, his wife Maria Yukiko said that it was because of what he had done in Lithuania. Sugihara went on to work in manual labor positions and completed his career as a manager for an export company.

In 1985, Sugihara was interviewed and asked about his actions in Lithuania:

You want to know about my motivation, don't you? Well. It is the kind of sentiments anyone would have when he actually sees refugees face to face, begging with tears in their eyes. He just cannot help but sympathize with them. Among the refugees were the elderly and women. They were so desperate that they went so far as to kiss my shoes. Yes, I actually witnessed such scenes with my own eyes. Also, I felt at that time, that the Japanese government did not have any uniform opinion in Tokyo. Some Japanese military leaders were just scared because of the pressure from the Nazis; while other officials in the Home

Ministry were simply ambivalent. People in Tokyo were not united. I felt it silly to deal with them. So, I made up my mind not to wait for their reply. I knew that somebody would surely complain about me in the future. But, I myself thought this would be the right thing to do. There is nothing wrong in saving many people's lives. . . . The spirit of humanity, philanthropy . . . neighborly friendship . . . with this spirit, I ventured to do what I did, confronting this most difficult situation—and because of this reason, I went ahead with redoubled courage.[2]

Sergei Pavlovich died in 1986 in Kamakura in relative obscurity after the loss of his diplomatic career. It seems that almost no one around him in Japan knew about what he had done. But it became known at his funeral. Large contingents of Jews arrived from around the world to pay their respects to this Orthodox Christian man from Japan.

Today, his diplomatic office in Kaunas is a museum where anyone can go and learn what this man did with what was given to him: He looked into the eyes of his fellow human beings and gave them mercy and hope.

---

2   Levine, *In Search of Sugihara*, 259.

CHAPTER 36

Through Communism to Freedom

W ITH WORLD WAR I AND its subsequent regional conflicts ending in 1920, Lithuania had stood independent for the first time in 125 years. It was not to last, however, for just twenty years later Lithuania again was caught between Germans to the west and Russians to the east.

In the beginning of 1944, Nazi Germany remained in control of Lithuania, and the Orthodox Christians of Lithuania were led by the Russian Metropolitan Sergei Voskresensky. He had not generally been well regarded by the Soviet government in Russia, yet they did not prevent his assignment to Lithuania and the Baltics in 1941.

When the Nazis moved into the Baltic countries that same year, he did not flee but remained at his headquarters in Riga. His position was difficult, however, as neither the Nazis nor Soviets favored him. So it was that on April 29, 1944, while on the road from Vilnius to Kaunas, unknown assailants stopped his car and murdered him. He was buried in Riga.

IN JULY 1944, THE SOVIET army returned to Lithuania, taking the eastern part of the country. Stalin soon annexed Lithuania and proclaimed it the Lithuanian Soviet Socialist Republic, and his army captured Klaipėda on the Baltic coast in January 1945. By September the Axis powers had fully surrendered, bringing World War II to an end.

With the dust settling on World War II, Lithuania found itself subject to the same nation from which it had emerged independent two decades before. The first time it was imperial Russia, and now this time it was Soviet Russia. That the first conquest by Russia was under an officially Christian government and the second was under an atheistic one did not much matter to the Lithuanian people. The long nightmare had begun again.

Yet those two decades of freedom had left their mark on the Lithuanian people. In 1944, while the Nazis retreated from Lithuania and the Soviets moved in, the Russians began forcibly conscripting Lithuanians to fight in the Soviet army, just as their imperial predecessors had done in the nineteenth century. In response, thousands of Lithuanian men left their homes and took up residence in the vast forests of their homeland. These guerrilla fighters, commonly known as *partisans*, were also called the "Forest Brothers."

From 1944 to 1953, the Forest Brothers of Lithuania waged one of the longest partisan wars in European history, with parallel movements in Latvia and Estonia, the sister Baltic nations to the north. Numerous partisan units operated all throughout the Baltic countries, eventually organizing into the Union of Lithuanian Freedom Fighters in 1948. The Soviets killed some twenty thousand partisans and captured another twenty thousand, as they gave their lives in hope of returning Lithuania's lost independence.

A whole culture sprang up around the partisans, and there was even a tradition of partisan songs that was passed down over the generations. Some were rousing and hopeful, celebrating the camaraderie of brothers-in-arms. Others were mournful and dark, carrying on the wistfulness of living in defeat. Singing societies were formed during the Soviet occupation, and many of these continue even today.

IN ONE OF THESE SONGS, titled "A Homeland Not Yet Free" (*Dar nesulaukęs laisvos tėvynės*), a dirge is lifted up for one of the partisans shot by the Soviets. His body is left in Cathedral Square in the heart of Vilnius, and no one dares approach—not his fellow Forest Brothers nor even his mother—for fear of the Soviets. His body is not given burial but is simply dumped in the Nemunas River:

A homeland not yet free,
Dear warrior, why did you fall asleep?

Your eyes went blind from the enemy's bullets,
You left your fighting friends.

They laid you on the stones,
And spilled blood surrounded you,
And neither your mother came,
Nor your brothers, the brave eagles.

And when they took you from the hard street,
They did not prepare the wood for your coffin.
They only buried you in the Nemunas River,
Because they would not share the black earth with you.[1]

While the conflict rolled on, the hope was that the Western powers would intervene and reestablish Lithuania as an independent country, but it became clear that the West was not interested in confrontation with the Soviet Union. Thus, though a few partisans would continue to soldier on for some years, in 1953 the Forest Brothers decided not to accept any more members, winding down the insurgency and leaving the fulfillment of the hope for an independent Lithuania to a future generation.

IT IS DIFFICULT TO SUMMARIZE the Soviet occupation of Lithuania, but one small comfort is that the repression of religion was not as extreme as it was in the early days of the Soviet Union. That said, religion was severely restricted, especially for Roman Catholics, many of whose churches were closed and clergy hampered from carrying out their duties. It was so difficult to train and ordain new clergy that secret instruction and even ordinations were often carried out in the middle of the night.

The Russian Orthodox diocese present in Lithuania was not as restricted, though of course the atheist Soviet state did not favor any religion. The advantage that the Orthodox had during this time was that, since their center of authority was in Russia rather than at the Vatican as it was for Catholics, and because the average Orthodox Christian in Lithuania was ethnically Russian, their church was seen by the Soviets as less of a threat. Further, the Soviet

---

1   Traditional, translated by Fr. Gintaras Sungaila.

237

government's posture toward the Orthodox Church had become considerably less aggressive after World War II.

It was in this context of relative freedom that in July 1948, the relics of the Three Martyrs of Vilnius returned from Russia, where St. Tikhon had taken them decades before, and they were received back at the Holy Spirit Monastery in Vilnius with great joy and fanfare. Interestingly, it is recorded that some of the services celebrated at this time included the Lithuanian language, perhaps a first in the history of Orthodox Christianity in Lithuania, though there are no records of the language being used again for decades following.

IN THE INITIAL YEARS OF the Soviet occupation, from 1944 to 1953 while the partisans were still operating, some 120,000 Lithuanians were deported, mostly to Siberia, including many intellectuals and Catholic clergy. Many more were taken as political prisoners. The infamous KGB headquarters in Vilnius housed many of them, and it even featured an execution room, where numerous dissidents were taken and shot in the head.

When we visited Vilnius in 2022, we went to this same building, which had been home to the Nazi secret police prior to the KGB use. It is now a museum, but much of the building remains as it was. We recall vividly being brought into the execution room. Even before we read the sign explaining what the room was, we could feel a malevolent presence there and signed ourselves with the Cross of Christ as we entered it. How many unfortunate souls were forcibly ripped from their bodies in that place, having committed the crime of resistance to the totalitarian atheist state?

In the countryside, villagers were rounded up and forced into collective farms, made to serve the economic machinery of communism for the glory of the Soviet state. The village life that had persisted in Lithuania for centuries was radically stripped away, and as in many places throughout the Soviet Union, there were shortages and starvation.

One can also see the mark left by the brutalist architecture of the Soviet Union in Lithuania. Almost anywhere you go, in between the stately imperial-era architecture and the sweeping baroque Catholic churches and municipal buildings of the Commonwealth period, if you find the ugliest building in view, it was most likely built during what all the locals call "Soviet times."

In Lithuania, the Soviets did not engage in the Russification efforts that the Russian Empire had undertaken, so while life in the Lithuanian Soviet Socialist Republic from the 1940s to the 1980s was much like the rest of the Soviet Union, it had a Lithuanian cultural flavor. It was nevertheless a totalitarian state, with criticism of the Soviet government severely punished, elections and economy tightly controlled, and statues of Lenin, Stalin, and other Communist leaders prominently displayed throughout the country.

The Baltic Way

ON AUGUST 23, 1989, THE fiftieth anniversary of the Molotov-Ribbentrop Pact—that secret agreement that divided Eastern Europe between the Nazis and the Soviets and gave Lithuania to the Soviets—two million people joined hands. They stood along 430 miles (690 kilometers) of highways, stretching from Vilnius in Lithuania to Riga in Latvia to Tallinn in Estonia.

As they stood there—Lithuanians, Latvians, and Estonians, the three Baltic peoples—they lifted up their voices and began to sing. It was one of the largest public protests in human history, and it represented one-fourth of the total population of the Baltic nations.

While there was a cultural distinctiveness between these three countries, there was a continuous sense among them for decades that they had been occupied and annexed, despite the official Soviet story that they had voluntarily joined the Soviet Union. The Soviets denied the existence of the Pact, yet the truth became public during the Nuremberg Trials in the wake of World War II. For the average Lithuanian, Latvian, and Estonian, the existence of this secret agreement was proof that their country had been annexed by force.

As the failures of the Soviet state became more apparent throughout the 1980s, there was a growing sense that something could change, indeed that something would change. The three Baltic sisters could be free again. Thus began what was called the "Singing Revolution" (Lith. *Dainuojanti revoliucija*), gatherings across all three countries in which ordinary people came together by the thousands to sing folk songs, religious songs, and patriotic songs. Together they sang, and together they remembered their common life, their common culture, their traditions.

The message was plain: *We are not Soviet. We are free.*

The Singing Revolution found its climax on that August day in 1989 in the two million voices lifted across hundreds of miles in what came to be called the Baltic Way (Lith. *Baltijos kelias*).

The sight electrified the countryside, and images of this protest spread throughout the world. The Soviets responded with strong rhetoric to what they said was "nationalist hysteria," and they called upon the workers to rise up against "nationalist, extremist groups" advancing an "anti-Soviet and anti-socialist" agenda.[2] Yet they did nothing. No one was arrested, no one was shot.

In the days following the Baltic Way, American President George H. W. Bush openly criticized the Pact, and West German Chancellor Helmut Kohl urged reforms. What would Lithuania do next? How would the West respond?

In December 1989, Mikhail Gorbachev, the leader of the Soviet Union, signed a report not only admitting to the existence of the Molotov-Ribbentrop Pact but condemning it. In February 1990, the first free elections to the Supreme Soviets (the local governing bodies of each Soviet republic) of the three Baltic states were held. Pro-independence candidates were elected to majorities in all three.

The following month, on March 11, 1990, the Supreme Soviet of Lithuania declared independence from the Soviet Union.

Four days later, the Soviet government demanded that the Lithuanians revoke their declaration, but the deed was done. In response, the Soviets imposed sanctions and an economic blockade of Lithuania, intending to starve out the dissidents.

Shortages arose in the country, and inflation increased rapidly, and many who had initially supported independence began to wonder if it were practically possible for Lithuania to survive on its own. A number of ideological and ethnic minorities staged protests against the pro-independence government. The Soviet army seized several public buildings, but there was little violence initially.

---

2   Imse, "Baltic Residents Make Bold New Push."

FINALLY, IN JANUARY 1991 THE Soviet army flew troops into Lithuania, and on January 10 Mikhail Gorbachev demanded that the country restore the Soviet constitution. When Lithuanian officials asked for assurances that the Soviet government would not activate armed troops inside their country, they received no reply. What followed is now known as the "January Events" (*Sausio įvykiai*).

On January 11, Soviet troops began seizing several buildings around Vilnius and in other parts of the country, particularly those dedicated to government and communication, while civilians organized, forming human barriers around them. The army shot a number of them, and in the two days that followed, the army focused its efforts particularly on two places—the Vilnius TV tower and the Seimas, the parliament of Lithuania. During the assault, fourteen civilians were killed and 140 hospitalized with injuries.

With communication cut off, an amateur radio operator named Tadas Vyšniauskas set up his gear inside the Seimas. He began frantically broadcasting what was happening in Lithuania, hoping that someone somewhere would hear and that the world would know.

Outside the Seimas, concrete barriers were erected, and they were spray-painted with various slogans in Lithuanian, Russian, and English such as "Communism = Fascism," "End the Occupation," and "Freedom for Baltic Countries." Most famously, one bore the phrase *Lietuvos Širdis*, "the Heart of Lithuania." This portion of the barricade still stands next to the Seimas.

When we visited there, we reached out our hands to touch the concrete and imagined the fear and determination of those who stood behind them in 1991. And we also thought about the lonely, desperate voice of Tadas Vyšniauskas, speaking into the silence. Would anyone hear? Would anyone respond?

Two American amateur radio operators, one in Indiana and one in Illinois, heard Vyšniauskas and they began to relay what they heard to other hobbyists like themselves. Through this informal network, various governments around the world learned what was happening.

AS SOVIET TROOPS ATTACKED IN Vilnius and other parts of the country, two Russian Orthodox Church clergymen went on Lithuanian television and began to speak about what was happening. One was a 24-year-old priest who pastored the Annunciation Cathedral in Kaunas, Hieromonk Hilarion Alfeyev:

> I would like to appeal to the Russian people of Lithuania, dear dear Russian people, brothers and sisters, in this terrible hour when the fate of Lithuania is being decided.
>
> When tanks surrounded the TV tower, the press house, and rush to the parliament, when the blood of innocent people is shed, I want to address you, my compatriots, with words of Christ's love and fraternal exhortation.
>
> I beg you once again, the Russian people of Lithuania, do not go against the fraternal Lithuanian people, do not support the bandits, do not allow a new disaster or the suffering of new human victims. It is painful and sad to see Russian people attacking the Supreme Council of Lithuania, advocating for the restoration of totalitarianism.[3]

The other clergyman who spoke out on January 13, 1991, was Archbishop Chrizostomas Martishkin, who had been appointed to the Vilnius diocese two months before the independence declaration in March 1990. At the time of the January Events in 1991, he had served in Lithuania for just a year:

> Yesterday I watched the TV. I saw how our president [Gorbachev] acted in the Supreme Council. I was really sorrowful, that we have such a head of state. Earlier I believed in the sincerity of this man. I believed that he is a true reformer. But now I see that he just lied to the society, he lied to us Russians.
>
> As it stands today, he represents a purely Communist position, and to be more precise, he is holding on to the Soviet variant of Marxism. He doesn't think about the fate of Russia, the fate of the country, of the Soviet Union—he just wants to put Communists back to power in the Republics, because they have no chance to achieve that through democratic election. And he does this all in our name, in the name of Russians! We will be the ones who pay the price![4]

---

3   Alfeyev, "Fr. Hilarion Alfeyev January 13th." This and the following quote are from television news broadcasts, translated by Fr. Gintaras Sungaila.

4   Martishkin, "Metr. Chrizostomas January 13."

Archbishop Chrizostomas went on to become active in the Lithuanian independence movement, and through his efforts Orthodox Christianity was enshrined in the new Lithuanian constitution as one of the nine traditional religions of Lithuania. The Lithuanian government awarded him a medal in memory of his efforts in January 1991. In 2000 he was elevated to the rank of metropolitan, and he governed the diocese until his retirement in 2010. He died January 6, 2025.

Despite the military action of the January Events, the Soviet attempt to crush the independence movement failed. In August 1991, the Soviet Union collapsed, and Estonia and Latvia followed the example of Lithuania, declaring their own independence. Throughout Lithuania, statues of Lenin and Stalin were toppled, and streets and buildings, often bearing the names of Communist leaders, were renamed to honor Lithuanian cultural figures. In September, Lithuania was admitted to the United Nations as a free, independent republic.

Many Orthodox churches that had stood empty or been restricted during Soviet times, along with Catholic and Protestant churches, were given back to their former owners. Lithuania emerged from over fifty years of occupation, and the Orthodox Christians of Lithuania, a community almost as old as the Lithuanian state itself, began a new era.

IF YOU GO TO VILNIUS today, you can see the exact place where the Baltic Way had its southern endpoint—in Cathedral Square—that same place where the Soviets laid many bodies of the Forest Brothers in mockery, daring their families to come pay their respects and face arrest and deportation. There between the bell tower and the national Catholic cathedral there is a single red-colored flagstone with a gold eight-pointed star in the middle. In a circle of letters is written a single Lithuanian word—*stebuklas*—"miracle."

CHAPTER 37

To Put Right an Old Wrong

FATHER ANDREW: I DON'T REMEMBER when I first heard about my great-uncle Bob. I never met him that I am aware, though I was eighteen years old when he died. He was the older brother of my grandfather Albert.

I don't know what exactly happened between them, but sometime in their forties or fifties they had a falling out, and as the story goes, they never spoke to each other again. Robert died in 1993 just a month shy of eighty years old, and no one was there with him.

As far as we know, he had never married. There is a tale that he perhaps had fathered a child out of wedlock in his youth, but if that is true or what that child's name might have been, we just don't know. I don't know if the authorities who took responsibility for his body reached out to my grandfather or not. My grandfather died ten years after his brother.

In a sad irony, the two brothers died within just thirty miles of each other and had never reconciled. Albert lived in Southington, Connecticut, while Robert lived in New Haven.

I don't remember when I learned their story, but even though I had never met Uncle Bob, the fact that this falling out had followed the two brothers into their graves bothered me for years. In my private prayers, I pray for the departed of my family, whatever their religious commitments, and I prayed for both Albert and Robert for a long time. And that is where I had left it.

A FEW YEARS AGO, I began to think again about my great-uncle. I began researching him again, to see what clues I could find about his life, and so I lit upon an entry on a cemetery website that a retired police officer named Frank had entered in 2017. It was sad to see such a terse entry, an icon of sorts of a life likely filled with a lot of sadness and ending alone.

In other records, Robert's last known profession was listed as "handyman" or "doing odd jobs," which basically meant he was unemployed. The family's impression of him is that he never really did much with his life, though that may just be my grandfather's unhappiness with his brother filtering to the rest of us. We may not ever know.

I contacted Frank (whose name I did not know at the time) to ask if the entry on the website could be transferred to me so that I could update it with whatever I could find. He was happy to do so, and thus began my correspondence with him. He told me much of the sad tale of that cemetery, a tale of neglect and even theft of headstones by the caretaker. It is in bad condition but does have a group of volunteers caring for it every so often. The cemetery is owned by a corporation that has no surviving members. So it is, legally speaking, abandoned.

IN THE SUMMER OF 2021, my grandmother Elizabeth died. Robert had been her brother-in-law, but of course she had not seen him in many years herself. She died in Colorado, where she had spent her last few years near other family, and her remains were sent to Middletown, Connecticut, for interment next to her husband. I joined my father and uncle in Connecticut for a memorial service and for the interment.

As I was making plans to journey to Connecticut, I remembered Uncle Bob. And I looked at the map and realized I would be only a half hour away from where he was buried.

So, over the weekend I was there, I went to the State Street Cemetery in Hamden, Connecticut, to see what I could see. There was, of course, no marker where my great-uncle had been buried, but in correspondence with Frank during my visit, he told me roughly the part of the small cemetery where the homeless and penniless had been buried. I paced along the rows of burials, wondering if I was walking near his bones.

I came upon a man who had been mowing some of the grass, and I spoke with him. I asked him if he was part of the volunteer group who took care of the cemetery. He told me that he was taking care of some of his own family's graves, and he complained that the city was not doing its duty in ensuring that the cemetery did not deteriorate. I told him about my uncle and a little of the family history.

"I hope you can find him," he said.

And that's when I decided that I would.

Frank suggested that I contact the funeral home that had buried him. My experience as a clergyman had taught me that someone always picks up the phone at funeral homes, so even though it was a Sunday afternoon, I called them. They were still in business, and they answered. The man on the other end of the phone said he remembered when they used to bury the indigent for the state, and he complained a little that they didn't get paid very much for it.

They did have a record of burying Robert, it seemed, and which cemetery he was in, but nothing else. No plot number was listed. I asked him what I could do about that. He said that the town clerk might have something, since a burial permit would have been issued, and those usually include plot numbers.

After the interment in Middletown that Monday morning, I called the Hamden town clerk to see if they had a record.

"What cemetery was that again?"

"State Street, ma'am."

"Oohhh, I am so sorry, sir."

"Yes, yes, I know."

"We get a lot of calls about that one. There probably isn't anything."

"Can you check anyway?"

"Of course. But don't get your hopes up, okay?"

"Okay."

Twenty minutes later, she called me back: "Sir? I found your uncle. And . . . I can't believe this, but . . . the plot is listed. It's C1. Do you want a copy of the record?"

I did, and thirty minutes later, I had a copy of the 1993 burial permit in my hand, and I was driving back to the cemetery. When I arrived, I walked around it to see if I could figure out where C1 might be. Using entries from the cemetery website that noted plot numbers, and matching them to headstones I found in the cemetery, I calculated where I was pretty sure it was. I sent one more note to Frank to ask if he knew. Sure enough, I had found it. And I was standing right next to where my great-uncle was buried.

It was just grass and leaves on the edge of this semi-abandoned cemetery. But I had found it.

ON MY WAY HOME, I called my dad to tell him what I had found. And I told him I wanted to buy Uncle Bob a headstone and put it there. He told me he wanted to pitch in, and he said I should tell my uncle (his brother) what I had found. So I did that, too, and he also said he wanted to pitch in.

When I got home, I started researching headstones. I found something modest but fitting, and I ordered it. Eventually it arrived at my home. It was heavy, but it was also just right.

So I drove back toward New Haven with the headstone in my trunk. I made a stop in Middletown to pray for my grandparents, and then I headed to the cemetery in Hamden. My old friend Fr. Gregory met me there, having driven down from Massachusetts. And so did Frank, whom I had never to that point met in person but whose care for the forgotten had helped me and my family to remember.

With my bishop's blessing, we prayed the prayers for the repose of a non-Orthodox Christian. I don't know what Robert might have thought about God in his life, but I am pretty sure that his mother had seen to it that he had been baptized a Lutheran, so perhaps there was something there. We placed the headstone and blessed it with holy water.

It was Uncle Bob's funeral, just twenty-eight years late.

IN THE ORTHODOX CHURCH, WE believe in prayer for both the living and the departed. Its purpose is for us to repent on their behalf. That does not mean we believe people aren't responsible for themselves and their relationship with God and His Kingdom, but it does mean that we believe we can affect that relationship. We also believe that God is merciful and hears our prayers.

As Christians, we are bound up not only with God and each other but with all of humanity. It is our task to pray for one another, to honor one another, and to work to heal hurts, participating in God's work of putting things right that have gone wrong.

I do not know what exactly went wrong between my grandfather and his brother in this life. I do not know what memory of angry words or bitter thoughts might have accompanied them into their graves.

I do know this, though: God loves us, and He desires that all of us should be saved and come to the knowledge of the truth. And so I pray that even by our meager prayers, what was broken in this life is now healed in the life that is to come.

MAY ALL THEIR MEMORIES BE ETERNAL.

PART VII

Holy Lithuania

Orthodox Christian Saints of Lithuania

CHAPTER 38

The Monarch and the Monk: Vaišvilkas and St. Eliziejus Laurušavietis

A LONG THE STEPS OF OUR pilgrimage we met a number of the holy people of Lithuania—among them the Three Martyrs of Vilnius, St. Athanasius of Brest, St. Leontijus Karpovičius, and St. Tikhon. While the map of our journey has been outlined by the rulers and the events of history as conventionally understood, the holy history of Lithuania—its truest history—is moved by holy people, those who exercise God's own government and move world history until its completion at the Day of the Lord.

To complete our pilgrimage, therefore, we are going to retrace our steps through that history to meet some of these holy ones whom we did not yet mention or whose stories we touched on only in passing. So let us return nearly to the beginning, to the time before the name of Christ was spoken throughout Lithuania—back to the thirteenth century, the time of the last pagans of Europe.

When historians try to tell the story of religious conversions, they often frame the narrative in terms of power dynamics and *realpolitik* (political pragmatism over moral or spiritual considerations). There is a certain degree of cynicism that underlies these accounts, as though people in the medieval world did not convert for genuinely religious reasons or as though a political factor necessarily precludes any other motivation. We would argue that, far from being the more "realistic" view, this approach to history actually belies the complexities of people's lives and motivations. Nowhere is this clearer than in the lives of the Lithuanian saints of the thirteenth century.

Although the Three Holy Martyrs of Vilnius were the first to give their lives as the ultimate testament of the gospel in Lithuania, the first Lithuanian saints come from a period almost half a century earlier. They have a few things in common: Each of them was from the nobility, each of them was forced to leave Lithuania proper for some reason—be it self-imposed exile or fleeing a hostile regime—and most importantly, each of them found rest, solace, and the true conversion of their souls in the Orthodox Church.

To tell their stories, we will begin with a figure who is not a glorified saint and who in fact was on the opposite side of a dynastic struggle from those who later turned out to be saints. But his life perfectly expresses the tensions and complexities of the time. It is the life of a man who was both monk and monarch, both Orthodox Christian and Grand Duke of Lithuania.

This is the story of the bloody thirteenth century. This is the story of Vaišvilkas.

Grand Duke Vaišvilkas and the Venerable Eliziejus Laurušavietis (Elisha of Lavreshev)

IN OUR FIRST CHAPTERS, WE mentioned King Mindaugas, the first and only crowned King of Lithuania and the nation's first Christian ruler. Around the year 1250, Mindaugas was baptized as a Roman Catholic. He died in 1263. What is less well known is the fact that his son and immediate successor, the Grand Duke Vaišvilkas (or *Vaišelga*), was an Orthodox Christian monk. This is that story.

Vaišvilkas first appears in the historical record when, at the age of thirty-one, he brokered a treaty between the then-Kingdom of Lithuania and the Kingdom of Ruthenia. As was common in those days, the treaty was sealed with a marriage—in this case, the marriage of Prince Shvarn of Ruthenia with one of King Mindaugas's daughters. As part of these arrangements, Vaišvilkas became the duke of the city of Novogrudok, in modern Belarus. By all accounts, he was as evil a ruler as can be imagined.

Concerning Vaišvilkas's life as a pagan, a chronicler writes: "Being a pagan, he began to shed much innocent blood, murdering three to four persons every day. If, on a certain day, he did not kill someone, he was greatly depressed, but when he did, he was happy again." This is generally interpreted to refer to ritual human sacrifices that Vaišvilkas, as a priest of the old religion, carried out each day.[1]

Vaišvilkas's story might have ended there, one more violent man lost to the annals of history, if he had not met the Elder Gregory. An Athonite monk and igumen of the monastery of St. George in Polonina, this Gregory was a man of such holiness that the Ruthenian chronicles say of him that, "there had never been such a holy person as Gregoij, nor will there ever be anyone like him again!"[2]

We cannot know what words passed between them, but after their meeting it is said that the fear of God entered Vaišvilkas's heart. After being baptized an Orthodox Christian, he turned away from worldly pursuits, abdicating his dukedom to live with the Elder Gregory at the monastery of St. Daniel the Stylite in Ugrovsk.[3] There, in the year 1254, he was "shorn into the black," receiving monastic tonsure and the name of *Lavr* (Laurence).

His father, King Mindaugas, was displeased. In those days, the small kingdoms of northern Europe were only as strong as their royal families, and to lose a son and heir to the monastic life could spell disaster for a dynasty. But the newly tonsured Lavr remained resolute, and after several years of monastic obedience under the Elder Gregory, he set out on a pilgrimage to the Holy Mountain of Athos, the epicenter of Orthodox monastic and spiritual life.

According to the most reliable sources, the prince-monk never made it to Mount Athos, being forced by the wars of those days to turn back once he had reached Bulgaria. However, in later days this pilgrimage led to the belief that Vaišvilkas had actually reached Athos, and that it was there he had been tonsured a monk. So it is that the Novgorod chronicle says concerning Vaišvilkas:

> Him the Lord chose as a champion of the true faith, for having gone to Mount
> Sinai [Athos], away from his father and his kindred, and from his pagan faith,
> he acknowledged the true Christian religion, and was baptized in the name of
> the Father, and Son, and Holy Ghost, and studied the sacred books and was

---

1   Goldfrank, "Lithuanian Prince-Monk Vojšelk," 44–76.

2   Perfecky, *Galician-Volynian Chronicle*, 82.

3   Maiorov, "The Cult of St. Daniel the Stylite," 345–366.

shorn into the monastic order on the Holy Mount; and having remained there three years, he went to his own country to his father. And his father being a pagan tried to persuade him to renounce the Christian faith and the monastic order, and to take up his rule. But he, armed with the power of the Cross, would not even listen to his father's persuasion and feared not his threats, but having gone away from his father built himself a monastery among Christians and remained there, glorifying the Holy Trinity, the Father, the Son, and the Holy Ghost.[4]

The monastery to which Vaišvilkas returned—and that he helped to build—was that of Lavreshev or St. Laurence, near Novogrudok, established by a monk named Eliziejus (Elisha). Eliziejus was himself of princely background and had been a high-ranking official in the court of King Mindaugas until he too met a holy man—in this case, St. Laurence, Recluse of the Kyiv Caves, Far Caves, and Bishop of Turov in the region of Minsk. According to one account, St. Laurence evangelized and baptized Eliziejus, afterward commissioning him to found his monastery. In another account, Eliziejus received Christian baptism and then retired to the wilderness to live as a hermit. Saint Laurence, hearing of his ascetic life, found him and ordered him to found the monastery of Lavreshev.

In either case, it seems that Lavreshev became a haven for the princes of the Kingdom of Lithuania to pursue instead the Kingdom of God in the angelic schema. This may at least partially account for the manner of Eliziejus's death.

In those days, jealous princes would sometimes try to remove their rivals through treacherous servants or hired killers. None now can say whether Eliziejus died at the hands of an old rival or as a result of the persecution of the Orthodox Christian Faith in the Kingdom of Lithuania. It is only known that on the night of October 23, in or about AD 1250, Eliziejus was murdered in his cell by one of his young disciples who had been bribed to betray his master.

But death is not the end for true servants of Jesus Christ, and after his death Eliziejus's sanctity was revealed through his relics, which became known for many healings and miracles. In one such account, a demoniac was healed after accidentally touching the bones of Eliziejus.

---

4   Michell and Forbes, *Chronicle of Novgorod,* 99.

The Old Testament book of 4 Kingdoms (2 Kings) chapter 13 relates the story of the time a dead man's body was hastily thrown into the tomb of the prophet Elisha. When the dead man's body touched the bones of the prophet, he was immediately restored to life. The obvious connection between these two accounts demonstrates two important things about Christ's holy ones and their ongoing role in the life of the Church.

The first is the clear continuity of God working through the saints, even in and through their bones, from the time of the Old Testament to the Orthodox Church today. That the grace of God that worked through them in their lives continues to be present even in their remains is the basis for the Church's preservation and veneration of the relics of the saints.

The second thing we can notice is that these accounts—one from the Old Testament, the other from the New Testament era—show the way the lives of the saints often "rhyme." The bones of Elisha restored a man's physical life; the bones of his namesake Eliziejus restored a man's spiritual life, liberating him from the forces of darkness and bringing him back into communion with Christ.

Such "rhymes" or "echoes" might seem like strange coincidences or even suspicious marks of potential plagiarism to secular historians, but they will not surprise anyone who has read the lives of the saints and understands the significance of names and patronage. The saints reign with Christ, after all, and when the Church bestows their names and patronage to persons and communities, part of that person or community's cooperation with life in Christ means that the personalities of those saints are expressed in their lives. The stories of Elisha and Eliziejus are but one of many examples of a "family resemblance" between saints and their own patrons.

There is another episode from the life of the prophet Elisha that is echoed in the life of his namesake. Some three centuries after his murder, Eliziejus delivered the Lavrashev monastery from the depredations of the Muslim Tatars. The latter, having devastated the region around Novogrudok, rode against the monastery, intending to lay siege to it and pillage it. As they approached, it seemed to them as though the Lavrashev monastery was surrounded by a great host of cavalry. Caught completely by surprise at this unexpected resistance, the Tatars broke and fled in terror. Those familiar with the story of the

Prophet Elisha will likely already have noticed the similarity to the account in 4 Kingdoms 6:

> Therefore sent he [the King of Syria] thither horses, and chariots, and a great host: and they came by night, and compassed the city about. And when the servant of the man of God was risen early, and gone forth, behold, an host compassed the city both with horses and chariots. And his servant said unto him, Alas, my master! how shall we do? And he answered, Fear not: for they that be with us are more than they that be with them.
>
> And Elisha prayed, and said, LORD, I pray thee, open his eyes, that he may see. And the LORD opened the eyes of the young man; and he saw: and, behold, the mountain was full of horses and chariots of fire round about Elisha. (v. 14–17, KJV)

Owing to this miracle, St. Eliziejus was formally canonized by the Orthodox Church at the Council of Vilnius in 1514. The Orthodox Church continues to celebrate his feast on October 23, the anniversary of his repose.

The Prince-Monk Vaišvilkas would outlive his saintly friend and contemporary, though only by a few years. As the chronicles relate, Vaišvilkas was forced out of his monastic retirement after his father King Mindaugas was murdered. The Kingdom of Lithuania was in tatters, with pagan rebels and Roman Catholic Crusaders eager to take advantage of the chaos of an interregnum. Therefore, with a heavy heart, and only after vowing to God that he would return to the monastery at the end of three years, Vaišvilkas returned to the world.

During those three years, his life was a study in contrasts. According to the *Chronicle of the Grand Duchy of Lithuania, Ruthenia and Samogitia*, he "dwelt pious in the law as a black man [monk]," wearing his monastic headdress on top of his princely robes and continuing to observe a monastic rule even as grand duke.[5] According to the *Chronicle of Novgorod*:

> Though undesirous to do so, but God inflicting him on them, the pagan Lithuanians, for the Christian blood, laid it in his heart, and he taking off from him

---

5   Quoted in Shumilo, "Svyatogorsk Trace."

his gown, vowed himself to God for three years, when he should resume his gown, and did not leave the monastic order. He gathered about him his father's soldiers and friends, and having prayed to the honourable Cross, he went against the pagan Lithuanians and defeated them, and stayed in their country all the year. Then the Lord repaid the accursed ones according to their works; for he took the whole of their country captive by force of arms, and there was joy everywhere throughout the Christian land.[6]

By all accounts, Vaišvilkas visited bloody vengeance upon the enemies of his nation and his faith. He also did what he could to strengthen the alliance of the Grand Duchy with the Orthodox Princes of the Rus', seeking to establish what one scholar has called "a strong union and a united Orthodox Rus'-Lithuanian state."[7] Then, at the end of three years, he handed the reins of the Grand Duchy over to his brother-in-law Shvarn and returned to the monastery.

Alas, the peace that Vaišvilkas had worked to establish was not to last. Not long after his return to the monastery, he was murdered by another one of his brothers-in-law, Leo (Lev) of Halych, Grand Prince of Kyiv, who was jealous of Shvarn and angry that Vaišvilkas had not left him the Lithuanian throne. Vaišvilkas had been a unifying figure for Christian Lithuania and the Princes of the Rus', and after his death, the fledgling alliances he had built fell apart, and the dynasty of Mindaugas came to an end. As for Vaišvilkas, he was buried in the Monastery of St. Michael in Volodymyr, finally achieving in death the rest and repose for which he had sought his whole life.

Unlike his friend and fellow-struggler St. Eliziejus, Vaišvilkas was never glorified as a saint by the Orthodox Church. But the arc of his life—from bloodthirsty pagan to Athonite monk, from monk to avenging Christian monarch, and from monarch to murdered monk—became the fodder for legends, folkloric retellings, and official chronicles well into the sixteenth and seventeenth centuries. Through the prayers of St. Eliziejus Laurušavietis, we pray that he found the true Kingdom for which he sought.

---

6   Michell and Forbes, *Chronicle of Novgorod*, 99.
7   Shumilo, "Svyatogorsk Trace."

CHAPTER 39

The Princess-Abbess: St. Charitina of Lithuania

A LTHOUGH ORTHODOX CHRISTIANITY WAS NEVER the major-ity religion in the Grand Duchy of Lithuania, the stories of people like Duke Vaišvilkas are examples of the way a strong Orthodox minority endured among the Lithuanian nobility throughout the Middle Ages. These nobles were caught between the warlike princes of the Rus' on one side and the bel-licose pagan Lithuanians on the other, and they often found themselves at the center of the dynastic struggles of the thirteenth century. But Christian virtue does not require peaceful times to flourish, as the life of St. Charitina shows.

Charitina was a princess, the grandniece of King Mindaugas and the daughter of Tautvilas, Duke of Polotsk. In those days, the life of a noble maiden was not her own. If all went well, she would be married to the prince of another noble house, becoming a peace-weaver who would raise noble sons and daughters and ensure the stability of the realm. But all did not go well for Charitina.

First, her father had a falling-out with his uncle, King Mindaugas. It seems that Mindaugas had promised him that if he invaded the lands of the Rus' on behalf of the Lithuanian crown, he could keep whatever lands he conquered. Duke Tautvilas was at first successful, but he eventually suffered a setback in the form of a military defeat at the hands of the Grand Duke of Vladimir.

Angry at his nephew's failure, King Mindaugas decided to seize all of Taut-vilas's lands for himself. With no other choice, Tautvilas received Roman Catholic baptism from the Archbishop of Riga and joined a coalition with the

Livonian Order, the pagan Samogitians, and other enemies of the Lithuanian crown in an effort to depose his uncle.

Things went poorly for the alliance when Mindaugas was also baptized and the Livonian Order switched sides. What was left of the coalition was utterly defeated by Mindaugas, forcing him to flee with his family into the lands of the Rus'. There, things continued to go poorly for Charitina and her family, for the Rus' of Novgorod had no love for the Lithuanian nobles who had so recently made war upon them.

Some say that to weave peace and preserve her family, Charitina agreed to marry the brother of St. Alexander Nevsky, Prince Feodor Yaroslavovich. It is perhaps around this time that she received Orthodox Christian baptism. But Charitina was not destined for an earthly spouse but for a heavenly bridegroom.

Before their wedding, her betrothed died suddenly and under mysterious circumstances. Seeing that this world now held nothing for her, Charitina renounced earthly power and royal privileges, entering into a women's monastery in Novgorod. There, she became known for her virtue, humility, purity, and strict asceticism, and she eventually became the abbess of the monastery.

She continued to labor there, leading those under her care into the everlasting Kingdom. She reposed in peace on October 5 in the year 1281, and her relics still rest in Novgorod at the Church of Ss. Peter and Paul. Through her prayers, may we pass through the suffering of this world to find our rest in Christ.

CHAPTER 40

The Exile Convert: St. Daumantas of Pskov

ISTORY IS COMPLICATED. THE LIVES of the saints are complicated. Sometimes holy people find themselves on the opposite sides of wars and political divides. The thirteenth century was a bloody time for the Grand Duchy of Lithuania, but it produced three Orthodox Christian saints: the Venerable Eliziejus, the Right-Believing Princess Charitina, and the third and perhaps least likely candidate for sainthood—Daumantas of Pskov.

We know that Mindaugas was the first and only Christian King of Lithuania. We also know that when he died at the hands of assassins, his son, Vaišvilkas (whom we have mentioned earlier) succeeded him as grand duke. It was Daumantas who killed Mindaugas.

At the time, Daumantas was the Duke of Nalšia, located somewhere on the northeastern border of Lithuania proper. He had been a staunch ally of King Mindaugas, and even married the sister of Queen Morta (Martha), the Christian wife of King Mindaugas.

Of Morta, the chronicles say many favorable things. She was a strong supporter of Christianity within the realm, actively working against her husband during his occasional relapses into paganism and always there to win him back to Roman Catholicism when enough ill fortune had beset him. When she died, Mindaugas missed her terribly and forcibly took her sister—Daumantas's wife—as his new queen. This, it is believed, is what caused Daumantas to turn against Mindaugas.

Colluding with Treniota, the pagan Duke of Samogitia who had long been causing trouble in the Kingdom, Daumantas killed—or more probably, ordered the killing—of Mindaugas and his sons. The death of Mindaugas and two of his sons threw the Grand Duchy of Lithuania into a decades-long dynastic struggle and is believed to have set back the conversion of the Grand Duchy to Roman Catholic Christianity by a hundred years.

With Vaišvilkas's return from his monastic exile to avenge the death of his father, Daumantas and his family fled in exile to Pskov, a city-state in northern Russia that had only recently won semi-independence from Novgorod. They were without a *knyaz* (prince) and, in order to assure their independence from the Livonian Order, which was pressuring them greatly at that time, they elected Daumantas to be their new ruler. When he had first come to Pskov, Daumantas had converted to Orthodox Christianity, taking the name Timothy in Holy Baptism. Now he began a rule that would be immortalized as the most glorious in the city's history, and the local Slavs knew him as *Dovmont*.

For thirty-three years, Daumantas would defend the city of Pskov against both the assaults of the Livonian Order and the meddling of the Princes of Novgorod. During this time, he married Maria, the granddaughter of St. Alexander Nevsky, who would later be glorified as the Venerable Schemanun Martha. He built up the ancient walls of the city, which continued to be called the "Dovmont" walls for centuries to come in his honor. He also built a great church in the Pskov Kremlin dedicated to the Holy Trinity. By the sixteenth century, the whole region of the "Dovmontov" town would be completely covered with churches.

In 1299, the warrior-prince would fight his final battle. After an engagement on the River Velika, the Livonian Knights raided the suburban regions around Pskov, destroying monasteries and killing men, women, children, and monastics, including St. Basil of Murozh. With no time to raise a large army, the aging Daumantas rode out with a small band of retainers and drove the Livonian Knights out of the lands of the Rus'. As he led them into battle, as he had done in times past, Daumantas encouraged his people, saying: "Good men of Pskov! Whoever is old among you is my father, whoever is young is my brother. Stand fast for the Holy Trinity!"[1]

---

1   "Blessed Dovmont (Timothy), Prince of Pskov."

Several months later, Daumantas reposed in peace. The people of Pskov wept for their adopted prince, whom they considered as one of their own. As one of the chronicles says, "there was then great sadness in Pleskov [Pskov] for the men and women and small children on account of their good lord, the noble Prince Timothy."[2] Although Daumantas's earthly rule had come to an end, his role as the guardian and protector of Pskov was just beginning.

In 1480, Pskov was besieged by a large army led by the Livonian Order. During the siege, St. Daumantas appeared to a citizen of the town and told him, "Take my grave cover, carry it three times around the city with a cross, and do not be afraid."[3] The people of Pskov did as St. Daumantas instructed them, and the Livonian army was defeated. They withdrew from the city and made peace with the Rus'. Following this deliverance of the city of Pskov, official services to the "Right-Believing Prince Dovmont-Timothy" were composed, although he had already been locally venerated as a saint immediately after his death.

Again, in 1581, Pskov came under siege, this time by an army of the Polish-Lithuanian Commonwealth led by King Stephen of Bathory. On the eve of the battle, a blind elder known as Dorotheus the Smith received a vision of the Mother of God standing above the corner of the city walls where the Polish army was set to attack the next day. She was there along with a number of other great saints of the Rus'—the holy Great Prince Vladimir, Anthony of the Kyiv Caves, Cornelius of Pskov, Euphrosynus of Spaso-Elazar and Savva of Krypetsk, Blessed Nicholas of Pskov, and Niphon, Archbishop of Novgorod. The two sainted Princes of Pskov, Vsevolod-Gabriel and Daumantas, also stood with her.

At the command of the Theotokos, her wonder-working Pechersk icon was set up at the place where she had appeared. The next day, no matter how hard they tried, the Poles were unable to breach the city's walls, and the city of Pskov was delivered. Although this vision took place on September 7, it is

---

2   "Blessed Dovmont."
3   "Blessed Dovmont."

celebrated on October 1 along with the Feast of the Protection of the Mother of God, owing to the great similarity between the two events.

In the life of St. Daumantas, we see the way in which the ministry of the saints, both while they are on earth as well as after their deaths, participates in God's ordering of the cosmos as they become protectors of cities and peoples. Through his prayers, may our days be filled with peace.

CHAPTER 41

Standing Firm: St. Macarius of Kyiv

VERY LITTLE IS KNOWN ABOUT the early life of Macarius. He was
born sometime in the mid-fifteenth century, a time of division and
struggle across Europe. Made a monk at the Holy Trinity Monastery in Vilnius, he was noted for his pious and ascetical life and was soon elevated to the
rank of archimandrite. He served as the abbot of the monastery until 1495,
when he was called upon to lead the Kyivan metropolis during a time of great
turmoil, both for the Orthodox Church, and for the city of Kyiv.

The fall of Constantinople in 1453 had sent shockwaves throughout the
Christian world, leaving much of the Orthodox Church under the heavy
Turkish yoke. The failed Union of Florence in 1439 had left wounds between
Moscow and Kyiv that had yet to heal. The then-Metropolitan of Kyiv, Isidore,
had agreed to the 1439 act of union, resulting in his rejection and deposition
by the bishops of the Ruthenian Church. His successor, St. Jonas, was made
Metropolitan of Moscow, signaling the rise of Moscow's importance at the
same time that Kyiv, then part of the Polish-Lithuanian Commonwealth, was
languishing as a center of cultural and religious importance.

A politically motivated man might have taken advantage of the situation,
playing off the rivalry between the Kyiv and Moscow Metropolises or seeking
to curry favor with the Roman Catholic rulers of the Commonwealth, as his
Ruthenian successors would a century later. Instead, Macarius proved to be a
true shepherd to his flock, seeking to preserve them in unity with the Orthodox Faith and striving against the promoters of the false union. His ministry

would be cut short, however, when the crown of martyrdom was added to his bishop's miter.

On May 1, 1497, while visiting the village of Strigolovo Macarius was celebrating the Divine Liturgy when Tatar raiders attacked the village. They desecrated the church, massacred the faithful, and slew the metropolitan. In his final moments, Macarius stood firm, offering himself as a living sacrifice and protecting the Holy Gifts until the end. Later, his relics were recovered, and within a few years of his death his sainthood was evident to all. His incorrupt relics now rest in the Cathedral of St. Volodymyr in Kyiv.

Through his prayers, may we find true unity in the ark of salvation, the Orthodox Church.

CHAPTER 42

Lithuanian Athonite: St. Anthony of Karyes

T HE SUPRAŚL MONASTERY OF THE Annunciation was founded in
1498 in what today is northeastern Poland. Its founding donor, Aleksandras Chodkevičius (Aleksander Chodkiewicz), was a Lithuanian-Ruthenian
magistrate of the Grand Duchy of Lithuania, a wealthy man who was part of
the small minority of Orthodox Christians among the nobility of the Polish-
Lithuanian state, prior to the formal union of the Commonwealth in 1569.
Within a year or two of its founding, a young man came knocking at the door
of the monastery, begging entrance.

The young man was named Onuphry. Although he had been brought up in
the Orthodox Christian Faith in the western Ruthenian lands in the Grand
Duchy, he had strayed into a life of crime and dissipation, culminating in the
heinous crime of murder. Now, with blood on his hands and a heart broken
like the Prodigal's, he begged to be allowed to begin a life of repentance in
the monastery. He was admitted and placed under obedience to a holy elder
named Paphnutius. Under his elder's guidance, he worked diligently at every
task that was given him and made great progress in the ascetic life. But still, it
was not enough to quench the longing in Onuphry's heart—a longing to atone
for the blood that he had wrongly shed, by offering his own blood for the sake
of Christ.

During the twelve years he spent at the monastery of the Annunciation,
Onuphry heard the stories of the Christians who were at that time being persecuted by the Turks in Eastern Europe. With each story he heard of their

266

excesses and indignities against the people of God, Onuphry's desire to go and seek martyrdom at their hands grew and grew. He begged his elder to bless him to go and die in Islamic lands, but the elder, who was wise and patient, instructed him to go instead to Mount Athos to seek further instruction and wisdom there. Before he left for the Holy Mountain, Onuphry was tonsured a schemamonk, and his name was changed to *Anthony*.

At Mount Athos, Anthony found a rule of life more strict than what he had known in the Grand Duchy. He was also prevented by the wise counsel of the monastic fathers from rushing headlong into his desire for martyrdom, being encouraged instead to continue to acquire the basic monastic virtues of humility, repentance, and obedience. His place of struggle was appointed to be at Karyes on the Holy Mountain, in the cell of St. Sava of Serbia. Anthony did as he was commanded, devoting himself to the rigorous monastic rule.

However, not long after his arrival at the Holy Mountain, a fresh persecution broke out against the Christians in the Ottoman Empire, and word reached Athos of the martyrdom of the New Martyr George of Kratovo. Once again Anthony desired to seek martyrdom. Having still not received a blessing to travel to Islamic lands to seek his death, Anthony went instead to Thessaloniki. There, he entered into a church of the Theotokos that the Muslims had turned into a mosque, and making the sign of the cross, began to pray. He was immediately arrested and put to torture.

After being imprisoned for ten days without food, he was brought before the local magistrate, who attempted to persuade him to renounce his faith and embrace Islam. Anthony remained immoveable, taunting the idolaters, calling them "dirty dogs" and "inheritors of eternal fire."[1] After being passed back and forth between magistrates, in a manner reminiscent of our Lord's own Passion, Anthony was finally condemned to death.

His body was burned, his bones ground to dust, and the dust and ashes were scattered to the winds so that the Christians would not be able to gather any relics of his body. The New Martyr Anthony thus won the crown he so deeply desired on February 4, 1516.

Through his prayers, may we be saved.

---

1   "Holy New Venerable Martyr Anthony of Karyes."

CHAPTER 43

The Protectress: St. Sofija Olelkaitė-Radvilienė

THE PRINCESS SOFIJA WAS BORN in 1585, the sole heir of the princely Olelkaičiai (Olelkovich) family that boasted direct lineage from Algirdas. Sofija's family had been Orthodox Christians for many generations, and her grandfather Yuri had charged his descendants with upholding the Orthodox Christian Faith no matter what persecution they faced.

It was not an easy time to be an Orthodox Christian in the Polish-Lithuanian Commonwealth. Sofija's family had once been wealthy, possessing vast properties and wielding great political authority in the Commonwealth. Owing to their Orthodox Christian Faith and therefore their ties—real or imagined—to the Grand Dukes of Moscow, their holdings and influence had been gradually stripped away from them.

Born an only child and an orphan by the age of one, Sofija was placed under the guardianship of relatives. She grew up in Vilnius, and then in Brest. While she was living with her guardian Hieronim Chodkiewicz, Governor of Brest, a marriage was arranged between Sofija and the son of the Governor of Vilnius, Janusz Radvila (Radziwill). Sofija was only eleven years old.

This arranged marriage was intended to settle some of the debts of her guardian, but negotiations broke down when it was discovered that Sofija's uncle had already squandered much of her dowry—and both sides actually gathered troops for a battle within the streets of Vilnius. Eventually, the city's senators convinced both sides to back down, but there were still other difficulties.

Sofija, though young, was a devout Orthodox Christian, and she refused to convert to Roman Catholicism to marry Janusz. Not only did Sofija insist on remaining Orthodox, she also insisted that her children would be baptized and raised as Orthodox Christians. This was unusual among the Lithuanian nobility, and it was especially controversial given the Union of Brest four years earlier, which had handed over most of the Orthodox churches in the Commonwealth to Rome.

Further complicating matters, Janusz, though from a historically Roman Catholic noble family, had privately converted to Calvinism. The question of their marriage actually prompted correspondence between the Roman pope and the Patriarch of Constantinople on the larger questions of marriage between Roman Catholics and the Orthodox. Eventually they both received the blessings of their respective prelates, and they were married in an Orthodox wedding service on October 1, 1600. Sofija was fifteen years old.

For the next eleven years, Sofija used all of her influence to protect the Orthodox inhabitants of her ancestral lands (located in modern Belarus). It was a difficult time for Orthodox Christians in the Commonwealth: They were expelled from their own churches and monasteries and forced to pay heavy fines for each service they wanted to celebrate. Sacraments such as baptisms, weddings, and funerals could be celebrated only with the approval of—and paying a fee to—a local Catholic clergyman. Orthodox burials could be conducted only at night.

Sofija's response to these injustices was quiet but firm. She gave generously of her own wealth to build new churches and monasteries for her people. Together with her handmaids, Sofija sewed new priestly vestments and adornments for the churches to replace those that had been seized by the Uniates. She also supported Orthodox churches in other regions by making pilgrimages on the days of their altar feasts.

Sofija died in childbirth at the age of twenty-six. Although he was not an Orthodox Christian, her husband ensured that the protections she had secured for her people were enshrined in law, preserving Orthodoxy in those lands. After her death, Sofija's relics were found to be incorrupt, and they now rest for public veneration in the Cathedral of the Holy Spirit in Minsk, Belarus, where she is known as *Zofia of Słuck*.

Of all the lives of the saints from the Polish-Lithuanian Commonwealth that we have learned about in this final portion of our tale, Sofija's story is perhaps the most moving. As a girl of eleven, she was defrauded by her uncle who wanted to marry her off to settle his debts. As a girl of fifteen, she was married to a man who did not share her faith, and she had to contend against the prevailing religious and political forces of her time. Although she was no monastic, she lived a life grounded in prayer and fulfilled the life of the "blessed" one described in the Beatitudes.

Through her prayers, may we inherit the Kingdom of Heaven.

Lithuanian Orthodox Christianity

W E RETURN AGAIN TO THE Baltic Sea, looking out across the cold waves to the west, in the direction of Sweden. It cannot be seen with the naked eye even on a clear day, but it is another world with its own life and legends just across those waters. Beyond that is the rest of Scandinavia, then Great Britain, then the Atlantic. For the pilgrim, however, with only the Baltic stretching out in front of him, the amber-jeweled seabed somewhere down beneath, he feels that he stands on the edge of the world.

Turning around to the east, he sees Lithuania with its little green hills, its old and rolling rivers, and its tall pine forests, the countryside dotted with white churches, standing crosses, and koplytstulpiai—the wayside wooden shrines of Christ and His saints. Christ has been named and worshipped here for over a thousand years, but what about the Orthodox Church?

Orthodox Christianity has survived in Lithuania even since the time of the pagan grand dukes, yet it has always been the religion of a minority. How will it continue through the twenty-first century?

ONE OF THE PRIESTS WE met and became friends with was Fr. Vitalijus Mockus. We asked him about his story, and he began this way: "In 1990, two great things happened for me. The first was the independence of my beloved Lithuania. And the second is that I became an Orthodox Christian." He was sixteen years old.

He told us how, when he was very young and living in a village in the Lithuanian countryside, a Russian woman moved to his community. He saw that she lived an earnest Christian life, not only on Sundays but all the time. She was very kind and helpful to his family. He had been baptized and raised a Roman Catholic, but his family did not practice their faith with any real earnestness.

Seeing this Russian woman's devotion as an Orthodox Christian, he wanted that for himself, and as a teenager he joined the Orthodox Church. As you just read in the previous chapters, his whole world was turning upside down, and a new chapter was dawning in the history of Lithuania.

In 1995, at the age of twenty-one he was ordained as a priest, serving under Metropolitan Chrizostomas. Like many Lithuanians raised in the Soviet period, he could speak Russian in addition to his native Lithuanian, so he was able to fit in well with the predominantly Russian-speaking Orthodox community in Lithuania, and he served in the Church Slavonic language as a priest.

As he served over the years, however, he always had it in his heart that this Faith, which had been present in Lithuania since at least the thirteenth century, should be accessible to ordinary Lithuanians. After having discussions with a small group of friends starting in 2003, he began to work on translating the Divine Liturgy of St. John Chrysostom. He made some reference to a nineteenth-century experimental text of the Divine Liturgy in Lithuanian using the Cyrillic alphabet that had been produced but probably never utilized in any church. Largely, however, he created the new translation from scratch, since the nineteenth-century work used outdated forms of the language. Father Vitalijus's friend, the composer and deacon (now archdeacon) Viktoras Miniotas—born in exile in Siberia to one of the many deported families—developed musical settings to fit the new translations. Even as he did this work, he did not prevail upon his bishop to create any initiatives but prayed earnestly to God, asking for His help in seeing the desires of his heart come to fruition.

Toward the end of 2004, without any prompting from Fr. Vitalijus, Metropolitan Chrizostomas came to him and said that he should consider making translations of the church services into Lithuanian so that the Orthodox Faith might live in the Lithuanian language. The bishop asked how long the work would take, expecting that it would take at least months. Overjoyed, Fr. Vitalijus told the metropolitan of his almost-completed translation work and asked to make use of a disused church building in Vilnius to hold services.

Then it happened on January 23, 2005, at the Church of St. Paraskevi in Vilnius, the very place where the Three Martyrs had been baptized, the very location of the first known Christian church in all of Lithuania, built on top of what had been a place of pagan worship. Father Vitalijus's voice rang out: *Palaiminta Karalystė Tėvo ir Sūnaus, ir Šventosios Dvasios, dabar ir visados, ir per amžių amžius.* The Divine Liturgy was served in the Lithuanian language for the first time in recorded history.

Since this initiative was so new and unheard of in the largely ethnically Russian Orthodox community in Lithuania, there was some resistance to the use of the Lithuanian language. There was even a petition circulated to ban the use of the language. But in the end, it attracted only eight signatures.

In the years that followed, the St. Paraskevi community attracted a number of converts from Lithuanian ethnic backgrounds, including a young man named Gintaras Sungaila and later his wife-to-be Justina Trinkūnaitė. Both were gifted liturgically—Gintaras as a scholar and translator (he is fluent in five modern languages and reads several ancient and medieval languages) and Justina as a conservatory-trained composer and choirmaster—and continued the work of translation and adaptation. Under the guidance of Fr. Vitalijus and with the work of this little community, Lithuanian-language Orthodox Christianity began to grow. In time, other services were translated, and in 2021 the community published the first Lithuanian-language Orthodox prayer book.

IN FEBRUARY 2022, WAR CAME to Ukraine, a land that for a time had belonged to the Grand Duchy of Lithuania and the Polish-Lithuanian Commonwealth. Debate over the role of the Moscow Patriarchate in the armed conflict resulted in fractures and controversy in the Orthodox churches in the Baltic states, including in Lithuania. As we made our pilgrimage in August 2022 and even in subsequent returns, this controversy was a live issue and directly impacted our new friends.

In 2023, connected with these controversies, the ecclesiastical presence of the Ecumenical Patriarchate returned to Lithuania for the first time since the years leading up to the Third Partition in 1795, when Lithuania became part of the Russian Empire. Now, as is the case in most places in the West and has been in Estonia since the 1990s, there are multiple Orthodox jurisdictions functioning in Lithuania.

The debates will no doubt continue. Yet when the Orthodox Christian tale-tellers and historians of the future look back on our time as their history, our prayer is that even while they acknowledge the context of historical controversy, most of all they will tell the tale of how Christ was glorified. We pray that they will tell the tale of how the Orthodox Christian Faith was open to people from every tribe, tongue, and nation.

Father Andrew: Our pilgrimage now comes to an end. We return to our homes, and we feel a certain sadness. We miss our friends.

Yet we also carry with us the saints, foremost the Three Martyrs but so many others. We cannot forget the beauty that we encountered. We carry with us a profound sense of having been changed forever, and this pilgrimage stands as an eternal monument in our hearts.

On our final night in Lithuania, we gathered together in the countryside for a meal. I stood up and raised my glass and said, "We are so grateful to you all. We are so grateful that in the midst of this time of difficulty and uncertainty you opened up your hearts to us and gave up your time and showed us true generosity and Christian friendship. My hope for your country is that the light of the Orthodox Faith would shine brightly, that your ministry in your country would be blessed by God and grow fruitful forever."

Father Vitalis, himself a Lithuanian convert trained under Fr. Vitalijus, who had assisted in the translation work, stood up to make a reply: "Thank you for everything you have said. But I want to correct something you said wrong."

I could not imagine what it might be. I felt that I was being grateful and gracious!

He continued: "You kept saying something—*your* country, *your* country. No. This is *our* country. You belong here as well. Please come back."

I did not know what to say. Certainly, while I am Lithuanian ethnically (along with many other things, like most Americans), I am not Lithuanian culturally. But I knew that here was a deep, open sense of sharing, of welcoming, of blessed hospitality.

I finally responded: "I came here hoping to learn something about my Lithuanian family. I hoped to meet them, if possible. That has not happened yet. But perhaps it has happened in a better, truer sense. You now are my Lithuanian family."

Father Gintaras said, "And you are our American family!"

AS I WRITE THIS, REMEMBERING everything, my heart is again full. The tears are in my eyes. I hope, dear reader, that you also know the love of Jesus Christ, the love expressed in Christian friendship, in Christian brotherhood and sisterhood. I hope that you received an image of this love in the course of our tale.

That is the tale of our pilgrimage. But we have a lot more stories to tell.

Garbė Jėzui Kristui! Per amžius! Amen.

Orthodox Christian Saints and Feasts of Lithuania

WHILE WE WERE NOT ABLE to include every saint or feast associated with Lithuania in our story, we list them here to show the richness of God's work in this land. While the borders are somewhat porous over history (particularly with regard to eastern Poland), our definition of *Lithuania* here is essentially the lands of the Grand Duchy of Lithuania from its earliest mentions in the eleventh century through to the Third Partition in 1795 (which included most of modern Ukraine and Belarus as well as parts of Poland and Latvia), then essentially the borders of modern Lithuania after that point. When in doubt, we decided to include a saint rather than exclude him or her.

The feast days listed are the standard calendar dates as found in the *Menaion*, which are drawn from multiple sources including purely local commemorations—as such, this list should not be regarded as having any official liturgical status. For those saints whose stories we did not tell in the main body of the text, we have added a note on their connection to Lithuania if it is not obvious from a location (e.g., Vilnius, Kyiv). (Note: The Orthodox Church calendar begins with September 1.)

September 5—Hieromartyr Athanasius of Brest (+1648)

September 7—Hieromartyr Macarius, Archimandrite of Ovruch, Pinsk, and Kaneva (+1678): resisted the Unia in Ruthenian lands

September 8—Icon of Our Lady of Trakai

September 8—Hieroconfessor Roman Medved (+1937): served as inspector of Vilnius Theological Seminary 1898-1900, spiritual son of St. John of Kronstadt

September 16—Cyprian, Metropolitan of Kyiv (+1406)

September 24—Venerable Leontijus Karpovičius (Leonty Karpovich) (+1620)

September 28—Right-Believing Princess Juliana Alšėniškaitė (Olshanskaya) (+1540): pious daughter of a noble Lithuanian-Ruthenian family who then ruled part of modern Ukraine but were originally from modern Lithuania and Belarus

October 3—Hieromartyr Agathangelus, Archbishop of Vilnius and Metropolitan of Yaroslavl (+1928)

October 5—Venerable Princess Charitina of Lithuania (+1281)

October 5—New Hieromartyr Gabriel (Igoshkin), Archimandrite of Melekess (+1959): stationed in Kaunas while in the military and sang in the cathedral choir, 1909–1913

October 12—Hieromartyr John of Riga (+1934): rector of Orthodox seminary in Vilnius and abbot of Holy Spirit Monastery, 1906–1911

October 23—Venerable Eliziejus Laurušavietis (Elisha of Lavreshev) (ca. +1250)

October 24—Hieromartyr Lawrence (Laurynas), Bishop of Balakhna (+1918): seminary rector in Vilnius (1912), auxiliary bishop to St. Tikhon (consecrated 1917)

November 19—Hieromartyr Eustratius (Grumkov) (ca. +1937): born in Vilnius in 1883, graduated from local Vilnius school

November 19—Venerable Martyr Mitrophan (Kvanin) (+1937): novice at Holy Spirit Monastery in Vilnius

December 4—Hieromartyr Nicholas Yakhontov (+1918): served as a parish priest in Kaunas, 1896–1902

December 26—Icon of Our Lady of the Gate of Dawn

January 1—Peter Mohyla, Metropolitan of Kyiv (+1647)

January 23—Venerable Gennadius of Mogilev, Wonder-Worker of Kostroma (+1565)

February 4—Martyr Anthony of Karyes (Antanas Supraslietis) (+1516)

February 12—Alexios, Metropolitan of Kyiv and Moscow (+1378)

February 12—George, Archbishop of Mogilev (+1795): resisted Unia in Ruthenian lands in years prior to the Partitions of the Commonwealth

February 15—Vilnius (Vilna) Icon of the Theotokos: icon of the Hodegetria type brought to Vilnius in 1495; original lost but copy is enshrined at Holy Spirit Monastery in Vilnius. Also celebrated April 14 (date of transfer to Moscow in 1472)

March 9—Hieromartyr Bruno Boniface of Querfort and his companions (+1009)

March 19—Right-Believing Princess Sofija Olelkaitė-Radvilienė (Sophia of Slutsk) (+1612)

March 25—Tikhon, Archbishop of Vilnius and Patriarch of Moscow (+1925): also celebrated October 9 and April 7

April 14—The Three Martyrs of Vilnius: Anthony (Antanas), Eustathius (Eustachijus/Eustatijus), and John (Jonas) (+1347)

April 20—Child-Martyr Gabriel of Białystok (Gabrielius Baltostogietis) (+1690): Białystok (now in Poland) was then part of the Grand Duchy of Lithuania

May 1—Hieromartyr Macarius, Metropolitan of Kyiv (+1497)

May 3—Venerable Martyr Paul of Vilnius (+17th c.): said to have been martyred by the Polish king

May 7—Zhirovits Icon of the Theotokos: appeared in the village of Zhirovits (Grodno province, now in Belarus) in 1470, then part of the Grand Duchy of Lithuania

May 20—Right-Believing Prince Daumantas (Dovmont) of Pskov (+1299)

May 23—Venerable Euphrosyne of Polotsk (+1167): abbess born in Polotsk prior to its incorporation into the Grand Duchy of Lithuania in the 13th c.; Cross of St. Euphrosyne is one of the symbols of medieval Lithuanian Christianity and modern Belarus

May 25—Commemoration of the conversion of three million Uniates to Orthodox Christianity at Vilnius in 1831

May/June, Second Sunday after Pentecost—Feast of All Saints of Lithuania (in the Lithuanian Exarchate of the Ecumenical Patriarchate)

June 16—Venerable Tikhon of Lukh in Kostroma (+1503): born in Lithuania and served in the military there

June 27—Cyril Lucaris, Patriarch of Constantinople (+1638): professor at Vilnius Seminary ca. 1596–1601, opposed Union of Brest, rector of Ostrog Academy

June/July, Third Sunday after Pentecost—Hieromartyr Nikephoros Kantakouzenos, Archdeacon of Constantinople (+1599): opposed the Union of Brest as Exarch of the Ecumenical Patriarch

July 2—Pažaislis Icon of the Theotokos

July 13—Transfer of the Relics of the Three Martyrs of Vilnius: feast of All Saints of Lithuania (in the Moscow Patriarchate)

July 20—Photius, Metropolitan of Kyiv (+1431)

August 2—Hieromartyr John Steblin-Kamensky (+1930): born to a Russian-Lithuanian family, raised in Vilnius during his childhood

August 11—Venerable Theodosius of the Kyiv Caves (Theodore, Duke of Ostrog) (+15th c.)

August 15—Surdegis Icon of the Theotokos

Bibliography

Primary Sources

"*Act of Independence of 16 February 1918*." Seimas of the Republic of Lithuania. https://www.lrs.lt/pls/inter/w5_show?p_r=5691&p_k=2.

Albinus, Petrus, and Georg Fabricius. *Chronicon Quedlenburgense ab initio mundi per aetates*. http://digital.slub-dresden.de/id287626156.

Alfeyev, Hilarion. "Kun. Ilarionas Alfejevas Sausio 13-ąją" ("Fr. Hilarion Alfeyev January 13th"). YouTube: Ortodoksas.lt. https://www.youtube .com/watch?v=1iqt-2CzhPQ.

Cross, Samuel Hazzard, and Olgerd P. Sherbowitz-Wetzor, trans. and eds. *The Russian Primary Chronicle: Laurentian Text*. The Mediaeval Academy of America, 1953.

Degutytė, Janina. "Neringa Pines." *All Poetry*. Translated by Dorian Rotten-berg. https://allpoetry.com/Neringa-Pines.

"Диариуш берестейского игумена Афанасия Филипповича" ("Diary of Afanasy Filippovich Abbot of Brest") in *Русская историческая библиотека. Т. 4. Памятники полемической литературы в Западной Руси. Кн. 1, СПб., 1878.*

Firkovičius, Simonas. "Ijisi baraśkiniń" ("The Smells of Friday"). Kara-ims of Lithuania. Translated by Karina Firkavičiūtė. http://www .karaim.eu/en/language/karaim-language-in-singing/karaim-song -the-smells-of-friday/.

Herodotus. *Herodotus*. Translated by A. D. Godley. Harvard University Press, 1920.

Hus, Jan. *The Letters of Jan Hus*. Translated by Matthew Spinka. Manchester University Press, 1972.

Kazimieraitienė, Gitana. "Neringa." In *Legendos pasakoja*. Šviesa, 2008.

Korecki, Tristan, and Philip Earl Steele, trans. *Union of Krewo (Act of Kreva)*. Polish History Museum. https://polishfreedom.pl/en/union-of-krewo-act-of-kreva/.

Kudirka, Vincas. "National Anthem of Lithuania." Seimas of the Republic of Lithuania. https://www.lrs.lt/sip/portal.show?p_r=38113&p_k=2.

Literae confirmationis articulorum Henrico Regi antea oblatorum. Translated from Polish using Google Translate. https://pl.wikisource .org/wiki/Literae_confirmationis_articulorum_Henrico_Regi_ antea_oblatorum.

Martishkin, Chrizostomas. "Metr. Chrizostomas Sausio 13" ("Metr. Chrizostomas January 13"). YouTube: Ortodoksas.lt. https://www.youtube .com/watch?v=xwS0GF2bZWM.

Michell, Robert, and Nevill Forbes, trans. *The Chronicle of Novgorod 1016– 1471*. Royal Historical Society, 1914.

Perfecky, George A., trans. *The Galician–Volynian Chronicle*. Wilhelm Fink Verlag, 1973.

Reunion Treaty of Brest. Eternal Word Television Network. https://www .ewtn.com/catholicism/library/reunion-treaty-of-brest-1474.

Rupyshev, Pontius. "Личные записи, запись 1923 г. Алтарь" ("Personal Notes, Entry 1923 Altar"). In *Понтий Рупышев. Избранное* (*Selections from Pontius Rupyshev*). Edited by A. Dobrotsvetova, et al. Поломник, 2017.

Rupyshev, Pontius. "Духовный дневник" ("Spiritual Diary"). In *Жизнеописание, духовное наследие Понтия Рупышева* (*Biography, Spiritual Heritage of Pontius Rupyshev*). Edited by A. Dobrotsvetova, et al. Поломник, 2016.

Savignac, David, ed. and trans. *The Pskov 3rd Chronicle*. Beowulf and Sons, 2016.

Semashko, Joseph. "Сочинение о Православии Восточной Церкви, начатое заседателем коллегии Иосифом Семашко в 1827 году, но только до половины конченное, – а также некоторые оставшиеся к нему заметки" ("A work on the Orthodoxy of the Eastern Church, begun by the board member Joseph Semashko in 1827, but only half finished, as well as some remaining notes on it"). In *Записки Иосифа, митрополита литовского*. Том 1. Санкт-Петербург: Типография императорской академии наук, 1883.

Slančiauskas, Matas. *Folk Tales of Northern Lithuania*. Translated by Robert J. Staneslow. Laughing Rabbit Productions, 2015.

Smith, Jerry C., and William L. Urban, trans. *The Livonian Rhymed Chronicle*. Indiana University, 1977.

"Sveika, Aušros Žvaigždė, šviesi." Transcribed and translated by Gintaras Jurgis Sungaila. Adapted for English meter by Andrew Stephen Damick, 2023.

von Jeroschin, Nicolaus. *The Chronicle of Prussia by Nicolaus von Jeroschin*. Translated by Mary Fischer. Routledge, 2016.

Zheleznova, Irina. *Tales of the Amber Sea: Fairy Tales of the Peoples of Estonia, Latvia, and Lithuania*. Raduga Publishers, 1974.

Secondary Sources

Arefieva, Irina. "Отсюда, от Литвы, вошел он в славу … (архипастырское служение Святителя Тихона в Литве в 1914–1917 гг.)" ("From here, from Lithuania, he entered glory … [Archpastoral service of Saint Tikhon in Lithuania in 1914–1917]"). Educational Orthodox Society. http://ricolor.org/europe/litva/1/tihon/.

Baronas, Darius. "Byzantium and Lithuania: North and South Look at Each Other." In *Byzantium, New Peoples, New Powers: The Byzantino-Slav Contact Zone, from the Ninth to the Fifteenth Century*. Edited by Miliana Kaimakamova, Maciej Salamon, and Małgorzata Smorag Różycka. Byzantina et Slavica Cracoviensia, 2007.

Baronas, Darius. "Christians in Late Pagan, and Pagans in Early Christian Lithuania: The Fourteenth and Fifteenth Centuries." *Lithuanian Historical Studies* 19 (2014): 51–81.

Baronas, Darius. "King Ladislas II Jogaila of Poland, Grand Duke Vytautas of Lithuania and the Roman Catholic and Greek Orthodox Church Union." In *Unions and Divisions: New Forms of Rule in Medieval and Renaissance Europe*. Routledge, 2023.

Baronas, Darius. "The Three Martyrs of Vilnius: A Fourteenth-Century Martyrdom and Its Documentary Sources." *Analecta Bollandiana* 122 (2004): 83–134.

Baronas, Darius, and S. C. Rowell. *The Conversion of Lithuania: From Pagan Barbarians to Late Medieval Christians*. Institute of Lithuanian Literature and Folklore, 2015.

Beresnevičius, Gintaras. "Sovijaus Mitas" ("Myth of Sovijus"). In *Dausos*. Taura, 1990.

Berezhnaya, Liliya. "Does Ukraine Have a Church History?" *Kritika: Explorations in Russian and Eurasian History* 10, no. 4 (Fall 2009): 897–916.

"Blessed Dovmont (Timothy), Prince of Pskov." Orthodox Church in America. https://www.oca.org/saints/lives/2008/05/20/101450-blessed-dovmont-timothy-prince-of-pskov.

Bliujienė, Audronė. "The Bog Offerings of the Balts: 'I Give in Order to Get Back.'" In *Archaeologia Baltica, Vol. 14: Underwater Archaeology in the Baltic Region*. Klaipėda University Press, 2010.

Buttar, Prit. *Between Giants: The Battle for the Baltics in World War II*. Osprey Publishing, 2013.

Butterwick, Richard. "How Catholic Was the Grand Duchy of Lithuania in the Later Eighteenth Century?" *Central Europe* 8, no. 2 (November, 2010): 123–45.

Cox, George W. *The Mythology of the Aryan Nations*. Longmans, Green, and Co., 1870.

Daumantas, Juozas. *Fighters for Freedom: Lithuanian Partisans Versus the U.S.S.R.* Translated by E. J. Harrison. Lithuanian Canadian Committee for Human Rights, 1975.

Davies, Norman. *God's Playground: A History of Poland, Vol. I: The Origins to 1795.* Oxford University Press, 2005.

Gimbutas, Marija. *Ancient Symbolism in Lithuanian Folk Art.* American Folklore Society, 1958.

Gimbutas, Marija. *The Balts.* Thames and Hudson, 1963.

Goldfrank, David M. "The Lithuanian Prince-Monk Vojšelk: A Study of Competing Legends." *Harvard Ukrainian Studies* 11, no. 1/2 (June 1987): 44–76.

Greimas, Algirdas J. *Of Gods and Men: Studies in Lithuanian Mythology.* Translated by Milda Newman. Indiana University Press, 1992.

"Holy New Venerable Martyr Anthony of Karyes (+1516)." Orthodox Christianity Then and Now, February 4, 2021. https://www.johnsanidopoulos .com/2021/02/holy-new-martyr-anthony-of-karyes-1516.html.

"Икона Богородицы Сурдегская" ("Icon of the Mother of God Surdegskaya"). Азбука веры. https://azbyka.ru/days/ikona-surdegskaja.

Imse, Ann. "Baltic Residents Make Bold New Push for Independence." Associated Press, August 27, 1989.

Kalik, Judith. "The Orthodox Church and the Jews in the Polish-Lithuanian Commonwealth." *Jewish History* 17 (2003): 229–237.

Kaszeta, Dan. *The Forest Brotherhood: Baltic Resistance Against the Nazis and Soviets.* Hurst & Company, 2023.

Kempa, Tomasz. "Kyrillos Loukaris and the Confessional Problems in the Polish-Lithuanian Commonwealth at the Turn of the Seventeenth Century." *Acta Poloniae Historica* 104 (2011): 103–128.

La Rocca, Francesco. "At the Crossroads: The History of the Greek-Catholic Church in Lithuania." *Occasional Papers on Religion in Eastern Europe* 31, no. 2, article 1 (February 2011): 1–9.

Laukaitytė, Regina. "The Orthodox Church in Lithuania During the Soviet Period." *Lithuanian Historical Studies* 7 (2002): 67–94.

Levine, Hillel. *In Search of Sugihara: The Elusive Japanese Diplomat Who Risked His Life to Rescue 10,000 Jews from the Holocaust.* Free Press, 1996.

Maiorov, Alexander. "The Cult of St. Daniel the Stylite Among the Russian Princes of the Rurik Dynasty." *The Slavic and East European Journal* 59, no. 3 (Fall 2015): 345–366.

Hieromonk Makarios of Simonas Petra. *The Synaxarion: The Lives of the Saints of the Orthodox Church.* Translated by Christopher Hookway. Vol. 1. Holy Convent of the Annunciation of Our Lady, 1998.

Markman, Kristina. "Hero or Villain? Mindaugas and the Image of Lithuanians in Medieval Chronicles." 25th Conference on Baltic Studies, University of Pennsylvania, May 26–28, 2016.

Markus, Anthony. "A History of Our Lady of Trakai." *All About Mary.* University of Dayton. https://web.archive.org/web/20241208211846 /https://udayton.edu/imri/mary/o/our-lady-of-trakai.php.

"Memorial of Saint Josaphat, Bishop and Martyr." Saint Vincent Archabbey. https://saintvincentarchabbey.org/ memorial-of-saint-josaphat-bishop-and-martyr-3/.

Meyendorff, John. "The Three Lithuanian Martyrs: Byzantium and Lithuania in the Fourteenth Century." *St. Vladimir's Theological Quarterly* 26, no. 1 (1982): 29–44.

Meyendorff, Paul. *Russia, Ritual, and Reform: The Liturgical Reforms of Nikon in the 17th Century.* St. Vladimir's Seminary Press, 1991.

Mickūnaitė, Giedrė. "Religious Debate and Visual Compromise: Interpreting Byzantine Murals in Lithuania and Poland." *Studia historica Brunensia* 66 (2019): 127–157.

Miknys, Rimantas. "Decisions of the Lithuanian Assembly (The Great Seimas of Vilnius) of 4–5 December 1905." *Lithuanian Historical Studies* 10 (2005): 145–154.

Mikos, Michael J., ed. and trans. *Polish Literature from the Middle Ages to the End of the Eighteenth Century: A Bilingual Anthology.* Constans, 1999.

Millar, John. *The Lithuanians in Scotland.* House of Lochar, 1998.

Mironowicz, Antoni. "Orthodox Church in the Polish-Lithuanian Commonwealth in the 16th–18th Century." *Białostockie Teki Historyczne* 14 (2016): 41–60.

Motieka, Egidijus. "The Great Assembly of Vilnius, 1905." *Lithuanian Historical Studies* 1, no. 1 (1996): 84–96.

Mouravieff, A. N. *A History of the Church of Russia.* Translated by R. W. Blackmore. John Henry Parker, 1842.

Plokhy, Serhii. *The Origins of the Slavic Nations: Premodern Identities in Russia, Ukraine, and Belarus.* Cambridge University Press, 2006.

Ralston, W. R. S. *The Songs of the Russian People: As Illustrative of Slavonic Mythology and Russian Social Life.* Ellis and Green, 1872.

Rowell, S. C., trans. *Christianity in Lithuania.* Aidai, 2002.

Rowell, S. C. "Whatever Kind of Pagan the Bearer Might Be, the Letter is Valid: A Sketch of Catholic-Orthodox Relations in the Late-Mediaeval Grand Duchy of Lithuania." *Lithuanian Historical Studies* 18 (2013): 47–65.

Savasis, Juozas. *The War Against God in Lithuania.* Manyland Books, 1966.

Shumilo, Sergey. "Святогорский след в судьбе монаха и Великого князя Литовского Войшелка (1223–1267)" ("The Svyatogorsk Trace in the Fate of the Monk and Grand Duke of Lithuania Voishelk [1223–1267]"). The International Institute of the Athonite Legacy. https://afon.org.ua/ru/publikatsii/svyatogorskij-sled-v-sudbe-monakha-i-velikogo-knyazya-litovskogo-vojshelka-1223-1267.html.

Staliūnas, Darius. "Assimilation or Acculturation? Russian Imperial Policy toward Lithuanians in the 1860s." *Central and Eastern European Review* 2 (2008): 1–20.

Stone, Daniel Z. *The Polish-Lithuanian State, 1386–1795.* University of Washington Press, 2001.

Straižys, Vytautas, and Libertas Klimka. "The Cosmology of the Ancient Balts." *Archaeoastronomy* 28, no. 22 (1997): 57–81.

Sugihara, Yukiko. *Visas for Life.* Translated by Hiroki Sugihara. Edu-Comm, 1995.

Sužiedėlis, Simas, ed. (1970–1978). "Mindaugas" in *Encyclopedia Lituanica*. Vol. III. Juozas Kapočius, 538–543.

Takala-Roszczenko, Maria. "The 'Westernisation' of the Eastern Orthodox Church Music Tradition in the 16th–17th Century Polish-Lithuanian Commonwealth." In *Europe–Evropa: Cross-cultural Dialogues between the West, Russia, and Southeastern Europe*. Uppsala Universitet, 2010.

Tsebenko, Andrii. "The Orthodox Church in the Context of State and Church Development in the Grand Duchy of Lithuania, Ruthenia, Samogitia and the Kingdom of Poland (1458–1509)." *Skhidnoievropeiskyi istorychnyi visnyk (East European Historical Bulletin)* 22 (2022): 24–32.

Valevicius, Andrius. "Orthodoxy in Lithuania Before Union with Poland." *The Greek Orthodox Theological Review* 45, nos. 1–4 (Spring 2000): 479–489.

Vėlius, Norbertas. *Sources of Baltic Religion and Mythology*. Vols. 1–4. The Science and Encyclopaedia Publishers, 1996.

Weeks, Theodore R. "Religion and Russification: Russian Language in the Catholic Churches of the 'Northwest Provinces' after 1863." *Kritika: Explorations in Russian and Eurasian History* 2, no. 1 (Winter 2001): 87–110.

Weeks, Theodore R. "Russification and the Lithuanians, 1863–1905." *Slavic Review* 60, no. 1 (Spring 2001): 96–114.

Weeks, Theodore R. *Vilnius Between Nations 1795–2000*. Northern Illinois University Press, 2015.

Weeks, Theodore R. "Vilnius in World War I, 1914–1920." *Nordost-Archiv* 2009, Bd. 17 (2008): 34–57.

Wereda, Dorota. "Reformation as an Inspiration for Reforms of the Eastern Churches in the Polish-Lithuanian Commonwealth." *Historia i Świat*, no. 7 (2018): 187–194.

Wlasowsky, Ivan. *Outline History of the Ukrainian Orthodox Church*. Vols. 1–3. Ukrainian Orthodox Church of the USA, 1956–1992.

Wooden, Anastacia K. "A Brief History of the Union of Brest and Its Inter-
pretations" in *Stolen Churches or Bridges to Orthodoxy?* Palgrave Mac-
Millan, 2021.

Žaltauskaitė, Vilma. "Catholicism and Nationalism in the Views of the
Younger Generation of Lithuanian Clergy in the Late Nineteenth and
Early Twentieth Centuries." *Lithuanian Historical Studies* 5 (2000):
113–130.

Zaroff, Roman. "Some aspects of pre-Christian Baltic religion," in *New
researches on the religion and mythology of the Pagan Slavs*. Lingva, 2019.

Zinkevičius, Zigmas. *Krikščionybės ištakos Lietuvoje: Rytų krikščionybė var-
dyno duomenimis (The Roots of Christianity in Lithuania: Eastern Rite
Christianity from the Data of Names)*. Katalikų akademija, 2005.

Subject Index

A

Act of Religious Tolerance (1905), 206
Adalbert of Prague, 146
Adomaitytė, Apolonija, 187
Aeneas, 126
Agathangelus, Archbishop of Vilnius and
 Metropolitan of Yaroslavl, 277
Albert, Bishop of Riga, 62
alcohol, 184
Alexander, King of Poland and Grand
 Duke, 95
Alexander II, Tsar of Russia, 178
Alexander III, Tsar of Russia, 181
Alexander VII, Pope, 170
Alexander Nevsky, 34, 64, 259, 261
Alexios, Metropolitan of Kyiv and Mos-
 cow, 43, 44, 277
Alexis of Wilkes-Barre, 110
Alfeyev, Fr. Hilarion, 242
Algirdas, Grand Duke of Lithuania, 42–44,
 45–49, 53–54, 65–66, 87, 114
All Saints of Lithuania (feast), 278
amber, 10, 140, 149–50
American Carpatho-Russian Orthodox
 Diocese (ACROD), 110
American Orthodoxy, 110–13, 117, 206
Anna, Queen of Poland and Grand
 Duchess, 90
Annals of Quedlinburg, 15
*Annals or Chronologies of the Illustrious
 Kingdom of Poland*, 129

Anne (Vytautas's granddaughter), 94
Anthony (Antanas). *See* Three Martyrs of
 Vilnius
Anthony IV, Ecumenical Patriarch, 93
Anthony of Karyes, New Martyr, 266–67,
 277
Antoniy Zubko, Vicar Bishop of Brest, 166
Apollonova, Klaudia Semionovna, 229, 230
Athanasius of Brest, 102–6, 276
Aukštaitians, 20
Aušrinė (morning star goddess), 25
Austria, 160–61

B

Baltic (term), 19
Baltic crusaders, 29, 61–62, 63–64, 66, 79,
 83. *See also* Livonian Order; Teutonic
 Order
Baltic languages, 20
Baltic paganism: beer rituals, 25–26; creation story, 26; end of, 49, 53; fragmentary sources on, 22–23, 27, 145–46; gods
 and goddesses, 24–25; human sacrifice,
 146, 253; integration into daily life, 27;
 Mindaugas and, 33; as mythological
 cultural inheritance, 27; neopagan
 reconstructions, 146–47; Soviets and,
 144; *Tale of Sovijus*, 23–24, 145; worship,
 26
Baltic Sea, 10, 271
Baltic tribes, 15, 19–20

Baltic Way, 239–40, 243

Baronas, Darius, 93–94

Bartholomew, Ecumenical Patriarch, 4

Basanavičius, Jonas, 180, 212, 213, 214, 215

Basil of Murozh, 261

Battle of Grunwald (Battle of Žalgiris), 71, 79–82, 88

Battle of Saulė, 30–31, 64

Battle of Vienna, 158–59

beer, 25–26

Bermontians, 192

Bernard of Clairvaux, 64

Berthold of Hanover, Bishop of Riga, 61

bodyguards, foreign, 76–77

Bogoyavlensky, Eleutherius, Metropolitan of Vilnius and Lithuania, 217

Boilo (liqueur), 184

Bolesław I the Brave, King of Poland, 58, 59, 82

Bolshevik Revolution (October Revolution), 192, 209, 214

Book of Roger, 145

book smugglers, 179

Brest, 102–3. *See also* Athanasius of Brest; Union of Brest

Britain, 126

brotherhoods, lay, 96, 97, 98, 99, 108

Bruno Boniface of Querfort, 15, 278

Brutus of Troy, 126

Buračas, Balys, 197, 199

Bush, George H. W., 240

Bychowiec Chronicle, 129

C

Canaanite religion, 24

Casimir III, King of Poland, 66

Cathedral of the Visitation of the Blessed Virgin Mary (Trakai), 72, 73

Catherine the Great, Empress of Russia, 160, 161

Catholic Church. *See* Roman Catholicism

cemeteries: Kudirkos Naumiestis, 187–88; State Street Cemetery (Hamden, CT), 245–47

Charitina of Lithuania, 258–59, 277

Chodkevičius, Aleksandras (Aleksander Chodkiewicz), 266

Chodkiewicz, Hieronim, 268

Christianity: comparison to paganism, 24; conversions, 126–27, 251–52; inter-Christian relations, 119–20; patronal feast days, 124; in post-communist Eastern Europe, 205; saints, 255. *See also* Orthodox Christianity; Roman Catholicism; Unia

Christmas Eve, 111–13

Chrizostomas Martishkin, Metropolitan of Vilnius and Lithuania, 242–43, 272–73

chronicles, 127–28

Chronicle of Novgorod, 256–57

Chronicle of the Grand Duchy of Lithuania, Ruthenia and Samogitia, 128, 256

Chronicle of the Grand Dukes of Lithuania, 128

Church of St. Euphrosyne of Polotsk (Vilnius), 162

Church of St. Paraskevi (Vilnius), 46, 273

cities, medieval, 74–75

Clement IV, Pope, 33

Clement VII, Pope, 99

coal mining, 183, 222–23

Commonwealth of Two Nations. *See* Polish-Lithuanian Commonwealth

Communism, 205. *See also* Soviet Union

Congress Poland, 165

Constantine the Great, 127

Constantinople, 127, 264

conversions, 126–27, 251–52

Cossack Hetmanate, 158

Council of Constance, 72, 94

Council (Union) of Florence, 95, 264

Council of Lithuania, 214–15

Council of Trent, 97–98, 164

creation story, 26

cremation, 24, 33, 36, 145

Crimean Tatars, 61, 74, 75, 76–77, 157. *See also* Tatars

crusaders, Baltic, 29, 61–62, 63–64, 66, 79, 83. *See also* Livonian Brothers of the Sword; Livonian Order; Teutonic Order

Curonian Spit (*Kuršių nerija*): about, 10, 139–40; churches at, 144–45; giantess Neringa legend, 124, 142–43; Hill of Witches, 143, 144; sand dunes and pine forests, 140–42

Curonians, 20, 29, 140

Cyprian, Metropolitan of Kyiv, 44, 93, 94, 277

Cyril Lucaris, Ecumenical Patriarch, 279

D

Damick, Albert, 222, 223–27, 244

Damick, Elizabeth, 222, 245

Damick, Fr. Andrew Stephen: family background, 184–87, 188–89, 222, 223–27; finding great-uncle's burial site, 244–47; at Hill of Crosses, 199–201; at Kudirkos Naumiestis cemetery, 187–88; Latvian cousins, 227–28; in Lithuania, 16, 71, 111, 274–75; surname, 226; *Sveika, Aušros Žvaigždė, šviesi* (hymn) and, 118–19; Three Martyrs of Vilnius and, 49–50

Damick, Robert, 244–47

Daniel, Prince of Galicia-Volhynia, 35

Dar nesulaukęs laisvos tėvynės ("A Homeland Not Yet Free"; song), 236–37

Daumantas of Pskov, 34, 35, 260–63, 278

Dausprungas (Mindaugas's brother), 28

Degutytė, Janina, 140–41

Deluge (Swedish invasion), 157, 158

departed, prayers for, 247–48

Dievas (father-god), 24, 26, 27

Dimitry of the Don, 68

Długosz, Jan: *Annals or Chronologies of the Illustrious Kingdom of Poland*, 129

Domeika, Antanas Petras, 16, 184–85, 186, 201, 222, 223, 224, 225–26, 227

Domeika, Jonas (John), 185, 222, 223

Domeika, Matas, 187

Domeika, Olga (née Weiland), 16, 184–85, 188–89, 201, 223–27, 228

Domeikaitė, Antanina, 185, 187

Dorotheus the Smith, 262

Dosithea of Kyiv, 117

E

East Prussia (Lithuania Minor), 158, 178, 179, 211

Eastern Europe, 205

Ecumenical Patriarchate, 3–4, 41, 42–43, 93, 96–97, 99, 109, 264, 273–74

Eglė, Queen of Serpents, 10, 131–38

Eleutherius Bogoyavlensky, Metropolitan of Vilnius and Lithuania, 217

Elizabeth the New Martyr, 208

Eliziejus Laurušavietis (Elisha of Lavreshev), 254–56, 257, 277

Estonia, 19, 29, 62, 236, 239, 243, 274

Euphrosyne of Polotsk, 162, 278

Eustachijus Valavičius, Catholic Bishop of Vilnius, 73

Eustathius (Eustachijus/Eustatijus). *See* Three Martyrs of Vilnius

Eustratius (Grumkov; hieromartyr), 277

F

Feodorovich, Alexei, 219

Feodosiev, Theodosius, Archbishop of Vilnius and Lithuania, 217

Firkovičius, Simonas, 77–78

food: alcoholic drinks, 184; Holy Supper, 111–13; Karaite and Tatar contributions, 77–78

Forest Brothers (partisans), 236–37, 243

Frederick William, Elector of Brandenburg, 158

G

Gabriel (Igoshkin), Archimandrite of Melekess, 277

Gabriel of Białystok (child-martyr), 278

Galicia, Metropolis of, 42

Galician-Volhynian Chronicle, 33

Galicia-Volhynia (Ruthenia), 28, 35

Gerhard von Rude (Teutonic knight),
  63–64

Gediminas, Grand Duke of Lithuania,
  37–39, 42, 45, 70, 128

Gediminas Hill, 37, 38–39, 124

Gennadius of Mogilev, Wonder-Worker of
  Kostroma, 277

George, Archbishop of Mogilev, 278

George II Rákóczi, Prince of Transylvania,
  158

Gerasim, Bishop of Smolensk, 128

Gerasim, Metropolitan of Kyiv, 95

Germany: Lithuanian independence and,
  214–16; Nazis, 230–31, 232–33, 235, 236,
  238

"Glory to Jesus Christ!" (greeting), 111

Golden Horde, 45, 67, 75, 76. See also
  Mongols

Gorbachev, Mikhail, 240, 241, 242

Goštautas clan, 89

Great Seimas of Vilnius, 211–13

Great Western Schism, 72, 94

Greek paganism, 25

Gregory Palamas, 44, 164

Grunwald, Battle of (Battle of Žalgiris), 71,
  79–82, 88

H

Hamden (CT): State Street Cemetery,
  245–47

Henry de Valois, 90

Hermann von Salza, Grand Master of the
  Teutonic Order, 63

Herodotus, 22–23

Hill of Crosses, 10, 197–201

Hill of Witches (Raganų kalnas), 143, 144

history, 82–83

Holy Cross Monastery (near Krakow), 93

Holy Lance of Vienna, 58–59, 82

Holy Roman Empire, 58–59, 62, 74, 158–59

Holy Supper, 111–13

"A Homeland Not Yet Free" (Dar nesulaukęs laisvos tėvynės; song), 236–37

human sacrifice, 146, 253

Hungary, 63, 68

Hus, Jan, 80

I

immigration, 183–84, 222–23

Innocent, Metropolitan of Vilnius and
  Lithuania, 50

Innocent III, Pope, 61, 62

Innocent IV, Pope, 32

Iron Wolf, 10, 38–40, 45, 124

Isidore, Metropolitan of Kyiv, 95, 264

J

Jadwiga, Queen of Poland, 68–69, 88, 93

James (apostle), 120

January Events (Sausio įvykiai), 241–43

January Uprising, 175, 176

Jaunė (Gediminas's wife), 45

Jaunutis, Grand Duke of Lithuania, 45–46

Jeremias II, Ecumenical Patriarch, 4, 97

Jesus Christ, 24, 111

Jews: Holocaust, 232–33; Karaite Jews,
  74, 75–76, 77–78; in Lithuania, 91, 231;
  Sugihara and, 232, 233–34

Job, Patriarch of Moscow, 97

Job Boretsky, Metropolitan of Kyiv, 100

Jogaila (Władysław II), King of Poland and
  Grand Duke: about, 60, 65, 127; Battle
  of Grunwald and, 79–81, 88; church
  union and, 72, 92–94; civil wars and,
  66, 67, 87, 88; at Council of Constance,
  72, 94; Crimean Tatars and, 76; death,
  89, 95; Trakai Castle and, 71; Union of
  Krewo and, 67–69, 79

John (Jonas). See Three Martyrs of Vilnius

John II Comnenus, Byzantine Emperor, 73

John III Sobieski, King of Poland, 158, 159

John of Kronstadt, 190, 191–92, 195, 196

John of Riga, 208, 277

John VIII, Byzantine Emperor, 94

John XIII, Ecumenical Patriarch, 42

John XXII, Pope, 33

Jonas, Metropolitan of Moscow, 264

Josaphat, Uniate Metropolitan of Kyiv, 166
Josaphat Kuncevich, Uniate Archbishop of
   Polotsk, 100–101, 109
Joseph Semashko, Metropolitan of Vilnius
   and Lithuania, 162, 163–67, 168
Juliana Alšėniškaitė (Olshanskaya), 277
Jūratė, Queen of the Sea, 148–50

K
Kallistos, Ecumenical Patriarch, 43
Karaite Jews, 74, 75–76, 77–78
Kastytis (legend), 148–50
Kaunas, 169, 171–72, 192, 208, 216, 221, 232,
   234
Kaup, 139–40
Kernavė, 36
Kęstutis, Duke of Trakai, 65–67, 70, 87
Khmelnytsky Uprising, 157–58
kibinai (meat pasty), 77
Kohl, Helmut, 240
Korčinskis, Fr. Jonas, 217–18
Kościuszko, Tadeusz, 160
Kražiai Massacre, 181–82
Krupnikas (liqueur), 184
Kudirka, Vincas, 180, 181, 182, 187
Kudirkos Naumiestis, 187–88
Kurkas (harvest god), 145

L
Laima (Laumė; goddess of fate), 27
Lance of Vienna, Holy, 58–59, 82
languages: Baltic, 20; Lithuanian, 20–21,
   24–25, 145, 207, 217, 218, 238, 272–73
Latgalians, 20
Latvia, 19, 20, 29, 62, 227–28, 236, 239, 243
Laurence, Recluse of the Kyiv Caves, 254
Laurušavas Monastery, 35, 254
Lawrence (Laurynas), Bishop of Balakhna,
   277
Layamon, 126
legends and stories: collective lore,
   123, 124–25, 126–27; Eglė, Queen of
   Serpents, 10, 131–38; Hill of Crosses,
   197–99; Iron Wolf, 10, 38–40, 45, 124;

Jūratė and Kastytis, 148–50; Myth of
   Sovijus, 23–24, 145; Neringa (giantess),
   10, 124, 142–43; Palemonid Dynasty,
   128–30; Swan Queen, 151–54
Lenin, Vladimir, 214
Leo (Lev) of Halych, Grand Prince of Kyiv,
   257
Leo XIII, Pope, 182
Leontijus Karpovičius (Leonty Karpovich), 108–9, 277
Leopold I, Holy Roman Emperor, 158
"Lietuva, Tėvyne mūsų" ("Lithuania, Our
   Fatherland"; Kudirka), 180
literacy, 127, 178
Lithuania: introduction, 1–5, 10–11;
   authors' pilgrimage to, 16–18; Battle of
   Grunwald, 71, 79–82, 88; chronicles,
   128; civil wars, 45–46, 65–67, 69, 87,
   261; earliest known mention, 15; Forest
   Brothers (partisans), 236–37, 243; gene-
   tic diversity, 20; Grand Duchy, 41, 45,
   46, 53–54, 65; Great Seimas of Vilnius,
   211–13; Holocaust and, 232–33; immigration from, 183–84, 222–23; interwar
   independence, 192, 214–16; language,
   20–21, 24–25, 145; modern nation-
   state, 19, 162; naming conventions,
   18–19; National Revival, 179–80, 182;
   Palemonid Dynasty, 37, 128–30; press
   ban, 178–79; Roman Catholicism and,
   53, 60, 69, 79, 87; Russification, 175–78;
   Singing Revolution and independence
   from Soviet Union, 240–43; Soviet
   occupation, 235–36, 237–39; unification
   under Mindaugas, 28–35, 60–61; Union
   of Krewo, 68–69, 79, 88–89; WWI and,
   207–9, 214; WWII and, 230–31, 235. *See
   also* Baltic paganism; legends and stories; Orthodox Church, in Lithuania;
   Polish-Lithuanian Commonwealth;
   Vilnius
Lithuania Minor (East Prussia), 158, 178,
   179, 211
Lithuanian paganism. *See* Baltic paganism

Lithuanian Wars of Independence (*Laisvės kovos* (Freedom Struggles)), 216

Livonian Brothers of the Sword, 29, 30–31, 61–62, 64

Livonian Order: background, 61–62, 64; Battle of Grunwald and, 81; Lithuania and, 34–35, 45, 66, 79, 259; Mindaugas and, 31, 32, 33–34; Pskov and, 261, 262*See also* Teutonic Order

Livonian Rhymed Chronicle, 29, 30, 31, 32, 33–35, 39, 62

Lizdeika (pagan priest), 38, 45

Louis I of Hungary, King of Poland, 68

Luzhinskiy, Vasiliy, Bishop of Orsha, 166

Lvov, Alexey Fedorovich, 171

M

Macarius, Archimandrite of Ovruch, Pinsk, and Kaneva, 276

Macarius, Metropolitan of Kyiv, 264–65, 278

Magdeburger Recht (Magdeburg Laws), 74–75

Manuel Paleologos II, Byzantine Emperor, 73, 94

Maria (Venerable Schemanun Martha), 261

Maria of Vitebsk, 46

Marienburg (Malbork) Castle, 66, 79

Martin V, Pope, 95

Martishkin, Chrizostomas, Metropolitan of Vilnius and Lithuania, 242–43, 272–73

Mary, Mother of God: Laima (Laumė) and, 27; national self-identity and, 114; Our Lady of Częstochowa, 91; Our Lady of Pažaislis, 169, 170, 171–73, 279; Our Lady of Surdegis, 219–21, 279; Our Lady of the Gate of Dawn, 10, 17–18, 114–17, 119, 124, 168, 169, 211, 277; Our Lady of Trakai, 73–74, 124, 276; Our Lady of Vladimir, 169; *Sveika, Aušros Žvaigždė, šviesi* (hymn), 118–19; Vilnius (Vilna) Icon of the Theotokos, 278; Visitation of the Blessed Virgin Mary,

72–73; Zhirovits Icon of the Theotokos, 208, 278

Matejko, Jan: *The Battle of Grunwald* (painting), 81–82

Maurice (saint), 58–59, 82

Medved, Roman (hieroconfessor), 277

Mėnuo (moon-god), 25

metathesis, 186

Michael Rohoza, Metropolitan of Kyiv, 97–98

Michalo Lituanus (Michael the Lithuanian), 76

Mikhnovo community, 193–96

Mindaugas, King of Lithuania: about, 28, 252; conflict with Tautvilas and Livonian Order, 33–34, 258–59; death, 34, 256, 260–61; Lithuanian independence and, 215–16; Roman Catholicism and enthronement as king, 31–32, 33; unification of Lithuania, 29–31, 60–61; Vaišvilkas and, 35, 253

Mindaugas II (Wilhelm Karl, Duke of Urach), 216

Miniotas, Viktoras (archdeacon), 272

Mitrophan (Kvanin), 277

Mockus, Fr. Vitalijus, 271–73, 274

Molotov-Ribbentrop Pact, 227, 231, 239, 240

Monastery of the Holy Spirit (Vilnius), 49, 50, 102, 107–9, 162, 208, 219

Mongols, 33, 37, 41, 42, 43, 76, 81. *See also* Golden Horde

moon, 25

Morta (Martha; Mindaugas's wife), 32, 33, 34, 260

Moscow, Grand Duchy of, 43, 67, 89, 95

Mount Athos, 253, 267

Myth of Sovijus, 23–24, 145

N

naming conventions, 18–19

Napoleon, 170

National Revival, 179–80, 182

Nazi Germany, 230–31, 232–33, 235, 236, 238

Neringa (giantess), 10, 124, 142–43
Nestor (priest), 46, 47
Nicholas I, Tsar of Russia, 166, 171
Nicholas II, Tsar of Russia, 208, 211–12, 214
Nikephoros Kantakouzenos, Archdeacon of Constantinople, 279
Norse paganism, 22, 24, 25, 40
November Uprising, 165, 174
Novogrudok, 42, 43, 252, 255

O
"The Oak Branches Were Bending" ("Užuolėlio šakos linko"; song), 177
October Manifesto, 212
October Revolution (Bolshevik Revolution), 192, 209, 214
Old Believers, 163
Old Prussian language, 20
Olga of Kyiv, 54, 55
Onesiphorus Divochka, Metropolitan of Kyiv, 97
Order of Dobrzyń, 63
Orthodox Christianity: American Orthodoxy, 110–13, 117, 206; Council (Union) of Florence, 95, 264; "Glory to Jesus Christ!" greeting, 111; Holy Supper, 111–13; inter-Christian relations, 119–20; reunion efforts with Catholicism, 92–95. *See also* Ecumenical Patriarchate; Polish Autocephalous Orthodox Church; Russian Orthodox Church
Orthodox Church, in Lithuania: introduction, 3–4; among nobility, 36, 258; Brest persecution, 102–3; as difficult story to tell, 201–2; in Grand Duchy, 35–36, 58, 60, 71–72, 88; inter-Christian relations, 119; interwar period, 192–93, 194, 216–18; Lithuanian language and, 207, 217, 218, 238, 272–73; Metropolis, under Ecumenical Patriarchate, 41–44; Mikhnovo community, 193–96; in Polish-Lithuanian Commonwealth, 96, 101; post-partition, 162–63; post-Soviet, 243; Russian imperial period, 158, 177, 182,
201; Russian invasion of Ukraine and, 273–74; Russian Orthodox Diocese, 168; saints and feasts, 276–79; Soviet occupation and, 237–38; Three Martyrs of Vilnius, 10, 46–50, 53, 107, 208, 238, 252, 278, 279; Tikhon, Patriarch of Moscow, and, 206–10; Unia incorporated into Russian Orthodox Church, 165–68, 177, 278; Union of Brest and, 92, 98–101, 269; during WWII, 235
Orthodox Church in America (OCA), 110
Ostrog, 97
Ostrogsky, Konstantin Vasyl (Konstantinas Ostragiškis), 97, 99, 100
Ostrov Peace Agreement, 88
Otto I the Great, Holy Roman Emperor, 58, 74
Otto II the Red, Holy Roman Emperor, 58, 59, 82
Our Lady of Częstochowa, 91
Our Lady of Pažaislis, 169, 170, 171–73, 279
Our Lady of Surdegis, 219–21, 279
Our Lady of the Gate of Dawn, 10, 17–18, 114–17, 119, 124, 168, 169, 211, 277
Our Lady of Trakai, 73–74, 124, 276
Our Lady of Vladimir, 169

P
Pac, Michael Casimir, 169–70
Pacas, Kristupas Zigmantas (Krzysztof Zygmunt Pac), 169
paganism, 24, 26. *See also* Baltic paganism
Palemonid Dynasty, 37, 128–30
Parnidis Dune (*Parnidžio kopa*), 141–42
partisans (Forest Brothers), 236–37, 243
Paul (apostle), 119–20
Paul of Vilnius (martyr), 278
Pažaislis Monastery, 169–71, 172
Pennsylvania, 139, 183–84, 222–23
Perkūnas (storm-god), 24–25, 27, 145, 149
Perun (god), 57, 58
Peter (apostle), 27
Peter, Metropolitan of Kyiv, 42, 44
Peter I, Tsar of Russia, 164, 220

Peter Mohyla, Metropolitan of Kyiv, 103, 277

Philaret, Metropolitan of Moscow, 165–66, 167

Philotheos Kokkinos, Ecumenical Patriarch, 43, 44

Photius, Metropolitan of Kyiv, 279

place, 123–24

Poland: Eastern Christianity and, 72; Teutonic Order and, 81; union with Lithuania, 68–69, 79, 87–89

Polish Autocephalous Orthodox Church, 194, 217

Polish-Lithuanian Commonwealth (Commonwealth of Two Nations): about, 91; Battle of Vienna and, 158–59; decline, partition, and dissolution, 159–61; elected monarchy, 89–90; establishment through Union of Lublin, 89, 95, 127; Khmelnytsky Uprising, 157–58; relations between Polish and Lithuanian cultures, 91; Swedish invasion, 157, 158

Pomponius Mela, 23

prayers, for departed, 247–48

press ban, 178–79

Primary Chronicle, 55–57

Protestants, 2, 75, 205

Prussia, Kingdom of, 158, 160–61

Prussians, 20, 33, 63, 64, 82, 139–40, 145

Pskov, 35, 261–63

R

Radvila, Janusz (Radziwill), 268–69

Radvilas clan, 89

Ragutis (beer god), 25–26, 46

Riga, 29, 61–62

Ringaudas (Mindaugas's father), 28

Rohlin, Dn. Seraphim Richard, 7, 17–18, 71, 77–78, 188, 199

Roman, Metropolitan of Lithuania, 43

Roman Catholicism: Baltic crusades and, 29; Council of Constance, 72, 94; Council (Union) of Florence, 95, 264;

Council of Trent, 97–98, 164; Great Seimas of Vilnius on, 213; Great Western Schism, 72, 94; Jogaila and, 60, 68–69, 79; Lithuania and, 53, 60, 69, 79, 87; Mindaugas and, 31–32; reunion efforts with Orthodox, 92–95; Russia on, 175–76; Soviet occupation of Lithuania and, 237; Visitation of the Blessed Virgin Mary, 72–73. *See also* Unia

Rome, 37, 126–27, 128–29

Romuva, 146–47

Rupyshev, Fr. Pontius, 190–92, 193–96, 217

Rurikid Dynasty, 56

Russia: Act of Religious Tolerance, 206; Bolshevik Revolution, 192, 209, 214; Cossack Hetmanate and, 158; January Uprising, 175, 176; Kražiai Massacre, 181–82; Lithuanian press ban, 178–79; November Uprising, 165, 174; October Manifesto, 212; partition of Polish-Lithuanian Commonwealth and, 160–61; Russification policy, 175–78; WWI and, 214. *See also* Soviet Union

Russian Orthodox Church: conversion of the Rus', 54–58; elevation to patriarchate, 97, 98; Kražiai Massacre and, 182; Lithuanian diocese, 168; "Living Church" and, 194; Russification and, 177; Unia incorporated to, 165–68, 177, 278. *See also* Orthodox Church, in Lithuania

Russian Orthodox Church Outside Russia (ROCOR), 110

Russian Primary Chronicle, 55–57

Ruthenia (Galicia-Volhynia), 28, 35

Ruthenians, 41, 54, 91, 97–99, 110, 164–65

S

saints, 255

Samogitians, 20, 21, 61, 63–64, 145

Saulė (sun-goddess), 25

Saulė, Battle of, 30–31, 64

Selonians, 20

Semashko, Joseph (priest), 163, 168

Semashko, Joseph, Metropolitan of Vilnius and Lithuania, 162, 163–67, 168

Semigallians, 20, 61, 64

Senyk, Sophia, 100

Seraphim of Sarov, 17, 117

Sergei Voskresensky, Metropolitan of Vilnius and Lithuania, 235

Sergius of Radonezh, 48

Shish-Stavitsky, Bogdan, 219

Shvarn, Prince of Ruthenia, 35, 36, 252, 257

Siege of Jasna Góra, 91

Sigismund II Augustus, King of Poland and Grand Duke, 89, 114

Sigismund III, King of Poland and Grand Duke, 97

Sigismund Kęstutaitis, Grand Duke of Lithuania, 95

Sigismund of Luxembourg, 94

Singing Revolution, 239–40

Skalvians, 20

Skirgaila (Jogaila's brother), 87

Smetona, Antanas, 214

Sofija Olelkaitė-Radvilienė (Sophia of Slutsk), 268–70, 278

Sophia, daughter of Dimitry of the Don, 68

Soviet Union: annexation of Lithuania, 235–36, 237–39; Baltic paganism and, 144; Molotov-Ribbentrop Pact, 227, 231, 239, 240; Singing Revolution and Lithuanian independence, 239–43; WWII and, 230–32. *See also* Russia

Sovijus, Myth of, 23–24, 145

space, 123–24

St. John's Night (*Joninės*), 143–44

St. Mary Magdalene Convent (Vilnius), 207, 208

Stanisław August Poniatowski, King of Poland and Grand Duke, 160, 161, 162

State Street Cemetery (Hamden, CT), 245–47

Steblin-Kamensky, John (hieromartyr), 279

Stephen of Bathory, King of Poland and Grand Duke, 90, 262

Stone, Daniel, 65

Sugihara, Chiune (Sergei Pavlovich), 229–30, 231–32, 233–34

Sugihara, Yukiko (Maria), 230, 233

sundials, 142

Sungaila, Fr. Gintaras, 18, 19, 75, 111, 140, 181, 200–201, 273, 275

Supraśl Monastery of the Annunciation, 266–67

Surdegis, 219; Our Lady of Surdegis, 219–21, 279

Sveika, Aušros Žvaigždė, šviesi (hymn), 118–19

Švitrigaila, Grand Duke of Lithuania, 95

Swan Queen, 151–54

Sweden, 91, 116, 157, 158

Synod of Polotsk, 168

Synod of Zamość, 164

T

Tale of Sovijus, 23–24, 145

Tamerlane, 37

Tatars, 42, 255–56, 265; Crimean, 61, 74, 75, 76–77, 157

"Tautiška giesmė" ("The National Hymn"), 180

Tautvilas, Duke of Polotsk, 31, 32, 34, 258–59

Teliavelis (blacksmith god), 27

Teutonic Order (Teutonic Knights): background, 62–63; Baltic crusades, 63–64; Battle of Grunwald and, 79–80, 81–82, 88; Council of Constance and, 94; Gediminas and, 45, 128; on Kurkas (harvest god), 145; Lithuania and, 66, 67–68, 79, 87; Livonian Confederation and, 29; Trakai Island Castle and, 70–71. *See also* Livonian Order

Theodosius Feodosiev, Archbishop of Vilnius and Lithuania, 217

Theodosius of the Kyiv Caves (Theodore, Duke of Ostrog), 279

Theognostos, Metropolitan of Kyiv, 42–43, 44
Theophanes III, Patriarch of Jerusalem, 100
Theophilus, Metropolitan of Lithuania, 42
Theotokos. *See* Mary, Mother of God
Three Martyrs of Vilnius, 10, 46–50, 53, 107, 208, 238, 252, 278, 279
Tikhon, Archbishop of Vilnius and Patriarch of Moscow, 206–10, 278
Tikhon of Lukh in Kostroma, 278
Trakai: Cathedral of the Visitation of the Blessed Virgin Mary, 72, 73; establishment, 70; as multicultural, 74, 75–77; Our Lady of Trakai, 73–74, 124, 276; Trakai Island Castle, 70–71, 72
Treniota, Duke of Samogitia, 33–34, 261
Trinkūnaitė-Sungailienė, Motinėlė Justina, 18, 273
Troy, 126–27
Tsemblak, Gregory, 95

U
Ukmergė, 30
Uliana of Tver, 68
Ulrich von Jungingen, Grand Master of the Teutonic Order, 81, 82
Unia: American Orthodoxy and, 110–11; Athanasius of Brest against, 102–6; Joseph Semashko and incorporation into Russian Orthodox Church, 163–68, 177, 278; Latinizations, 164; Monastery of the Holy Spirit (Vilnius) and, 108–9; Union of Brest, 92, 98–101, 269; use of term, 99
Union of Brest, 92, 98–101, 269
Union (Council) of Florence, 95, 264
Union of Krewo, 68–69, 79, 88–89
Union of Lithuanian Freedom Fighters, 236
Union of Lublin, 89, 95, 127
United States of America: American Orthodoxy, 110–13, 117, 206; immigration to, 183–84, 222–23; protests by Lithuanian-Americans, 174, 182

Urban VI, Pope, 72, 93
"Užuolėlio šakos linko" ("The Oak Branches Were Bending"; song), 177

V
Vaišvilkas, Grand Duke of Lithuania, 31, 34–36, 71, 252–54, 256–57, 258, 260, 261
Valančius, Motiejus, Catholic Bishop of Samogitia, 179
Varangians (Varangian Guard), 56, 76
Vasiliauskas, Artūras, 129–30
Vasiliy Luzhinskiy, Bishop of Orsha, 166
Velnias (Velinas; god), 25, 27
Vienna, Battle of, 158–59
Vikings, 140
Vilnius: Church of St. Euphrosyne of Polotsk, 162; Church of St. Paraskevi, 46, 273; Great Seimas of Vilnius, 211–13; Jewish population, 231; John of Kronstadt in, 191; KGB headquarters, 238; Monastery of the Holy Spirit, 49, 50, 102, 107–9, 162, 208, 219; origin stories, 38–39, 129; St. Mary Magdalene Convent, 207, 208; Three Martyrs of Vilnius, 10, 46–50, 53, 107, 208, 238, 252, 278, 279
Vilnius (Vilna) Icon of the Theotokos, 278
Virgil, 126
Vitalis, Father, 274–75
Vitebsk, 100–101
Vladimir (Volodymyr) of Kyiv, 54–58
von Jungingen, Ulrich, Grand Master of the Teutonic Order, 81, 82
von Salza, Hermann, Grand Master of the Teutonic Order, 63
Voruta, 32
Voskresensky, Sergei, Metropolitan of Vilnius and Lithuania, 235
Vydunas (Wilhelm Starost), 146
Vyšniauskas, Tadas, 241
Vytautas the Great, Grand Duke of Lithuania: Battle of Grunwald and, 79–80, 81–82; *Chronicle of the Grand Dukes of Lithuania* and, 128; church union and,

92–93, 94; conversion, 67; at Council of Constance, 72, 94; Crimean Tatars and, 76–77; death, 89, 95; as grand duke, 69, 88; Jogaila and, 66, 67, 69; Karaite Jews and, 75–76; Metropolis of Lithuania and, 44; Trakai and, 70–71, 72, 73

Vytenis, Grand Duke of Lithuania, 39

W

Weeks, Theodore, 175–76

Weiland, Theodore (Ted), 185, 225, 227

Wilhelm Karl, Duke of Urach (Mindaugas II), 216

Wilkes-Barre (PA), 174, 222–23

Winged Hussars, 91

women, 212

Wooden, Anastacia, 96

World War I, 207–9, 214

World War II, 230–34, 235

Y

Yakhontov, Nicholas (hieromartyr), 277

Yaroslavovich, Feodor, 259

Yotvingians, 15, 20, 22–23

Z

Žemyna (earth-goddess), 25

Zhirovits Icon of the Theotokos, 208, 278

Zubko, Antoniy, Vicar Bishop of Brest, 166

About the Authors

THE VERY REV. ARCHPRIEST ANDREW STEPHEN DAMICK is Chief Content Officer of Ancient Faith Ministries, the former pastor (2009–2020) of St. Paul Antiochian Orthodox Church of Emmaus, Pennsylvania, the author of several books from Ancient Faith Publishing, and the host or cohost of multiple Ancient Faith Radio podcasts. He resides in Emmaus with his wife, Kh. Nicole, and their children.

THE REV. DEACON SERAPHIM RICHARD ROHLIN is a philologist, medievalist, and deacon in the Orthodox Church in America. He is the cohost and producer of several podcasts on Ancient Faith Radio, a frequent guest on The Symbolic World podcast and YouTube channel and cohost of its popular Universal History show. His work focuses on mythology, history, folklore, and traditional storytelling in the Orthodox Christian tradition. He resides near Dallas, Texas, with his wife and six children.

We hope you have enjoyed and benefited from this book. Your financial support makes it possible to continue our nonprofit ministry both in print and online. Because the proceeds from our book sales only partially cover the costs of operating **Ancient Faith Publishing** and **Ancient Faith Radio**, we greatly appreciate the generosity of our readers and listeners. Donations are tax deductible and can be made at **www.ancientfaith.com.**

To view our other publications, please visit our website:
store.ancientfaith.com

ANCIENT FAITH
RADIO

Bringing you Orthodox Christian music, readings, prayers,
teaching, and podcasts 24 hours a day since 2004 at
www.ancientfaith.com

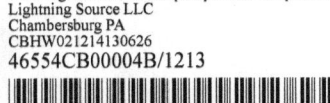